Breaking Up Blues

Pacific

WITHDRAWN

University

Breaking Up Blues is a reassuring and practical self-help book for those going through break-up and divorce.

Breaking up is much more painful, much harder to manage well, than anyone expects. There are many pitfalls – of ongoing battle and bitter self-righteousness; of refusing to 'mind'; and of being stuck in depression and guiltiness. Time on its own does not heal all.

Written by a psychoanalyst, who has her own experience of break-up, this book has great authority. Denise Cullington is sympathetic but challenging. She takes you gently but firmly through the areas we would rather not know about – feelings of failure and of guilt; of hatred and envy; of sadness and loss – and suggests that just pushing them out of conscious mind may keep you stuck. Facing up to emotional pain can be healing and helpful for the future.

Remaining together in a strengthened relationship; breaking up, but doing it as well as possible; helping children face love and loss; learning from experience; awareness of defences that may get in the way of intimacy: all of this is packed into this readable, wise book that will prove indispensable to all those experiencing a break-up.

Denise Cullington is a psychoanalyst living and working in Oxford. She trained at the Institute of Psychoanalysis; the Tavistock Clinic, London; and as a Clinical Psychologist.

D0031995

Breaking Up Blues
A Guide to Survival and Growth

Denise Cullington

Routledge
Taylor & Francis Group

LONDON AND NEW YORK

First published 2008 by Routledge
27 Church Road, Hove, East Sussex BN3 2FA

Simultaneously published in the USA and Canada
by Routledge
270 Madison Avenue, New York NY 10016

Reprinted 2008

Routledge is an imprint of the Taylor & Francis Group, an Informa business

© 2008 Denise Cullington

The right of Denise Cullington to be identified as the Author of this Work
has been asserted by her in accordance with the Copyright, Designs and
Patents Act 1988

Typeset in New Century Schoolbook by Garfield Morgan,
Swansea, West Glamorgan
Printed and bound in Great Britain by TJ International Ltd
Padstow, Cornwall
Paperback cover design by Lisa Dynan

British Library Cataloguing in Publication Data
A catalogue record for this book is available from the British Library

Library of Congress Cataloging in Publication Data
Cullington, Denise, 1952-
Breaking up blues : a guide to survival and growth / Denise Cullington.
p. cm.
Includes bibliographical references and index.
ISBN 978-0-415-45546-6 (hardback : alk. paper) – ISBN 978-0-415-45547-3 (pbk. :
alk. paper) 1. Man-woman relationships. 2. Separation (Psychology) 3. Rejection
(Psychology) 4. Divorce–Psychological aspects. 5. Interpersonal relations. I. Title.
HQ801.C83 2008
306.89–dc22
2007046308

ISBN: 978-0-415-45546-6 (hbk)
ISBN: 978-0-415-45547-3 (pbk)

For Katie and Max
and for my parents, Helen and Derek

Blues is fundamentally a music that fights self-pity and even holds it up to ridicule, scorning all deceptive attempts at ducking responsibility for at least part of the bad state of affairs.

US jazz critic, Stanley Crouch, *Always in Pursuit*, 1999

Contents

Acknowledgements

This book would not have been thought without my experience of my own analysis, my training at the Adult Department of the Tavistock Clinic and the Institute of Psycho-Analysis – and the supervisors, colleagues and patients who all, in their own ways, taught me over the years. There are many to whom I owe deep respect and gratitude, but in particular I would like to acknowledge the wise, tough and forgiving presences of Martin Miller and Edna O'Shaughnessy.

Several dear friends put up with me when I was deep in the blues and helped me feel pleasure – and joy – in tough times. Susannah Taffler hung on – invaluably. Charlie Knight, Alex Josephy, Erika Bard and Sue Weaver were generous and loving.

My family gave me quiet, steadfast support. Marge van Walwyk was gold. My children put up with my preoccupation with impressive courage and pulled me back into life.

This book would not have been written without the generosity of Jennie Karle, who partnered me in thinking through my ideas, and making them readable. Mary Ayres and Jane Bingham offered companionship and feedback in the otherwise solitary, preoccupied world of writing.

Many read the work at various stages and provided me with tactful combinations of support and challenge: in addition to those mentioned above are Melinda Oswald, Veronica Gore, Mike Simm and Margot Waddell. Trevor Burton gave me help on the legal chapter. The editorial team at Routledge were patient and helpful.

Many spoke to me about their experience of break-up and I hope they feel that their confidence has been honoured and used well in describing the painful struggle for all who break up. Thanks too to the children who talked to me and allowed me to use their drawings and poems.

Finally, this book would not have been written without the many good years with Tom, the ending of which left me with the curious problem of how to grapple with, and move on from, them.

To all those – and more – I offer grateful thanks.

Permissions acknowledgements

Every effort has been made to source material and obtain permission from the copyright-holders and the publishers. If inadvertently any permissions have been missed, we would be pleased to be informed. The author is grateful to the following for permission to reprint their work.

From *Life after Marriage* by Al Alvarez, with permission of the author. From *Experience* by Martin Amis, published by Jonathan Cape. Reprinted by permission of The Random House Group Ltd. Excerpted from *Experience: A Memoir* by Martin Amis. Copyright © 2000 by Martin Amis, reprinted by permission of Knopf Canada. From Sister Wendy Beckett, with permission of the author. From *Loss* by John Bowlby, published by Chatto & Windus. Reprinted by permission of The Random House Group Ltd. From *The Artist's Way* by Julia Cameron, published by Pan Books. Reprinted by permission of Macmillan Publishers Ltd. From *Nights at the Circus* by Angela Carter, published by Vintage Books. Reprinted by permission of The Random House Group Ltd. From *On Men: Masculinity in Crisis* by Anthony Clare, published by Chatto & Windus. Reprinted by permission of The Random House Group Ltd; reprinted by permission of A P Watts Ltd on behalf of Professor Anthony Clare. Poems by Polly Covell, printed with permission of the author. From *Always in Pursuit* by Stanley Crouch, published by Vintage Books. Reprinted by permission of Knopf Publishing Group; and by permission of Georges Borchardt Inc. From *The Standard Edition of the Complete Psychological Works of Sigmund Freud*, Volume XIV (1914–1916) by Sigmund Freud, published by Hogarth Press. From *Complete Poems in One Volume* by Robert Graves, published by Carcanet Press Limited (2003). 'Breaking Up Is Hard To Do'. Words and Music by Howard Greenfield and Neil Sedaka. © 1962, Screen Gems-EMI Music Inc., USA. Reproduced by permission of Screen Gems-EMI Music Publishing Ltd, London W8 5SW. From *A Farewell to Arms* by Ernest Hemingway, published by Jonathan Cape. Reprinted by permission of The Random House Group Ltd. From *Fever Pitch* by Nick Hornby, published by Penguin Group, (USA) Inc. (First published by Victor Gollancz 1992, Penguin Books 2000). Copyright © Nick Hornby, 1992. Reproduced by permission of Penguin Books Ltd. From *Atomised* by Michel Houellebecq, published by William Heinemann. Reprinted by permission of The Random House Group Ltd. From *What I Loved* by Siri Hustvedt, published by Sceptre. Reprinted by permission of Hodder Headline. From *Intimacy* by Hanif Kureishi. Reprinted with the permission of Scribner, an imprint of Simon and Schuster Adult Publishing Group, from *Intimacy: A Novel* by Hanif Kureishi. Copyright © 1998 by Hanif Kureishi, first published in Great Britain by Faber & Faber Limited, all rights reserved. From *An Unquiet Mind* by Kay Jamison, published by Picador. Reprinted by permission of Pan Macmillan. From *What do Women Want?* by Erica Jong, published by Bloomsbury. Reprinted with permission of Ken Burrows. From *Love Secrets of Don Juan* by Tim Lott, published by Viking. From When there is talk of War by Ruszard Kapuscinski, published by *Granta*. From *In Search of Lost Time* by Marcel Proust, published by Vintage Classics. Reprinted by permission of The Random House Group Ltd. From *Love Story* by Erich Segal, published by Hodder & Stoughton. From *Self Abuse* by Jonathan Self, published by John Murray. From *Unless* by Carole Shields. Reprinted by permission of HarperCollins Publishers Ltd. © Carole Shields (2003). From *Pick of Posy*. Reprinted by permission of PFD on behalf of Posy Simmonds. © Posy Simmonds, 1982. From Jill Tweedie, published by Guardian News-

PART 1

Prelude to break-up

Reality, however terrible, is bearable if others allow its reality. When they refuse you that, when they skip round you, pretending you've got it wrong, that's rock-bottom time.

Jill Tweedie[1]

papers. Copyright Guardian News and Media Ltd, 1982. From *No Future without Forgiveness* by Desmond Tutu, published by Rider. Reprinted by permission of The Random House Group Ltd. From *Black, White and Jewish* by Rebecca Walker, published by Riverhead Books. Reprinted by permission of Penguin Group (USA).

1

Introduction

Don't take your love away from me
Don't you leave my heart in misery
If you go then I'll be blue
'Cause breaking up is hard to do.[2]
Howard Greenfield and Neil Sedaka

Breaking up is a 'normal' life event: soon more marriages may end in divorce than will last – and that doesn't include the break-up of long-term non-married partnerships.

Because it is so common, we hope that break-up can be got over easily. We see photos of celebrities, who one moment are tearful and bedraggled, going into a detox unit or getting into yet another fight – and the next, lounging on a beach or glittering at an Event with a shiny new lover. Surely that's how we're all supposed to manage it – painlessly, glossily?

At the same time, gossip pages – and being around anyone who is in the middle of breaking up – reveal that there is a darker, more dangerous side: that it is easy to get into crazed, vengeful battles which spiral and end in chaos. There are wives who throw paint over their husbands' Mercedes, cut up their suits, or, memorably, one wife who cut off her partner's penis. There are husbands who are in such despair and rage that they kidnap their children, or kill their children and then themselves. And behind these head-lines there are all the unnewsworthy, everyday accounts of withholding, rage and misery. As in the 1960s song above, you may suspect that breaking up is hard to do: but it is not until you do so yourself that you discover how much – much – harder it is than you ever expected.

Many couples who decide to break – with whatever mixture of sadness, despair and outrage – expect to do so in a way that is reasonably *civilised*. We all *know* that children need to be protected; that their relationship with both parents should not be harmed; that too much time and money should not be wasted on legal battles.

But in the event, you suddenly find yourself caught up in treacherous emotional rip-tides that pull you off your feet; suck you dangerously far out to sea; throw you over and over in the waves before smashing you on the sand – or the rocks. Divorce – like its partner, the legal process – is a giant beast that feeds on the unwary, grinding you with gnashing jaws and spitting – or shitting – out a terribly battered *you*.

And though you may know, logically, that you need to resist the pull into this exhilarating maw of outrage, accusation and counter-accusation, it can happen so quickly and unexpectedly that it can be hard to resist, and hard to find your way back from.

Divorce is an everyday disaster – the biggest one many of us will face. Most of us don't face war, famine, civil breakdown, death of children, complete powerlessness – thankfully. We are so privileged.

But emotionally, divorce has the shattering impact of civil strife and breakdown. And the enemy is the one you once loved and with whom you once shared so much. Your sense of security has gone – of feeling (more or less) loved and (more or less) loving. The loss of any sense of companionship in a shared journey is highlighted in the extreme isolation of the gaping loss you suddenly face.

One of the loneliest things in facing divorce is the belief that everyone else manages it quickly and relatively painlessly. If the impact of break-up hurts like hell for a long time, you can feel a failure – on top of everything else – for not breaking up as well as you think you should.

In fact studies that followed adults and children in the years after divorce found that breaking up is far from easy for anyone.[3] After the initial immense shock and disruption dies down, a minority were able to use their divorce as a *window of opportunity*; they were able to learn from their painful experience and found a new sense of self-worth, often – but not always – in a new relationship; they continued to parent well.

Many did well enough and many found a new relationship to replace the old one – but they did not change or learn from their experience. The same difficulties that had created problems in the previous relationship now put pressure on the new one – and some foundered as a result.

Others had particular difficulty: they had been able to do well enough within the framework of their marriage – but not without it. Continued bitter fighting could be a way of managing the hurt and humiliation of loss, but was an obstacle to settling and moving on. Close to one third of former couples were still caught up in hostilities even ten years after breaking up in one study – mostly over access to children and money. These parents' capacities to attend to the needs of their children were severely impaired and the children suffered as a result in the short term – and often in the long term too.

Men were at more risk of doing poorly after a break-up. In break-up men often lose more: for many men the loss of their children in their daily lives is an unexpectedly devastating blow. In addition men are likely to lose the structure of family life, their role and their home – and they are less likely to have a network of friends to whom they can turn to for support. Men are also more likely to deal with emotional pain by shutting it down – and this has its pitfalls.

We don't get taught, or shown, how to leave a marriage – nor how to be left. You may want to end up with *no baggage* – but what does this mean? If the baggage in question is not spending the rest of your life preoccupied with *what went wrong*; or with *how pathetic / terrible / . . . your ex is* – then yes, it would be good to be free of that.

Do you airbrush out that past shared history as though it had never happened – a bad mistake that it's a relief to be out of? But if you rid yourself of memories, you will leave yourself emotionally empty. You can't have good memories, which might be a source of pleasure, since awareness of the loss of those good times will expose you to grief.

Protecting yourself from bad memories, which might cause guilt, means you can't know why the relationship foundered and what your part in it might be. It means you can't learn for the future.

Truth is painful, but evading reality is not the way to a full life. Just putting the past behind you, being positive and not dwelling on regrets are not enough: in fact in the long term they can make it worse. Pushing painful feelings out of sight does not get rid of them – however much we all might wish it would. And there is a cost: you shut down a part of your personality; your capacity to know yourself, to learn from experience and to respond to others. It leaves you with constricted, no-go areas of your personality: it affects the relationship you have with children, friends, family – and with possible future partners.

To be able to learn from your experience; to have memories of that period of time you shared with your former partner; and to feel emotionally free to engage with life and – in time – the possibility of a new partner, you need to mourn the loss and notice your part in it as well as your ex's.

But the more vulnerable you (we all) feel – stressed, hurt and panicked after a break-up – the more tempting it is to avoid looking at anything which could be upsetting or undermine your already-tattered self-worth. It can feel so much easier to keep to the apparent reassurance of a state of mind where pain and hurt *should not happen*; that if they do, *someone else is at fault* and deserves to be *punished*; and that any share in blame is *intolerable*, because it is so damning.

You can attempt to reverse your feelings: you are no longer sad at the loss of your partner but *only* glad, and he (or she) is *only* hated and unwanted. You can also hope to rid yourself of unwanted feelings by provoking them in your ex: so, if you feel guilty, you provoke rage in them – and they become the *bad* one.

Rage helps you feel powerful. Blame helps you feel innocent of any fault of your own – but blame and rage can whip you, and your former partner, into a cycle of attack and counterattack which – without a deliberate and determined decision to stop – can keep on going, with all its resultant damage.

The emphasis in this book is on the emotional difficulties, which interfere with moving on, rather than the strictly practical ones.

The point is not to end a marriage in some ideal or especially virtuous way, but what is in your best interests and – if you have them – your kids. When breaking up – no matter who *started it* – you need to do it as best you can. It is not in your interests to be still caught up in bitterness and anger ten years after breaking up, nor in passive resentment and hopelessness. You need to be able to pause and catch your breath. Rather than just swirling in panic and desperation, you need to think a bit; notice why you get caught up in endless battles – and why your ex might be behaving as he or she is. It can help to hold on to support – but you will need to do more than just cling on: in time, there is emotional work that only you can do.

Facing up to feelings – such as those of loss and sadness; of having some share in responsibility for the breakup; of helpless fury when life does not always go the way you wish it would – is painful and shameful. But it can also be relieving and empowering. Rather than feeling helplessly swayed by panic and impulse, you may find you have more of a mind to think, and decide what is in your best interests. It leaves you less likely to get caught up in perpetual battle; or to become chronically depressed.

The more you can digest the emotional impact of breakup, the freer you will be internally to move on. If you have children it is especially important to do this – because it leaves you more emotionally open to help them. If you are less caught up in rage and resentment it is easier to cooperate with your former partner – as you need to if you are to help your children best.

Rather than just endlessly examining the faults of your ex, it helps in the end to learn from your experience, and from your mistakes. It is worth knowing more about what breaks a marriage – and what sustains it; more about yourself and the emotional resources, difficulties and expectations that *you* bring to a partnership. It is important to find a way to manage alone – though with the support of others – or you will be at risk of rushing into a new relationship out of panic, and not able to choose carefully. It helps to find a capacity within you to know, parent and protect yourself.

This book is a map of the emotional territory. Like all maps it is important to know where the different paths lead and the whereabouts of the sheer cliffs, the minefields and the bogs. The choice of which path to take is yours – but I hope that this map will help you at least pause before the almost irresistible pull into headlong action and reaction. If you find one path leads to a dead end, having a reasonably reliable map – and a willingness to look at it – increases your chances of finding your bearings and moving off in the direction you wish.

I wish I could cheer you with how relatively easy and straightforward it can be after breaking up and offer easy short-cuts – but the only ones I know of are all traps. The territory, as I see it, is painful and difficult – but it is possible to find a way through.

I write from experience as a psychoanalyst and before that a clinical psychologist, working over the years with many whose emotional problems interfered with their capacity to trust and be close; some had broken up as a result of their difficulties; others had never got close; some had experienced their parents' break-up. I have spoken at length with men and women whose partnerships have broken; some had made the decision to leave and others were left. I tell many of their stories here, in somewhat disguised form.

Most important of all, my own marriage broke up and I learned an immense amount from finding my own slow way through that miserable experience.

This book is for those who think of leaving – and want to consider the possible risks and benefits of breaking up. It is for those who are breaking up and want to manage it as best they can. It is for those digesting the emotional aftermath of break-up and feel still burdened by anger, guilt and grief.

The book is for those who want to learn from the past so that they can do better in future relationships. For those who are breaking up from a formal marriage or from living together, I describe the emotional difficulties of those breaking up from heterosexual relationships – but I think that gay couples will find it useful too. I hope this book speaks to men as well as to women – particularly since there is evidence that men are more at risk of shutting down feelings and then are less able to use the opportunity to learn from their experience.

The break-up of your marriage will change everything – whether you find a new partner, remain single, or even if you get together again. It involves unavoidable loss and pain. But there are many valuable things that can be learned along the way. I hope that you will find in the long run that you can retain a memory of the good times as well as the bad. The marriage may have failed – but failure can be recovered, and learned, from.

It is not a sprint, but a marathon. Take the long view. Protect yourself in the worst moments. Enjoy the view when you have moments to do so. Maybe, with luck and effort, you can end up saying as Mr Valiant-for-Truth does at the end of *Pilgrim's Progress*, when all the trials, including the Slough of Despond, have been faced:

> though with great difficulty I am got hither, yet now I do not repent me of all the trouble I have been to arrive where I am.[4]

I hope this book will help you in that.

Notes

1 Tweedie, Jill (1982) The vision of life seen in depression has the truth in it, the bare-boned skeletal truth. *Guardian*, 17 April.

2 Greenfield, Howard and Sedaka, Neil (1962) *Breaking Up Is Hard To Do*. RCA 8046, © 1962, Screen Gems-EMI Music Inc., USA.

3 Wallerstein, J.S. and Blakeslee, S. (2004) *Second Chances: Men, women and children a decade after divorce*. Boston, MA: Houghton Mifflin.

   Hetherington, E.M. and Kelly, J. (2002) *For Better or for Worse: Divorce reconsidered*. London: Norton.

   Amato, Paul and Keith, Bruce (1991a) Parental divorce and adult well-being: A meta-analysis. *Journal of Marriage and the Family* 53(1): 43–58.

   Amato, Paul and Keith, Bruce (1991b) Parental divorce and the well-being of children: A meta-analysis. *Psychological Bulletin* 110(1): 26–46.

4 Bunyan, John (1678–1684) *The Pilgrim's Progress*. London.

Should you leave?

> When someone loves you, the way they say your name is different. You know that your name is safe in their mouth.
>
> Billy, age 4

There are also times when your name no longer feels *safe* in your partner's mouth. Sometimes it may be temporary and resolved by a good row, good sex, a bit of good luck, a good holiday or a good night's sleep. But sometimes it just isn't. You find yourself with someone who is no longer – and however imperfectly – basically lovable and loving: instead you find yourself with someone who seems only hostile, suspicious – or worse, just plain uninterested.

When a marriage starts to founder there is an absence of life: of energy lost as a result of countless, barely perceptible withdrawals that erode the foundations, drip by drip.

What do you do? What if making a fuss doesn't work for long – but not making a fuss means you stay stuck? You may hope that by withdrawing, your partner will come searching for you – but what if he (or she) just becomes more distant. If you are attentive and your attention is not reciprocated, you are left feeling even more emptied and angry. Feelings of resentment and mistrust may have grown to such a pitch that discussion or fights don't lead to any reconciliation – but only add further to feelings of hurt, rage and grievance.

You may wish to be close but your partner is so full of grievance and complaint that you can feel that to get close again, means only submitting to his (or her) barrage of complaint – and you no longer have the strength or the will to do so.

How long do you wait, hoping that things will somehow get better? Do you stop expecting anything any more from your partner – but keep your eye open for a possible fling, or for a new long-term partner? Do you leave anyway and hope that in time you will find a better partner? If things are so bad and you don't act first, your partner might – in which case it might feel less humiliating to be the one to leave, than to be left.

The impact of external stress on break-up

Some partnerships break in response to serious emotional difficulties in one or both partners – such as chronic depression, violence or alcoholism. It may take time to decide to leave but the one who leaves has generally thought it through carefully.

A surprisingly large number of couples who break up do so almost on impulse.[1] These couples are not necessarily more unhappy than those others who remain together: they report no higher levels of boredom with their partner, nor infidelity, loneliness, loss of sexual interest, depression or alcoholism.

But those who break up are more likely to have had to deal with a significant external stressful event: a stress such as the death of a parent or close friend, a life-threatening illness of a child or themselves, a redundancy or a mid-life crisis.[2] This stress acts as an emotional *trigger* to break up. And if such acute stresses can trigger a break-up, what about the impact of stresses which are chronic such as poverty, ill-health or long-term unemployment? Maybe it's no surprise that poor families are twice as likely to break up.[3]

Under stress we revert to an earlier style of mental functioning: a more infantile one. Our need for nurture goes up and our capacity to offer care and appreciation will go down. We hope that our partner will make us feel better – cheer us up, boost our confidence, give us good advice, help us take our mind off things – as our mother or father may once have done. And just as you may have blamed your parents when they failed back then to make everything completely all right – so now you may resent your partner when they fail.

Some stresses (such as the death of a parent or redundancy) may affect one partner more than the other – and the one less burdened may still be able to offer support. Some stresses, such as middle age, may strike you both – though not necessarily in the same way. Some experiences – such as the death of a child – can put such a burden of grief and helpless rage on both parents that neither has much to offer the other.

Some couples have to manage in chronically difficult circumstances, coping with financial, housing and employment difficulties; many can feel themselves helpless, overwhelmed and resentful at their lives – and it is no surprise that more marriages break down in those groups.

Certain couples have more capacity to withstand the increased external pressures which topple other marriages: those who have an emotional 'bank account' of mutual support and goodwill have more resources to withstand such stressful times; and recognise the impact of stress on their partner – rather than taking his (or her) irritability as a personal attack.[4]

For other marriages – which might have lasted in good-enough circumstances – the additional stress can be sufficient to splinter it along the fault-line: there may no longer be sufficient will, or capacity, to attend to the increased needs of one partner when he (or she) is more needy:

Nick was involved in a shocking accident when he was working away from home: he just missed being killed, but others were not so lucky. He felt overwhelmed and in great need. He wanted his partner, Jane, to really listen and help him bear his intense distress.

But Jane resented him being away so much: she was busy with her life and their young children. She had little spare capacity anyway to absorb his distress – but she also angrily felt that since he was around so little when *she* needed *him* – she really didn't see why she should.

What breaks marriages is the anguish of being emotionally abandoned by a partner who is oblivious to their needs. Eventually it leads to . . . depression and rage.[5]

It is hard to live with a partner who is chronically stressed, and possibly depressed. His (or her) needs and self-preoccupation go up; your partner wants more and is able to offer less. If nothing you do seems to make any difference, your initial feelings of sympathy may turn to impatience and anger.

- Is he (or she) just wallowing?
- Why don't they just pull themself together!
- Will you be permanently lumbered with a depressed spouse?

You might sympathise with your partner – but still not be prepared to wait forever:

Sally had had enough of her husband, Alan. She could see that he was a good man in his own way, but he had been so low, moody and passive for several years – since a car accident in which a friend had lost his life. She had tried to get him to go for some treatment but he wouldn't. Their sex life was non-existent.

Sally had tried to be patient, loving and supportive – but finally she could bear it no longer. She felt sorry for Alan and worried how he would be without her. She worried for their kids. She worried whether she would meet a good man with whom she could make a better life. But she felt she just had to take that risk: staying would just mean suffocating, slowly.

External stresses – which we can do little to actively make better but can only slowly digest – leave us feeling helpless and useless: they stir up intense anxiety and often-unrecognised depression. In an effort to pull yourself out of this stuck position, you can cast around for what is possible to change and one thing to change – which might make a difference – is your marriage.

When wondering about breaking up you may recognise the external pressures on you – but it can still be hard to know whether your dissatisfaction with your partner is largely a response to that outside stress – or if the pressure has highlighted faults in the partnership that are past mending, and is a useful spur to change. (I describe some of these pressures more fully in Chapter 20 on stress and stages of life.)

When facing a significant emotional strain, some retreat to alcohol or drugs to cope. One addictive drug is the incredible adrenalin rush of falling in love and of leaving the familiar and the resented.

An affair

An affair offers hope, excitement, sex and the zest of revenge for all the angers of the marriage – expressed and not. It also offers company, encouragement and the reassurance of touch, at such a bewildering time. An affair can be entered into as a *fling* – something exciting, transgressive and sexual – rather than as a deliberate attempt to leave the marriage, but the feeling of being suddenly, blissfully *special* may be overwhelming after the mutual taking-for-granted of a long partnership.

Caro slowly felt more and more despairing of getting her husband, Paul, to listen to any of her complaints. It was not that he was a bad man – but she felt he always made himself feel big by putting her down. She allowed herself to have an affair with a family friend and was amazed to find someone who put her first. She had forgotten that she could ever feel like this. Caro felt wonderful, loved, special – and she decided to leave: to do anything else would have felt like giving up hope of anything more than the mediocre.

Even if you may *know* that this initial period of intense, sexual, romantic love has a relatively short shelf-life, how can you turn your back on a new lover who seems so wonderful? How do you find out whether your lover's appeal is more to do with their novelty – or whether you really are better suited?

- If you stay, will you always regret your choice?
- But if you go, will you always feel guilty?

It is difficult in all this upheaval to give yourself time to think: to find out what is true and what is not. It can seem easier to take action and make the move before doubts creep in. You may fear that if you stop and think you'll never have the courage to leave, and you'll spend the rest of your life regretting your cowardice.

At one moment you feel you just can't leave, at the next everything feels constricting and you have to get away. Staying for the known and the familiar can seem timid compared with a brave, bold move for change. You can feel like a sullen adolescent for whom leaving home seems the answer to all problems – but at the same time is unthinkably terrifying.

Leaving is often less the result of careful thought, but of *not thinking* – and the result can be almost as much of a shock to the one who leaves as the one who is left.

Martin enjoyed how admiring and appreciative Lucy was of him – so unlike Suzie, who could be bossy and who, in any argument always seemed to end up in the right. He felt like a rebellious schoolboy. His affair with Lucy was partly about showing Suzie who was boss.

When Suzie found out about the affair, she was outraged and full of contempt. Martin was surprised to notice that she was also devastated– he had assumed she might not be that bothered. He was sorry now: he might have wanted to hurt her – but not as much as he could see that he had. In a way he wished that he could make it all right – but it would mean a humiliating back-down – and he would not do that. It was exciting too, being wanted by the two women.

Only when Suzie finally told him she wanted a divorce, did it suddenly seem more than a weird kind of game. He looked around at his house and his boys playing in the garden. He looked at Suzie, so much part of his life for so long – and realised he would never have her or their boys in the same way again. Martin felt sick. He was losing virtually everything he'd worked for, for years. He felt frightened and very sad. It wasn't supposed to have happened like this. Then he felt angry – which made him feel better.

Some months later, he advised a friend not to let the same thing happen in *his* marriage.

Dealing with the impact of external stresses by breaking up and attempting to settle into a new life is a brave thing to do – even if in retrospect it may seem fool-hardy. Throwing everything in the air may be a way of addressing the need for substantial change – but if you don't attend to those other issues too, breaking up on its own won't make everything better long term – and if you expect it to, you may set yourself up for tremendous disappointment.

In the initial period after break-up you may feel immensely excited, because you are taking action: there is the novelty of the change and much to attend to. But when things begin to settle, it is likely that you will find yourself facing the same difficulties that you had before the break-up. Breaking up brings additional emotional demands, on top of the ones you had before, which you may have hoped to resolve by leaving. In that sense you are a double invalid – managing the underlying problem as well as the demands of breaking up.

Reality check

So is life really better for most people after break-up? Judith Wallerstein, who has studied divorcing families in depth, comments how the adults have a 'palpable need to put their best foot forward, to cover their failures, and to disguise their unhappiness'.[6] In other words we may be hearing a sunnier version of break-up and divorce than the reality warrants.

It is helpful – but sobering – to learn from two very in-depth studies led by clinicians in the United States which followed up adults and their children in the years after break-up,[7] – and whose findings have been supported by large-scale surveys in the United States,[8] and in the UK.[9]

I don't want to be disheartening – but being realistic is useful. If you are going to break up you need to know the downside as well as the up: a whirl of excited dreams alone may give you the courage to leave – but then offer a long fall.

How many of the following 'facts' do you think are true?

- Divorce is tough in the short term – but after a short time you will move on.
- You and your ex won't fight in the ridiculous way that some people seem to.
- Your children are resilient.
- They will do better with two happily separated parents than if you remain together, somewhat unhappily.
- You will have more time for yourself.
- You won't make the same mistakes as last time.
- A new partner will appreciate you much better than the old one.

The disheartening answer is that none of the above is true – without a lot of effort.

Children whose parents break up suffer in the immediate, traumatic aftermath – and after too. Compared to peers from families where the parents have similar marital dissatisfaction but remain together, in adolescence children of divorce have more emotional, behavioural and educational problems. In young adulthood they have more difficulties forming and maintaining close romantic relationships.[10]

These effects are greater when parents continue to fight; if they are less able to provide attentive, concerned care; and if the parent looks to their child to parent them. Children from a chaotic or abusive family are helped by their parents' divorce – but only if the resident parent is able to settle and provide a stable base for them.[11]

I don't propose to say more about children at this stage – though I do in considerable detail later in the book. Of course it matters how your children do, and if you stay or leave it is important to think about what will help them best. But if you decide to stay *for the sake of the children* and do so in a long-suffering way, you are probably not doing anyone any favours.

Only if you decide it might be in *your* long-term best interests to see if you can make your partnership work better, are you likely to put in real effort.

So does divorce bring all the advantages that adults hope for? Not surprisingly there is an initial period of trauma – which takes a lot longer to settle than many might expect. In that first eighteen months after break-up, adults feel volatile mixtures of panic, dread, hopelessness, rage, loneliness, grief and exhilaration. Many show loss of impulse control – acting out destructively and self-destructively. They put their feelings into action, using drink and drugs to self-medicate; provocation to whip up anger, violence and excitement; and casual sex as an attempt to reassure themselves of their worth. Adults suffer physical ailments as their immune systems are overstressed.

During and after break-up, physical violence occurs in a quarter of the families. Men are more likely to be violent when they are the ones left, as a desperate attempt to regain control and self-esteem. Many – particularly men – rush rapidly into further relationships, hoping to ease their loneliness: many of these rapid remarriages collapse – often initiated by the new wife.[12] If so, the men face considerable despair.

As couples begin to settle, do they find what they had been looking for? For about three out of ten adults life after divorce is significantly better than before: they had been able to use the break-up as a *window of opportunity* and their confidence had grown. There were more women in this group. Some of these were in new, more satisfying, partnerships – and if so, this was a great boost to their happiness. Others were single but had developed resources of friendship, work, community and interests which made life satisfying: they were less at risk of rushing into a new relationship out of loneliness.

Between a quarter and a third of divorced adults were seen as *losers* after break-up – in particular those who continued to fight bitterly even ten years on, over access to children and money and others who held on to a more hidden, but still bitter sense of grievance. Some of these adults had been impulsive and explosive within the marriage and its breakdown made this worse. But others seemed to have coped well enough within the marriage: it was its ending which had stirred up such feelings of hurt and hatred that spiralled destructively.[13]

Less than half the fathers paid child-support regularly or in full – which was not related to income, but was seen rather as an expression of power and retaliation. If new relationships did not work out, men and women both were at risk of feeling defeated, isolated and reliant on drink or drugs to maintain their mood.

What stressed new partnerships – and contributed to the 60 per cent rate of divorce for second marriages – was for women the stresses between their children and the new partner.

For men it was when they had replaced their partner, but had not considered their contribution to the previous difficulties. They had turned to an affair hoping to find the sense of being valued rather than criticised, and the sex that was absent in their marriage. But if they did not learn about their part in what had gone wrong in the past relationship, their new partner was likely to change from a loving, appreciative one to one who was increasingly nagging.

External factors make it easier for some to adjust after a break-up than others: those who have more support from family, friends and social groups find it easier. It is easier for those who have a training to get better-paid jobs; having sufficient money helps. Being attractive helps.

But there are also personality factors that make it easier or harder to break up. Being irritable and explosive not surprisingly makes things more difficult. So does acting on impulse rather than planning. Some manage to push concerned others away – either out of pride or by being too demanding – while others find it easier to reach out for, and use, help.

If divorcing couples can manage to make agreements and stick to them – over issues such as money and access to children – this is enormously helpful. And it takes tact from both sides.

Conclusion

Don't expect that breaking up and beginning a new relationship will automatically lead you on to a better new life. It will take hard work and compromise to achieve that.

There is no right answer. Inevitably – leaving or staying – you will have certain regrets. Long term it may be worth the heartache and effort of breaking up – but it is possible too that if you had put the same effort into the relationship you already had, that one too might have improved.

Notes

1 Wallerstein, J.S. and Kelly, J.B. (2004) *Surviving the Breakup*. New York: Basic Books.
2 Wallerstein and Kelly, *Surviving the Breakup*.
3 Hughes, Rt Hon Beverley and Cooke, Graeme (2007) Children, Parenting and Families. In Peace, N. and Margo, J. (eds) *Politics for a New Generation*. (IPPR).
4 Wallerstein, J.S. and Blakeslee, S. (1995) *The Good Marriage: How and why love lasts*. London: Bantam.
5 Wallerstein and Blakeslee, *The Good Marriage*, p. 244.
6 Wallerstein, J.S. and Blakeslee, S. (2004) *Second Chances: Men, women and children a decade after divorce*. Boston, MA: Houghton Mifflin, p. 27.
7 Wallerstein, J.S., Lewis, J.M. and Blakeslee, S. (2002) *The Unexpected Legacy of Divorce: A 25 year landmark study*. London: Fusion.

Hetherington, E.M. and Kelly, J. (2002) *For Better or for Worse: Divorce reconsidered*. London: Norton.

8 Amato, Paul (2003) Reconciling divergent perspectives: Judith Wallerstein, quantitative family research, and children of divorce. *Family Relations* 52(4): 332–339.
Amato, Paul and Cheadle, Jacob (2005) The long reach of divorce: Divorce and child well-being across three generations. *Journal of Marriage and the Family* 67(1): 191–206.

9 Cockett, M. and Tripp, J. (1994) *The Exeter Family Study: Social policy research findings*. York: Joseph Rowntree Foundation.

10 Amato, Reconciling divergent perspectives.
Paul Amato, personal communication (July 2007).

11 Amato, Reconciling divergent perspectives.
Amato and Cheadle, The long reach of divorce.

12 Wallerstein and Kelly, *Surviving the Breakup*.

13 Johnston, J.R. and Campbell, L.E.G. (1988) *Impasses of Divorce: The dynamics and resolution of family conflict*. New York: Free Press.

3

Should you stay?

Leaving your options open

You may wish that you could be decisive. You may even act decisive, hoping that once a decision has been made you can get on and adjust to the new life. It might seem foolish and weak to be unsure, but the reality is that, if your partnership has been under pressure for a while, you may just not know. Psychological closure comes at the end of a process of mourning for what has been lost. Rushing into making the decision doesn't make that end point come quicker – it just cuts down the possible available options.

Attempting to make things better

A half-hearted attempt at improving things just wastes time and will be frustrating for everyone involved. A serious effort at making things work may well be helpful – whether you find good reasons to stay together, or you become clearer why you no longer want to do so.

Trying again does not mean miserably accepting the less than good: it means making active efforts to make things better. If you want to do so, you will need to look at things from your partner's point of view as well as your own – in which case you will almost certainly find that, as well as your well-known complaints about him (or her), they have some justifiable complaints about you. You will probably have heard these complaints before, but have chosen to deal with them by ignoring them.

The more accurate your partner's complaint is, the more uncomfortable it will feel. It is easy to become defensive and attacking, but if you do so, your partner will become defensive or attacking in turn – and you will be back again in the cycle of mutual recrimination.

You don't have to be *convinced* that it's the best thing to do to *try again*; you will probably have very mixed feelings. Deciding to do so doesn't mean that you are trapped forever. It may be easier to think of trying one day at a time, as Alcoholics Anonymous and Narcotics Anonymous advise: doing your best to see if you can make your relationship work better for now – and then see.

You do need to be straight with yourself and with your partner: if you don't know what you want, or you lurch from one position to another – say that. Don't pretend. If you are seeing someone else, don't hide the fact.

Some are pleased to have stayed and made things better:

> Jack was away a lot on business – his work was creative, exciting. Coming back to his wife, Sara, and daughter, felt dreary in comparison. Sara could get depressed and resentful. If truth be told, he rather despised her.
>
> When he was away he had various affairs and felt he deserved the break. Jack was amazed when a lovely, bright, younger woman fell for him and wanted to be with him. He could see the great life they could have together. It was almost too great: he was not sure that he could quite keep up with her.
>
> A cautious bit of him also knew she'd want a child – and he didn't want to go through family life again. What was so appealing about her was her freedom, her time for and pleasure in him. But oh, she was lovely!
>
> Jack realised that he just could not leave his marriage – and particularly his daughter. He felt rather ashamed: that he was being weak and boring not to choose the daring, romantic, sexy path.
>
> Since he was not going to leave, Jack decided that he'd better make his marriage as good as possible. He and

Sarah went into marital therapy. He'd been before but had felt trapped and reluctant. He took it more seriously now.

Things got better. Sara became happier and became more confident in her work. They made an adventurous trip together. Their daughter moved into a fierce adolescence and Jack was pleased to be there for her. He felt calmer, less frenzied. He had less need to rush around proving how great he was.

Jack thought sometimes, with a terrible tug, of the lover he'd given up. Life wasn't perfect – but it had its deep satisfactions.

The advantages – and the risks – of separation

Separating may help you find out for yourself whether it is your partner and the marriage which feels unbearable, or whether there is something in you – your doubts and difficulty – which needs attention. The trouble is that finding out more about yourself on your own, and what you may have been getting in an unacknowledged way from your partner, takes time: more than just a few weeks. It is easy to want to return just because being alone is so new and alarming.

There is a real risk that if you leave, your partner may not want you back – and that you only find out too late what the partnership, and family life, does offer. If you may want to try to make things better in the future, there are things to bear in mind when you are leaving – so that you don't do irreparable damage on your way out the door.

Neil felt fed up with his life. He had his own business and, though it went well enough, he was bored and fed up. The best time of day was meeting up in the pub in the evening with his mates.

His home life felt constricting: the house seemed full of kids and his wife, Gill, would be angry when he returned: he felt like an increasingly coiled spring. Their rows became more bitter and sometimes Neil ended up smashing things. He'd left home for a few nights – but had always gone back. It made him feel he'd blown off steam and for a while Gill was subdued – which suited him. He was drinking more heavily.

When Neil left after yet another furious row, Gill would not let him back. Because of his threats of violence, a police injunction was taken out against him. He was drinking more and his work was suffering badly. He felt angry and defiant – but he was also very frightened about what was to become of him.

When Neil noticed that Gill and the kids were suffering, he was pleased – but guilty too. When they seemed to do OK without him, he hated them and felt it wasn't fair. What made it more intolerable was that he knew how much he'd contributed to the collapse of his marriage.

Neil couldn't see how to get his life back on course: he felt that he'd lost the one thing – his family – that had really meant something to him. He just hadn't noticed till now.

A few months later, he made a serious suicide attempt.

Why discussion doesn't help

When you share a common goal – such as a wish to find a way to make things work or break up as well as possible – discussion can be a useful way of sorting out difficulties. But if one of you wants to split up and the other doesn't, discussion is pointless and may be destructive. It is simply not relevant at this moment who is at *fault*, or what would have made a difference.

If your partner is leaving he (or she) needs to prove why they are right to leave: they have no interest in why it went wrong – except probably to prove that it is not their fault.

If you are leaving, your partner might want to persuade you to stay; dispute your reasons to leave; or get rid of their pain by proving to you how worthless you are.

Unless you decide at some future point that you both want to attempt to make your partnership work, 'discussion' is about apportioning blame. It can only hurt and inflame.

The problem of guilt

Guilt can pull you one way and then another. You may think that your partner – and you – will be relieved and that breaking up will be relatively easy: in fact if he (or she) were only relieved, you might feel hurt and angry too. You may suspect that they will be devastated; you don't know for how long. You may long to leave and punish them, but they are also the one you fell in love with and shared years with.

At one moment you can struggle to be friendly to the one you are leaving; at the next moment you can't stand them a second longer. But there is no escaping: however much you wish to avoid it, the impact explodes and shatters everything – inside and out.

Martin Amis described his feeling on leaving his first wife and children:

> Only to [my father] could I confess how terrible I felt, how physically terrible, bemused, subnormalised, stupefied from within, and always about to flinch or tremble from the effort of making my face look honest, kind, sane. Only to him could I talk about what I was doing to my children. Because he had done it to me.[1]

Bearing your partner's hurt can feel almost intolerable and it may be a relief if he (or she) rages at you – because then you can feel angry back, which makes you feel less guilty.

Sometimes the more guilty you feel, the more aggressive you may be – for if you succeed in provoking your partner to fury you can hope to get rid of any feelings of guilt. But if you try to put all the blame on your partner, he (or she) is likely to feel that you are being doubly *cheating* – leaving and not acknowledging any guilt: their fury, distress and mistrust of you will increase – which matters, whether you stay away or if you try again.

If you can resist going on the attack as a way of managing your guilt, it makes separation less likely to spiral into uncontrollable rage. If the break-up becomes permanent, you are more likely to have some basis for cooperation over money and your children. If you were to try again to make your partnership work, there would be less sense of a betrayal to overcome.

The fear of losing face if you return

Frank had a secret which ate away at him that he had hidden away from his wife, Nuala. As a result of a brief affair, he'd got a girl pregnant – and she had the baby. Of course it was stupid, he bitterly regretted it, but he just could not find the right moment to tell Nuala about it: and the longer it went on, the more foolish and stupid he felt he was being. If back then he had not told her for fear that she might walk out, how much worse would she react now if she ever found out?

Frank did his best to put it all out of mind and, though he paid child support, he had no contact with his daughter or her mother. He concentrated on his work and his family. He was terrified that his daughter might sometime try to find him. Leaving seemed the only alternative.

In the anger and recriminations during the break-up the truth finally came out. Nuala was devastated by the fact that Frank had not told her all these years: that was a much more important betrayal to her than the affair or the child. Did it mean that everything that had meant so much to her had been a sham for him, all this time?

Frank was mortified: he felt exposed as such a coward. He found work out of the country for a number of years. He found a series of new partners – as did Nuala – but sometimes he still wondered whether, had he found a way to face the hurt and the lies, even at the end, it might have saved his marriage.

Some couples do find their way back, after time apart:

Lily left her husband Graham after several years of marriage because she found his infidelities too wounding.

She had plenty going on: work; interesting friends; she lived abroad for a time; had a couple of relationships.

Life seemed rich and full – but she missed Graham all the same – and he did her.

They got back together six years later. Both were very independent people, who found it alarming to be too close – but they were able to make a much more solid commitment to each other. They had children. Their careers flourished.

They acknowledged that they did not fill all of each other's needs and were more accepting of that. Each knew that their marriage formed a solid bedrock for their lives. They were pleased they had found a way back to each other.

Note

1 Amis, M. (2000) *Experience*. London: Jonathan Cape, p. 99.

4

Being left

Animals, when threatened or wounded, go on the attack. And your partner's wish to leave or his (or her) affair is a threat and a wound. You may panic and desperately want them to return so that everything can be just as it was before. You may feel relieved that they are going. You're also likely to be outraged, hate them and want to hurt them as much as you can − hoping to get rid of your feelings of shock and trauma and to feel powerful instead. All the wounds and complaints from when you were together − as well as from your past before you knew each other − are likely to get thrown in the pot. You can feel compelled to rush into action, kick your partner out and file for divorce.

It can seem impossible to sort out what you want. You may know you are furious. You may want to punish your partner because he (or she) has hurt you so much. You may try to bully them to stay. You may want them only because anything else feels too frightening − but you probably can't yet know. It is particularly hard to manage these feelings if your partner has someone else's arms to hold them and reassure them of their lovableness − and you don't.

The problem is that your feelings are responses to the shock and stress. They are little to do with the reality of what your partner offers you or how much you might hope for the opportunity to make the marriage better. You probably can't yet know, particularly if your marriage has been in the doldrums. Rushing into action gives you a sense of being in control of things, but the result may not be in your long-term best interests.

Some who divorced their partner later regretted that they had not risked waiting to see if they might have sorted out their difficulties. Men in particular have difficulty tolerating their partner's infidelity.[1] Feelings such as pride, rage, resentment, fear of looking foolish or being further hurt can all get in the way of giving the partnership a proper second chance.

> When his rage died down, Paul thought sadly that if he had been less furious with his first wife Penny, following her affair, they might have worked things out. He could begin to see he hadn't always been a great partner to her.
>
> His life was all right. His new marriage was pretty happy – but, deep down, he missed Penny and wished that they'd managed to sort it out. When Christmas came and their grown-up children and their young grand-children stayed with her, and only came over to visit him, he wished he could be part of it too. He felt he'd been stupid.

Who is the *real* leaver?

It is not always as clear as it first looks, who is the leaver and who is the one left. In the emotional withdrawal from a marriage the one who leaves, as well as the one who is left, can feel that they have lost the love of their partner. In Chapter 3, the ones who left all did.

> When Amanda's long-term partner told her he was leaving, among the many reactions she had, was 'Phew!' She had known all along really that their relationship wasn't quite right, but hadn't done anything about it – although if an interesting and interested potential part-ner had shown up, she might well have responded to the opportunity.
>
> It didn't stop her feeling gutted and deeply wounded.

She was *left* but her partner may also have been right, to feel that he was not being loved in the way he hoped.

Is an affair unforgivable?

The general assumption is that an affair is probably unforgivable and the only honourable, gutsy thing to do is to get rid of your errant partner for good. You may have used the – implicit or explicit – threat of such action as a way of keeping your partner *in line*. If your partner does have an affair, it can seem as if your prior assumptions leave you no choice but to go. And if you accepted your partner back to see if you could make it work better, you might worry that you no longer have that same threat of leaving to ensure they don't hurt you in the same way again.

If you've seen the classic film *Brief Encounter* (1945), with the characters played by Trevor Howard and Celia Johnson who are torn between their love for each other and their commitments to partners and family, you are likely to put yourself in their shoes and wish they would free themselves to go off together, and feel their agony when they turn back to their partners.

It's only when you find yourself painfully in the shoes of one of the partners that you decide that falling in love with someone else and leaving is obviously outrageous. Your partner having an affair is horribly painful, and undermining of your sense of worth and trust. But, however painful, it is *understandable*.

Have you never been tempted to have a fling, or had one – or two or even more – thinking it would not *count* if your partner did not know about it? Might you not have done so, if you had had the opportunity? It is one thing to expect your partner to be completely faithful to you – and less easy when you find yourself tempted.

Men and women are both more likely to have affairs, or to leave, when they feel insufficiently appreciated by their partner. An affair can be an expression of resentment or hopelessness – a wish to hurt the partner, or provoke a response from him (or her) – as much as who, and what, is turned to.

A partner's affair, which leaves you feeling cheated and deprived, need not only be a sexual one. Men can feel that the excited coupling his partner has is with their children –

and that he is now an also-ran. Women may feel that all their partners' liveliness goes elsewhere – into work, or sport, computer games or the pub. These, and others, can feel like wounding betrayals too – and can stir up feelings of resentment and wish for revenge.

If your partner has an affair, your response to it is likely to have a significant impact on whether you find a way to remain together, or not.

Does an affair mean your partner hates you?

> You don't stop loving someone just because you hate them.
>
> Playwright and novelist, Hanif Kureishi[2]

It is easy to assume that, if your partner is having an affair or wants to leave, he or (she) must only *hate* and *despise* you.

> When Mary's long-term partner left, she knew he adored their three children – who were still quite young – and his house. How then could he do this? The only explanation that made any sense was that he hated her so much, and could not wait to get away.

It is true that, having decided to leave, your partner will be trying to muster every argument he (or she) can find for why they should leave: why they are right to do so and why they should not feel guilty. This is of course not the *whole truth*, but what your partner needs to believe to be able to leave.

But the more angry, critical and blaming you are, the more you fit into the image of the *horrible you* which your partner wants to believe. By going on the warpath, you may succeed in getting rid of some of your feelings of hurt and helplessness. But if all you are offering your partner is a version where you are uniquely virtuous, and he (or she) an unforgivable sinner, it is sad – but not surprising – if your partner stays away.

Trying to be clear what you want, and therefore what your strategy is, is important. In Siri Hustvedt's *What I Loved*, when Lucille's husband, Bill, left his lover and returned to her, she nagged and complained:

> nagging is a strategy of the powerless, and there is nothing mysterious about it . . . the dreary sound of Lucille's domestic complaints . . . I suspect that whether she knew it or not, a part of her pushed Bill away.[3]

In contrast Violet, the lover, responded with

> blazing awareness of purpose . . . Violet didn't look 'devastated'. She didn't even look sad. She was wearing a small, navy blue dress that hugged her body. Her lips were shining with red lipstick and her hair had been artfully tousled . . . she responded to the sympathy in my voice with a cool crisp tone that warned me I had better remove all traces of pity from mine. 'I'm fine . . . I'm delivering a letter to Bill . . . Speed and strategy. That's what matters now' . . .
> The letters . . . 'had to be sincere but they couldn't be maudlin. They had to be written without a shred of self-pity, and they had to be sexy without being pornographic'.

The most important part of Violet's strategy – *hair artfully tousled* or not – is that she refused to retreat to a hurt, angry demand that Bill should stay, but rather she expressed her wish for him to do so. If you decide to fight for a second chance then – male or female – you too might be better advised to show your partner what they are losing in you, rather than all the reasons they are better to stay away.

Waiting versus action

If you can find a way to do so, it might be helpful to give yourself a bit of time and space to find out what you might want for yourself. It is not easy, but your partner's leaving is a chance to do some reality testing, and maybe some growing, on your own.

Waiting, and not knowing what will result from it, is very hard – but then so is breaking up. What you would wait for is not just to find out whether your partner finds that their version of you and the marriage – that you offer *nothing*, or only something *unwanted* – is true or not.

You would also be giving yourself the opportunity to calm down – and find out more what your partner has, or hasn't, offered you. You might find out the advantages – and the drawbacks – of living alone. You might find out what another relationship offers you: ways in which it could be more satisfying – and ways in which it might be less so.

Only if your partner were to want a reconciliation – and of course they might not – would you then really be in a position to choose whether or not to work to make things better. If you genuinely want to give your marriage a second chance you need to discover what you want, and fight for it – accepting the risk that you won't necessarily *win*.

Making a second attempt after separation

An attempt at reconciliation is risky: you will have to open yourself up to the hope and wish to make things better – and it might not work. You may find that you really are better apart than together: you may have too much resentment and mistrust to let go of; you may realise you have grown apart and just don't meet each other's needs.

You risk renewed hope, and possible further hurt and disappointment – but arguably that risk of further hurt is a reasonable one given the alternative of letting your marriage crumble out of fear and pride. Making a second attempt may settle doubts that otherwise might linger, about whether you could have made it work, had you tried a bit harder.

In the following example the couple did find their way back to each other after eight months apart – in large part as a result of the courageous refusal of Alice, who was *left*, to turn to self-pity and vengeance:

David could see retirement over the horizon. He felt exhausted, dispirited and old. His marriage felt stale. He was intrigued when a junior colleague flirted with him and he ended up going to bed with her, thinking it would be a one-night stand. He was amazed to find himself head over heels in love with her; she was young, adventurous, bold. With her he felt energised, sexy, alive. He decided he must follow this new relationship that offered so much more hope than his marriage. He left his wife, Alice, and moved in with his lover.

Alice still believed that at heart they had a good marriage, and one that they could make better. She believed that he was *mad* more than *bad*: this view of David made Alice less enraged. She still wanted him. She did not berate him. All she could do was wait, attempt to look after herself as best she could, and hope David would discover that his romantic dream had its own downsides.

Eight months later David asked her whether they could meet to discuss his returning to her. He felt foolish, vulnerable and exposed. He trusted that if Alice agreed to let him return she would not just rub his nose in it all. She agreed to his return.

They worked hard over the next months at their relationship, with a marital therapist, and also a lot on their own.

Eight years later they are pleased to be together; they take each other less for granted and look after each other better. In the separation – however painfully – they had managed to reinvigorate their partnership in a way which friends, who had stayed together, had not had the opportunity to do. Things are not perfect – but they are both grateful and accepting.

It's only worth giving your partnership another go if you both – however ambivalently – decide it's worth it, rather than one of you pulling the other reluctantly along. In that case you've got to let go of blame and fault; who's *right* and who is in the *wrong*. Bullying, coercion and moralising won't work. If you can talk about your feelings, without making the other entirely responsible for them, that can help. It can be useful to wonder whether some of your expectations of your partner are unreasonable; or whether your assumptions of them are more to do with your past than with who they are. You need to find ways of listening to your partner when he (or she) expresses complaints and give up your wish to be always *in the right*; you need to find ways to negotiate and make concessions.

What if you wait too long?

There is the risk that waiting, and hoping for reconciliation, can keep you in a limbo, never quite accepting the fact of the break-up and stopping you from being able to free yourself and move on.

On the other hand, if you don't stay frozen and passive as a way of hoping to ensure your partner's return but use the time to discover more about yourself and life in the meantime, then you are keeping your options open, and not foreclosing out of pride and vengeance.

In your threatened marriage you have some, but not complete, control of whether you end up together or apart. The result may not be just what you hoped it would be. But if you can learn from this painful time, and emerge knowing yourself better and appreciating your relationships more – with an intimate partner or with others – that's a goal well worth working for.

Notes

1 Hetherington, E.M. and Kelly, J. (2002) *For Better or for Worse: Divorce reconsidered*. London: Norton.
2 Kureishi, Hanif (1999) *Intimacy*. London: Faber & Faber, p. 108.
3 Hustvedt, Siri (2003) *What I Loved*. London: Hodder & Stoughton, p. 61.

PART 2

The trauma of break-up

Happiness is the lucky pane of glass you carry in your head. It takes all your cunning just to hang on to it, and once it's smashed you have to move into a different sort of life.

Writer, Carol Shields[1]

5

Loss

You might think that if a relationship is stressed and poor that it should be easy to let go of; that feelings of relief and pleasure should outweigh any sense of loss – and at some moments they probably do.

But the break-up of a long-term partnership is shockingly painful. It stirs you fundamentally. You are crazed. You are mad – in both senses of the word. You are not in control of yourself – or the situation. You feel terrified, like a helpless, panicked baby. You swirl from despair to rage to exhilaration to grief to utter panic.

One moment you feel excited and determined, with endless energy. The next moment you are yelling at the bus driver, or having a near miss in the car. Your body feels as if it is locked into overdrive, with the accelerator pedal stuck and revving wildly, without engaging. You wake in the night with terror that you will never find a way through.

You want someone to make it all better, to hold and soothe you, as a parent does a child, when you wake from this nightmare – to reassure you that everything is all right, that it's only a dream. But of course it's not. And the one who up till now, however imperfectly, would still have been there for you, is there no longer. That is the disaster.

You are in shock – like the survivor of any other sort of crash. In this state you can feel full of energy so that you can do anything. But you need to be careful with yourself: you are wounded – even if it's hard yet to know quite what the damage is.

It is easy to stay in this traumatised state, like a rabbit transfixed in the headlights, rehearsing and reliving each moment; being so much still inside the experience that it is not possible to think about or digest it. And then it can feel that the only option is to act quickly, to get the hurt out and turned back on the one who is seen to have caused it – as is typical of victims of other traumas.[2]

You can prowl round this loss, snarling – round and round – but still, in the end, it needs to be digested. If you can hold on to some capacity to think as well as to feel, and protect yourself rather than flailing wildly, then you can begin to tease out not only *who* is lost, but also what are the associated losses – some of which may be lost for good, and others which may be recoverable.

Panic

When your partnership breaks up, the loss of your partner and your familiar way of life stirs up something primitive, biological: it has as much to do with your partner's physical presence – his (or her) smell, their tone of voice, maybe their touch which, whatever else, could make everything feel familiar and safe, their presence in your mind – as much as what they did, or did not, offer.

As infants, maintaining a bond to our first familiar figure – generally our mothers – is a matter not just of reassurance but of life or death. To be abandoned as an infant spells disaster. Adults too, in situations of extreme danger or pain, can revert back to that early, terrified, disintegrated state, desperate for someone to *make everything all right* – and soldiers who are wounded or dying in a war zone may call out to the mother of their infancy for comfort.

This primitive, biological need for connectedness, from a time before there were words to represent the experience, underlies our adult intimate partnerships and which is why it can be so painful to pull away from the relationship – even if it is unfulfilling; even if it is destructive.

Polly Covell addresses this aspect of loss:[3]

My daughter asks if
I miss anything about her Dad and
I tell her 'Oh
I miss him to share things with –
When he was here to share – he
Could be fun'.

'I miss everything about him'
She said.
'I might get him 48 hours alternate weeks but
I'd rather the two in the old way'.

She's right
Yet again, my daughter.
Straight to the heart of it –
No 'independent' crap.
And the truth?
I can barely remember life before him.
He was in every cell.

When the wound is so profound, *in every cell*, you can't
make it better by just cutting it out – because if you do, you
will be left with nothing.

EXTERNAL LOSSES

Partnership will have provided much in the way of security
– even if it may sometimes feel irritatingly constricting.
Partnership provides a role – as a contributor to the household, maybe as a parent – which offers a sense of stability,
when much else around feels less certain. Being one of a
couple may have many difficulties but you were, however
imperfectly, accompanied – and suddenly you are no longer.
All the domestic chores are yours alone, the practical decisions, the bill-paying, the responsibilities – all are yours.
One loss – that may not even be noticed or valued – is the
effortless, taken-for-granted presence of your partner, his
(or her) familiarity and companionship.

You may lose much that is familiar – your family house,
neighbourhood, income. Two external losses in particular
can be hard to bear: loss of children and friends.

Loss of children

The loss of daily contact with children for the non-resident parent – most of the time the father – can be unexpectedly devastating. Martin Amis describes a father's *atavistic despair*; his sense of *exile* which in the past was a result of warfare, and now is more often an inadvertent result of parents' break-up.[4]

A father generally loses his role in his children's daily lives – the closeness from being regularly around. He may not be there for comfort or advice when it is needed, and as his contact with them is less frequent he may find it harder to set limits.

Jonathan Self described his experience of separation from his sons as a result of his break-up:

> I miss my children. Not in an abstract, intellectual way. Physically I retch when I contemplate the enormous distance between us. I am consumed by vast, ill-defined fears for their safety and well-being. The thought of something dreadful happening to them, of not being there to protect them, makes me nauseous . . . Detached not just from my boys, but from the world itself, I exist in a trance-like state, struggling to make sense of what is happening around me.[5]

Some men try to protect themselves from the pain of intermittent contact with their children, and of the humiliating need to maintain some sort of cooperative contact with their children's mother, by withdrawing – sometimes physically but also by emotional blunting.[6] This may offer a protection of sorts, but it is a desperate loss for children and is a self-inflicted injury by the father, which is likely to increase his sense of *exile*.

Mothers too can be devastated by the absence of their children when they are with their fathers.

Loss of friends

You lose the company of those who are more your partner's friends, colleagues or family. With other friends, you may feel like the bringer of bad tidings, threatening the otherwise unquestioned assumption that the marriages of those we like do not break.

Mark had been close to both Nick and Jo for many years. He loved their lively, affectionate, sparky relationship and hoped he would find one as good as theirs. Ten years later he was horrified when they broke up. He could not bear to see their tense faces; their grief and rage.

He also felt let down by their failure to remain a perfect couple for him. If their marriage had broken up, could his be at risk too? Mark could not bring himself to keep contact with either of them. He was concerned, he was terribly sad, but it was just too upsetting. And he had so much else to attend to.

Some friends won't approve of your break-up:

While married, Penny and her husband regularly got together with friends. When she ended their marriage these invitations stopped: instead her women friends would suggest meeting up separately, for lunch. Penny enjoyed this but missed the mixed company – she felt hurt and suspicious that she was seen as having less worth than before. But the other husbands' sympathy was with the man she had left, and this was hurtful to her.

It is easy to feel hurt and wounded by the ways that friends are lost – but there may be more to it than that. Friends can feel in a no-win situation. You want your friends to support your point of view; to take your side and agree with you all the ways your ex was *rubbish*. But if they do, you may well feel hurt that they don't understand why parting is so hard. If they continue to see anything good in your ex you may feel hurt and resentful. It is dangerous territory for them.

When you are stressed and deprived, you can have very mixed feelings towards what your friends still have: whether an intact partnership, the advantages of joint parenting and a joint income, or a settled, single life. In comparison with your friends you can feel suddenly like a poor relation. *It's not fair that you are suffering as you do – and others aren't.* If you hide such feelings from yourself, you feel irritable – but not know why. If you admit to any such feelings, you feel miserably ashamed – and wonder whether anyone could like you if they knew.

You can lose friends because you are simply too pre-occupied and crazed: you have virtually nothing to offer friends for a long while. It is shocking, threatening – and also boring – for friends to see us so maddened, for such a long time. What is impressive is those friends and family who *do* stay and share with us – some of the time – in the bad times as well as the good: those who put up with us when we are grouchy and inaccessible; crazed and manic; panicky and hopeless.

You may wish they could be a fairy godmother and make everything all right. They may wish it too – but they can't. What they can offer is their support: it doesn't make everything *all right*, but however imperfect, it is a real consolation.

Be grateful. Honour them. Protect them from too many demands.

INTERNAL LOSSES

As well as these external losses there are internal wounds, which can be even harder to make sense of and manage.

Feeling connected

A spider constructs an intricate web that sways in the breeze and yet is held in place by stretching filaments between various tethering points in the branches. So we too – and often taken for granted – feel held by attachments to family, friends, work, a community of others with shared interests – as well as by attachments to others who reach out to us through religion, music, writing and the arts: all these connections may make us feel part of a larger whole.

When one of our main tethering attachments, the one to our partner, snaps the whole structure of that web – of our sense of worth, and of hopes and resilience in bonds of any sort – can feel at risk of collapse.

Loneliness

> I'm lonely and sometimes I'm desperate and want to die. But it passes . . .
>
> Writer, Tim Lott[7]

In the sunny moments breaking up can feel freeing, an adventure, a new start – but it also leaves you exposed to icy winds where you suddenly feel devastatingly alone.

The loneliness that Lott refers to is not only the need for company, but also the need to feel connected in any way at all. The web of everything that connected you: the *you* who you had felt yourself to be – who matters, what matters – is torn apart. You lurch between heights of excitement – and despair. At your lowest, loving sympathy and support barely touch you. You are in a separate universe, utterly alone.

> A few weeks after her husband left, Jane signed on at a local gym where, among a series of questions, they asked about her next of kin in case of an emergency.
>
> She looked blank: She had no one. Her children were too young. Her parents were too old. She felt cut off from friends. The one she was still centrally bound to, and had been for years, had left.
>
> If she had a heart attack in the gym she was not sure whether her estranged husband would be concerned enough to help. She thought he would probably be pleased if she died.
>
> Because she would be pleased if he were to drop dead.

You may recognise, sometimes for the first time, your need for firm connections and without them how alone and at risk you are. In your anxiety you can want to cling on to your attachment to your lost partner – when what may help you more is to firm up your connections with those who are still there for you, and to reach out to others. Individual friendships are very important as can sharing in a community activity of some sort.

It's easy, when your self-esteem is low, to withhold your full effort – because you are fearful of failing. But if you are reaching out to others, and do so half-heartedly, you are likely to invite a less than whole-hearted response – which can then seem proof that you are unlikable and unwanted.

Letting others matter to you is a risk – but so is protecting yourself by not letting anyone be of real value to you.

Loss of self-worth

Some of the shock and loss of a partnership are shared by those who lose a partner through their death. They too face the gaping sense of loss, loneliness and insecurity in the absence of their mate. But there are important differences: losing a partner through death is likely to stir up greater sadness, but the loss of your partner as a result of loss of love leaves both of you doubting your worth.

Consider a couple who have been together a number of years: not a perfect couple but one with the normal combination of satisfaction and frustration. If one dies unexpectedly, the partner will probably be devastated. He (or she) will go through all the stages of mourning – of disbelief, pining, anger and sorrow. They may remember difficult times – the disappointments, rows or betrayals – which will be a source of distress and guilt. But they are also more likely to remember the good times they shared: what they loved about their now-lost partner and all the ways in which they had felt loved. They will think of all that they might have shared in the future had the partner not been so cruelly taken. The sorrow is agonising: the world will feel a less safe place. But his (or her) fundamental feelings of trust and self-worth are likely to remain intact.

This is not so if you leave, or are left.

Leaving

> I just can't stop thinking about it. I just can't get it out of
> my mind.
>   There's nothing you can do with things like that.
> You can only hope to co-exist with them. They never go
> away. They're always with you. They're just – there . . .
>   Martin Amis[8]

To leave you will need to selectively perceive the reality and
you will remind yourself of the worst version of your marriage: how bad things were; all your partner's faults and
failings; why what you feel for them is not love, sympathy
or appreciation – and maybe never really was.

  Focusing on the difficulties in the partnership helps to
justify your leaving – and enables you to feel less guilty –
but leaves you with a shrivelled version of the past. It
makes leaving less painful, but at the cost of destroying
something essential to your well-being: of a view of yourself
as having ever been loved and loving.

  If you have any good memories of the lost partnership –
which would bolster your self-esteem – it leaves you vulnerable to agonising guilt and sadness. If you can push
your partner into outrage, it will support your view of them
as *bad* and *worth leaving*. But in all the mud they will fling
at you, some is likely to stick – and to contribute to your
sense of having done something unforgivably *bad*.

If you are the one to leave, you have to face all the responsibility of being the *bad* one – which can seem horribly
unfair:

> Penny left her pleasant but passive husband: she felt that
> he had never really had his heart in making their rela-
> tionship work. She deeply resented it that, yet again, she
> was the one who had to take the action: she had to bear
> all the guilt and doubt – while others felt sorry for her ex,
> who was seen as the victim.

Being left

When you lose your partner through death, you may face desperate loneliness; life may feel very unfair – but you still have a memory of your partner's love and commitment to you, however imperfect.

When your partner chooses to leave, he (or she) – who once loved you and who knows you so well – no longer does. You are *unwanted*: the one who is too old, boring, angry, passive, controlling, absent, depressed; too selfish; insufficiently loving, fun, serious, sexy; too flighty; too demanding; too busy . . .

Your partner may have similar feelings of self-doubt – but in leaving, he (or she) can hope to leave all the painful feelings of being *unwanted* in you.

If your partner leaves for a new lover, it is agonising. In your fantasy – and maybe in reality – they are having an exciting sexual time without you. If they think of you at all, you believe, it will only be with pleasure at being away from you. If you suffer, they will probably be pleased and triumphant.

You might believe that it would be easier to bear if your partner was alone too – but a partner who leaves, not as a result of an affair but because he (or she) simply doesn't want to be with you any more, is no less agonising.

Becky supported her husband going away on a trip with some men friends of his: she could see he could do with a break from the demands of life with their two young children. She was horrified that he returned only to tell her that he wanted to live apart. There was apparently no one else involved. He just did not want to be with her any more. Annie felt that losing her husband to a new partner would be less wounding than having to face the fact that he just did not want to be with her.

Sometimes facts emerge which were previously hidden – and which can seem to make a mockery of any belief that the marriage was ever any good.

Pete's view of his apparently happy-enough marriage was overturned by finding out that his wife had had a long-term affair with one of his best friends – and that mutual friends had known about it, but not told him.

What was so hard for him to come to terms with was not so much the fact of the affair, but that his wife – and those he had thought were his friends – had kept it from him for so long. He felt that he could not rely on any good memory at all – he assumed it must have all been a complete sham. It wasn't only his sense of having been loved that was snatched away, but his trust in his own judgement too.

Shame

The loss of worth in your partner's eyes is painful enough, but you also lose any secure sense of your own worth, which is even more disabling. You feel preoccupied, and caught up in a state that is shameful and humiliating for you and – you assume – shocking and repellent to others.

It is such a terrible blow to your pride and self-worth, of being part of a joint endeavour that has failed. However much you know of the number of marriages that come to an end, you may well have believed that you *would* succeed – and humiliatingly you have not. You may have felt – more or less – in control of your life. Instead you feel powerless and desperate, and it may feel that the only thing you can do is to hide this hatefully, shamefully, needy *you* away. The trouble is that this leaves you at risk of not being able to be close to anyone – and increasingly isolated.

Sharing shock and devastation with fellow travellers can be invaluable. Like survivors from a plane crash, or like the Ancient Mariner, you may need to talk about this disaster endlessly in an attempt to make some sense of it. It is a great help, and often creates a tremendous bond, to find that there are others out there in the world who face – or have in the past faced – something similar: that you are not entirely alone. It can be so helpful to feel supported and understood.

At the same time it is a risk if all those you connect with have the same experience as you. When it comes to moving on from this blow, it can be helpful if one of you has left and the other been left; if one of you is a man, the other a woman; if one of you went through it in the past but has since settled. It can shift the one-sided assumptions that can otherwise seem so tempting to cling on to – such as that:

All men are so . . . or
Women are such . . .

Sally was devastated when her husband left her for another woman. Her friends were immensely sympathetic and many railed at her husband on her behalf. But what helped her most of all was to talk to those – women and men – who had been the one to leave their partner. It helped her to know – however uncomfortably – that people she liked and admired could make the decision to leave, and to know how painful it was for them to have done so.

At this early stage, it didn't make her less furious with her ex – but it made his leaving, potentially understand-able – not just the action of a fool, a madman or a cruel monster.

Loss of innocence

Until your marriage unravelled you are likely to have had a certain innocent view – that *lucky pane of glass*[9] – that, despite any imperfections you are basically loved, lovable and loving. Then suddenly you are not: you find yourself reacting in all kinds of petty, vengeful ways. And the one who was your partner is probably showing you just how hateful and bad you are. You believed in some version of *happily ever after* – and it didn't work out like that.

If you let any of this hateful stuff in, you may dread that you will never recover from self-hatred. If you keep it out and go on the warpath, you are likely to find yourself doing and being all that seems hateful.

You can replace the *lucky pane of glass* with one distorted now by cynicism and mistrust. If you can't resist the excitement offered by self-righteousness and blame, you risk smashing the once *lucky pane of glass* into even more irrecoverable pieces. Or you might, in time, replace that glass with one which allows you to see more clearly: your strengths but also *your* vulnerabilities, difficulties and unrealistic expectations as well as those of your partner. And that could be a basis for a less innocent, but sturdier, view.

Notes

1 Shields, Carol (2003) *Unless*. London: Fourth Estate, p. 1.
2 Garland, Caroline (ed.) (2002) *Understanding Trauma: A psychoanalytical approach*, 2nd edn. London: Karnac.
3 Polly Covell, Missing (unpublished poem).
4 Quoted in Cooke, Rachel (2006) The Amis papers. *Observer*, Review, 1 October.
5 Self, Jonathan (2001) *Self Abuse: Love, loss and fatherhood*. London: John Murray, p. 219.
6 Wallerstein, J.S. and Blakeslee, S. (2004) *Second Chances: Men, women and children a decade after divorce*. Boston, MA: Houghton Mifflin.
7 Lott, Tim (2003) *The Love Secrets of Don Juan*. London: Viking, p. 3.
8 Martin Amis describing the pain of leaving his first wife and children, in Amis (2000) *Experience*. London: Jonathan Cape, p. 159.
9 Shields, *Unless*, p. 1.

6

Rage

Rage is the earliest way we have of dealing with frustration, threat or hurt. A baby who has to wait too long, becomes distressed, arches his back, tenses all his muscles, yells and flails and – if he had the physical capacity – might smash and destroy. His automatic, physiological reaction prepares him for action: for fight or flight.

And as adults under threat – such as when a marriage breaks – we too attempt to get rid of hurt, in any way we can. Creating mayhem can seem exhilarating and such a relief. And if you can't get your way, at least you can hope that by making your partner feel terrible, you can succeed in getting rid of your own pain and panic.

Events that leave you with such painful heartache *shouldn't be allowed*. Maybe *if you scream loud enough . . . somehow everything will be made all right!* Rage makes you feel powerful rather than feeling helpless and hurt. It helps you feel energised instead of feeling despair and grief. Raging at the one you are breaking apart from makes them hateful – and then, with luck, you will be only pleased to see the back of them, not hurt and sad. It allows you to provoke and condemn your ex, rather than notice any doubts about yourself.

When a marriage breaks, it is easy to believe that it doesn't matter if you do the most damage you can, because there is nothing left to protect, or that only your ex will be hurt, and not you too. If in the past battles resolved things or died down, you may assume that current battles will too – and if they don't die down, it does not matter anyway. Why bother to restrain yourself?

But battles are more dangerous than you might expect. Warfare is easy and can be fun to start but – once started – it is much harder to stop than before. It can unravel in shocking ways – in the dirtiness of the bombs used, and the extent of the collateral damage.

The rules have changed. In the past the relationship was based on wanting to find a way through and stay together – and now at least one of you doesn't. In the past you might have taken time out from an argument, calmed down and reflected on your partner's point of view. A hurtful remark, or a blatantly biased point of view, could be quickly challenged. Now both of you are left to stew in isolation.

When any discussion is renewed – even if one of you is ready to compromise – the other may be still in a state of outrage. Subtle provocations – a look, a tone of voice, a taunting disregard – can whip the frenzy up once more. Hatred now is all too easily inflamed – and it burns a long time.

The end of the partnership removes many of the constraints that, up till now, had supported you both. This territory is new and lawless. You can feel so full of hurt and venom. It's like drivers playing *Chicken* on the roads:

They will pull back before there's a head-on crash – won't they?

Don't count on it. In this inflamed, dangerously wounded, frame of mind, killing your former partner – physically or emotionally – could seem the ultimate victory and killing yourself could feel a not-so-bad solution to the problem of how to go on living.

Betrayal

It was not an enemy that reviled me
or I might have borne it:
it was not my foe that dealt so insolently with me
or I might have hidden myself from him.

But it was you a man like myself
my companion and my familiar friend.[1]

(Psalm 55)

In break-up, part of the immense hurt and outrage is that
the one who is rejecting is someone who knows you so
intimately, who could not have been a more *familiar friend*.

A particular betrayal is if the one who leaves – to avoid
guilt – *reviles* the past relationship and his (or her) partner
as having never been of value. This is a dangerous strategy
– for a partner who feels that he (or she) has been made
vile is likely to explode in retaliatory rage – which all too
easily spirals. That is when fury is likely to curdle into
hatred and a wish for vengeance.

> Jo had plenty of resentments of her husband, Nick, as he
> did of her. She knew things were very difficult between
> them, but thought that when outside pressures calmed
> down, they would find each other again. She still had in
> mind the man she had fallen in love with, years ago: of
> the many good times they had shared; what good com-
> panions they could be; their shared investment and pleas-
> ure in their children.
>
> But Nick now claimed that it had been wrong from
> the start – all those years ago. Jo looked at him aghast.
> How could he so coolly deny all the countless good times?
> The Nick she had known had been honourable: surely he
> would have acknowledged the good things he was
> leaving as well as the bad? He might have left – but not in
> this sleazy way.
>
> Jo felt stolen from, betrayed, and that was when she
> started to hate Nick – rather than just hating the hurt he
> was causing. She despised him. He was weak and pathetic.
> She would fight for all she could get: if he lived in penury
> – he deserved it. She didn't care if all the money went to
> the lawyer – anything was better than Nick getting more.

Hatred

Hatred is different from anger. When you are angry you
still want the other to hear you. You may be furious with

him (or her), but you still want to reach them: they are worth the effort. There is still some hope.

Hatred is more dangerous, more malignant than anger. When you hate your ex, you lose any awareness of anything good in them: they are useless, worthless, contemptible. You aren't interested in negotiation or compromise: you want to control, punish and humiliate them; you want vengeance.

Hurting the one by whom you feel so hurt becomes more important than protecting yourself. It is addictive: exhilaratingly black and white. There is the thrill of self-justification and virtue; the pleasure of superiority, power and contempt; the satisfaction of demolishing the other. There is the immense buzz of the fight – as those who play *space invaders* know – even when the *enemy* is only a blip on a computer screen. And when you hate, your adversary means nothing more to you than a crudely represented *space invader*, a worthless blip to blast away.

But just as you wish to destroy your enemy, so they will you – and you will need to protect yourself rigidly against attack, and prepare to shoot them down before they do you. Feeling so full of hatred, you are implacable, intractable.

Polly Covell wrote of the explosive power of her rage following the break-up of her marriage:

I rammed concrete
round. Underpinned
arms, legs and anywhere
more dangerous.
Coolant steamed
round my core. No-one
remembered to connect
the Geigers.
I feared I'd melt
the permafrost and burn right through
the arse end, out
in hissing distance
of Uluru.
A nugget,
glinting, black, immensely dense,

almost certainly
lethal.[2]

The poet's hatred contaminates everyone she is within
hissing distance of: she is *almost certainly lethal.*

If no *coolant* or *concrete* is applied, the effects can be catastrophic – as they are in *Othello*. Othello, who believes his
wife Desdemona is unfaithful to him, cries out:

She's gone; I am abus'd; and my relief
Must be to loathe her . . .[3]

All my fond love thus do I blow to heaven:
'Tis gone. –
Arise, black vengeance, from the hollow hell!
Yield up, O love, thy crown and hearted throne
To tyrannous hate![4]

The impact is catastrophic in this play where Othello kills
his wife but often – if less dramatically – in everyday life
after break-up. In the aftermath of a broken partnership
there is so much opportunity for sabotage and mayhem.
Resentment and provocation can be expressed in many
ways: from the subtly irritating, such as managing to be
late *again*, or paying, but never quite on time; sniping at
the other parent or a pained silence at the mention of their
name. It is so easy to criticise directly or undermine your
ex's attempts to parent well; to be subtly bullying – or to
use overt intimidation and violence.

He lashes out. She is witheringly scornful. He withholds
payments. She creates difficulty with access. He is unreliable visiting. She slags him off. He does her . . . They
continue to rehearse the wrongs done by their ex in court, if
they can afford it – or to anyone else who will listen. Your
partner suffers – but so do you; and so do your kids. And it is
so hard to stop.

The impact of ongoing hatred on children

Fathers who punish their ex-wives by not paying child
support regularly or in full – as many don't – punish their
children too.[5] Mothers who are frantic about paying bills

don't mother well. Nor do those who have to work additionally long hours away from home and are exhausted.

Mothers who are embittered at their children's father are not able to help them have any balanced view of him. And the impact on their children is poignantly and extensively documented.

A father's exclusion from seeing his children – sometimes out of anxiety, whether realistic or over-anxious, about the harm he may do but also sometimes for reasons drummed up by a vengeful mother – is a source of desperate sadness for the father and for the children.[6] But a father who deals with this threat by bullying is even more likely to alarm the mother – and possibly the authorities too – about his capacity to parent his children well.

About half of parents manage a low-level truce by simply ignoring the presence of the other; only a quarter of parents have managed to sufficiently let go their enmity that, ten years after breaking up, they can be flexible and discuss issues concerning their children together in their children's best interests.

The impact of ongoing hatred on you

You have only to look at international conflicts that persist over years and generations – which look back to past grievances to justify fresh outrages and counterattack – to see how easy it is to go along with the inflaming of conflict and how hard it is to accept compromise and restraint. Each attack justifies the next counterattack: casualties create increasingly desperate enmity. Hatred and bitterness grow. Peace does not automatically break out with the passage of time.

It is easy to believe that if only you can dominate, outwit and subdue your now-unwanted partner sufficiently they will collapse, admit defeat, take all the blame – and you will be *justified, vindicated: the victor! Triumphant!*

But you know, really, that the world does not work like that – whether in personal or in international relations. Unjust settlements have provided the justification for further wars throughout history and when power is unequal, retaliation comes in hidden ways – through sabotage and terrorism.

You may have immense sympathy with the multiple traumas that led to the emergence of Israel, and its need to feel secure – but many fear that its strategy of retaliating immensely hard at any attack, hoping to intimidate its opponents, has made it less secure rather than more so.

You may understand the trauma that 9/11 had on the American people, and the wish to punish the perpetrators and ensure that such an attack does not happen again – but few would argue, with hindsight, that going to war without a clear strategy for an enduring peace is helpful.

Similarly when a partnership breaks, you need to keep in mind the end game – not just the brutal opening salvos.

I am tempted to edit out the last three paragraphs, aware of the acute sensitivities on all sides. And similarly when a marriage breaks passions run desperately high – and there can be a pressure on friends, family and professionals too, to *only* sympathise with you and take your side, hiding any dismay about the impact of your implacable view.

In fact, however infuriatingly, what might be more helpful is to hear not only that your ex may be an *absolute bastard/bitch* but that they may have reasons to behave the way they do – sometimes in response to your actions.

American clinicians working with couples caught up in intractable battles after divorce found that what could be very effective was to see divorced couples in two groups, mixing men and women, leavers and left.[7] It was so helpful to have someone who could see and express the view of the so-hated ex – while not being caught up in the passionate battle.

The support you need from your friends and family – and your lawyer – is to be there for you, but not to add fuel to your outrage and hatred of your ex. And it can help you to get him (or her) to stop.

The cost of holding on to grievance

When it comes to managing life after break-up, you have some choice in continuing to extract your pound of flesh –

or you can choose to let go of the grievance – and make it easier for both of you to move on.

> Paul was devastated when his wife, Caro, left him. At first he pleaded with her to come back. He could see that he had not been responsive in many ways to her and he promised to try so much harder.
>
> When Caro did not come back, Paul became angry. His feelings of grievance did not change as the years passed – not even after he settled down with a new partner.
>
> His behaviour did have an impact – as he hoped it would: it was hard for Caro to bear. It also made it more difficult for their children, who felt they were living in a cold war state.

Paul had moved away from the state of mind where he was able to acknowledge any responsibility for the break-up – and in that way he felt relieved. But as well as being a terrible cost to his kids it almost certainly was to him too – for living in a state of grievance is sapping of energy and liveliness.

> Peter described himself as having 'no baggage' from his marriage. He was bright, attractive, funny, was a good dancer, sharp – a bit uncomfortably sharp. When he had drunk a bit he got on the subject of his former wife, and how much maintenance he paid her after a relatively short marriage. It didn't seem he could really like or trust women very much.

Peter's apparent 'lightness' covered over something he still felt bitter about. And, despite his other attractive qualities, it got in the way of him developing a relationship with someone new.

Corrosion of self-worth

> 'War . . . deforms not only the soul of the invader, but also poisons with hatred and so deforms the souls of

those who try to oppose the invader . . .' Yes, to leave war behind meant to internally cleanse oneself, first and foremost to cleanse oneself of hatred . . .

We know that it does not only begin with bombs and rockets, but with fanaticism and pride, stupidity and contempt, ignorance and hatred. It feeds on all that, grows from that.

Journalist, Ryszard Kapuscinski[8]

Despite all that you may hope, warfare doesn't leave you happy, powerful and *innocent* – or only brittley so. And it has a devastating cost.

You are contaminated: the battle disrupts your sleep, colonises you as you prepare for the next attack, saps the energy that you need for moving on in life. How can you feel yourself as potentially lovable by anybody, when you are so full of poison and bile?

If you feel full of hatred, hurt and the wish to punish, then you must assume that your ex harbours similar, if not worse, feelings towards you. Feeling hateful towards and hated by the one you once loved and felt loved by is an uneasy state of mind. Not only do you feel that your ex is out to cheat and hurt you, you can become suspicious of the whole world.

Wishing for the other's death

Divorce: the incredibly violent thing. What parent, involved in it, has not wished for the death of the once-loved one? This is universal. And this is why your heart feels gangrenous inside your chest. This is why (as I put it to myself) you want men in white to come and take you away and wash your blood.

Martin Amis[9]

Probably all couples who break up wish the other would just die – and some of the satisfaction of the battle is the possibility that your partner could be sufficiently provoked to have a heart attack or drive into a motorway bridge.

It seems as if it would be so much easier to mourn a partner who has died. If he (or she) had died, it would not be such a terrible blow to your self-worth. You would be able to remember fondly all the good memories of the partnership now lost, letting any irritations and difficulties slip out of sight.

Rather than having to leave your partner and feeling guilty and *bad*, their death would have freed you – but you would be supported by sympathetic well-wishers and friends; you would still be *good* in their, and your, eyes. Rather than facing the hurt and the humiliation of being left, your partner's death would leave you bearing equal loss and loneliness – but not the agony of feeling unwanted.

If only your partner had died, there would not be the same practical and financial difficulties to face: family income would not need to be divided between two households. There might be no need to move from the family home. The impoverishment – emotional as well as financial – would be so much less.

If your partner had died, he (or she) would not remain out there in the world as a potential irritant: their success or happiness would not stimulate your feelings of rivalry or envy; their difficulties would not make you feel concerned or guilty – even if you felt triumphant too.

But harbouring such deadly feelings towards the one who was your partner contaminates your sense of your worth: why your *heart feels gangrenous*; why you want someone to *wash your blood*.

In fact, your partner dying might not have turned out to be quite as easy for you to deal with as you might believe. Those studied after the death of a partner, where the relationship had been hostile, had more difficulty mourning and were more likely to get caught in chronic mourning and depression.[10]

It may help to know too that – if you can recover from the blow of break-up – there are advantages of your partner *not* dying.

When Annie's husband left her and their young children she was gutted. Nothing could be worse than this! Five years on, she was not so sure. A friend's husband had died shortly before her own break-up. She could see how hard it must be for her friend's son never to see his father again.

Her kids came back from seeing their father, and although they missed him and his daily presence in their lives, they still gained a lot from him: she was glad he was around to offer them his support. She also began to appreciate the freedom it gave her when her kids were staying with their Dad.

Though the pain of her marriage breaking up had been much greater at the time than being widowed, looking back – and in certain moods – Annie thought the additional pain was offset by advantages of her ex still being alive. It made Annie feel better no longer wishing her ex had died: she felt less 'gangrenous'.

The downside of blame

There are many advantages of identifying your partner as the *wrong* one, whose *fault* it all is. But there are downsides too.

If your world view is so black and white, so full of moral fervour; if mistakes and being at fault are so *unforgivable*, so *contemptible*, then how can you accept yourself if *you* are anything less than entirely perfect? If, even momentarily, you recognise any faults of your own, your sense of moral triumph becomes shaky. You might have to face feelings of doubt, guilt, shame and worry about the damage you have contributed to – and if you are so scathingly unforgiving, how can you possibly face up to that?

Only if you are less viciously condemnatory of all your partner's faults, will it feel safe enough to notice you have any faults of your own.

Blaming the other and refusing to take any responsibility is the stuff of all battles. If you have any real interest in finding a way through, then – like international peace negotiators – you need to begin to listen, however grudgingly, to your partner. You need to face the fact that –

irritatingly, threateningly – your partner may have a point too.

If it is not only your partner that was *bad* (selfish, mean, unfair . . .) but there are ways in which you were too – and may continue to be – the world becomes less black and white: there are more shades of grey. In one way this can feel a relief: you are no longer in a terrifying war zone but rather in a dispute where arguments can be made and some sort of compromise worked out. But it can feel dreary and disappointing to have to abandon the pleasure and the thrill of complete virtue and self-justification.

Peace may be calmer than warfare. Life can resume – but it also faces everyone with the more mundane struggles and disappointments of everyday life. And when some sort of peace formula *is* painfully arrived at, how easily an assassination or a terrorist bomb can smash it up. Look at Northern Ireland, at Israel/Palestine, former Yugoslavia, Iraq . . .

We all of us have suicide bombers inside us, all too ready to respond to the thrill of mayhem and sabotage: all too ready to focus, once again, on our ex's outrages as a way of not having to face our own difficulties and sadness.

If you can allow a cease-fire to happen and when it is broken, as it will be, by bombs – inadvertent or deliberate – and manage to hold your fire and think, rather than rushing into frenzied overkill then you start to slow this spiral of violence and make a – sometimes uneasy but ongoing – peace more likely.

You can play some part in restraining your partner's hatred. If he (or she) is the equivalent of a crazed gunman holding a shotgun at your head, you are unlikely to get them to put their *gun* down by yelling: they are more likely to pull the trigger. You are more likely to defuse things if you are calm; genuinely attempt to understand their point of view; and point out what is in their best interests and your children's – as well as your own.

If you won't listen when your partner tries to tell you something important, what other way can he (or she) get you to attend but to yell or threaten? If you yell and threaten them, they are more likely to lash out or retaliate

– physically or indirectly, but no less infuriatingly. If you want to try to get off this treadmill:

- Be clear as you can about ground rules.
- Be straight.
- Don't criticise – ask for what you want.
- If you or your partner get infuriated, stop. Say you're willing to talk tomorrow when you're less furious.
- Wait. Don't retaliate straight away. Sleep on it.
- Think back to your long-term goal.
- Keep your children's best interests – for a good relation with both parents – in mind.

Rage and hatred, up to a point, may be necessary in letting go of the one you once loved. It can be a self-protective defence – but it is limiting if you never let that guard down and allow yourself to experience other feelings such as guilt and grief. If you really can't or won't bear to know about these other feelings, you will need to keep on fanning the red hot embers into a permanent conflagration – and that is dangerous.

In the meantime, if you can't yet let go of your fury, it might help to channel your rage as constructively as possible:

THE BEST REVENGE IS TO HAVE A GOOD LIFE.

Not to show him (– or her): but for you – because you deserve it.

Notes

1 Psalm 55, 12–13.
2 Polly Covell, Lethal (unpublished poem).
3 Shakespeare, *Othello*, III. iii. 267–268.
4 *Othello*, III. iii. 445–449.
5 Child Support Agency figures suggest that one-third of fathers don't pay.
  Hetherington and Kelly suggest that less than half of fathers pay in full: Hetherington, E.M. and Kelly, J. (2002) *For Better or for Worse: Divorce reconsidered*. London: Norton.

6 O'Connor, Matt (2007) *Fathers 4 Justice: The inside story.* London: Weidenfeld & Nicolson.
  Rayburn, Tina and Foster, Timothy (2007) *I Want to See my Kids! A guide for dads who want contact with their children after separation.* London: Fusion.
7 Johnston, J.R. and Campbell, L.E.G. (1988) *Impasses of Divorce: The dynamics and resolution of family conflict.* New York: Free Press.
8 Kapuscinski, Ryszard (2004) When there is talk of war. *Granta,* 88. Reviewed in *The Independent,* Review, 4 January 2005.
9 Amis, Martin (2000) *Experience.* London: Jonathan Cape, p. 257.
10 Bowlby, John (1998) *Loss: Sadness and depression.* Volume 3 of *Attachment and Loss.* London: Pimlico.

7

Legal battles

The impossibility of a *fair* share

After break-up, there are many reasons to feel deprived and cheated – and demanding more. Financially, making the family budget – which once covered one family – now stretch to two households, and maybe two mortgages, is a shocking loss.

Although legally divorce is now *no fault*, emotionally we still expect it to be so: the more you are angry with your *guilty*, *bad* partner, the more you want to deprive and punish him (or her) and have everything yourself. Even when the financial sums involved are not extreme, they can represent much more than money alone – but what is *fair*; who is *good*; and who is getting *cheated*.

But there is no *fair* share of children, when both parents love them and don't want to lose them. Should children's time with each parent be divided down the middle to be scrupulously *fair* to both parents? This is almost certainly *unfair* to children, who need a stable, secure base – as well as the best possible relationship with the non-resident parent.

When there are not huge assets it is far from clear how these assets should be fairly divided up. If there are children at home, the primary parent – generally the mother – often gets a larger share in order to provide a family home for the children. If this is *fair*, what, quite, should that bigger share reasonably be? How *deprived* should a father be expected to be, so that his ex and their children remain in relative comfort?

A mother with children still at home may be given maintenance for herself, as well as financial support for the children. While this may reflect a continuing need for her to be available for children, it can feel *unfair* to her former husband, who no longer directly benefits from her efforts in running the home. He may fear that his ex may avoid looking for a job more from a wish to deprive him, than from a real concern for the best needs of their children. The mother may feel that she is being pushed into earning – regardless of any needs their young children have of her – more to satisfy her ex's need for *fairness* than for any other reason.

If there is a new partner living with one parent, should his (or her) income be put into the pot to be divided up between the two new households – or should it be ignored? There is no *fair* answer. And for those who were not legally married, the lack of clarity and room for battle is even greater.

Legally the fair balance is not as clear as it first looks. Technically in England and Wales family assets are now divided equally, regardless of who contributed what (since a ruling, White v. White); there is a formula for calculating child support developed by the (now abandoned) Child Support Agency (CSA), based on a percentage of earnings, the number of children and the amount of time they are with the non-resident parent. Even so, one Mayfair divorce lawyer described a divorce settlement as a *'moveable feast'*.[1]

When one of the partners is a footballer, a rock star, or a dot.com millionaire, there may be much to fight for. For the rest of us it would be much more helpful to have clear guidelines for what the *fair share* should be – as happens in other parts of Europe.

The absence of such guidelines may have dubious advantages of flexibility, but in practice the lack of clarity invites participation in a dangerously addictive game. And those who get caught up in a legal battle can often feel caught up in a giant system, which seems more in the interests of the legal profession, rather than the hurt and angry clients.

Access to children

There is much room for hurt, fear and fury about access to children after break-up. If one-quarter of men resort to physical violence around the time of break-up, particularly in response to a partner's wish to leave;[2] and if most men and women react to the stress of break-up by becoming volatile, dishonest and punitive – in big and small ways – there is all kinds of evidence to assume that you are suddenly seeing the *real* side of your partner that you had never noticed so clearly before, and they the *real* you.[3] It can leave each of you with fears about the other's capacity to offer any sort of safe parenting for your children.

In addition to that concern, you will have other motives that drive you: wanting to punish and hurt him (or her); wanting to be powerful when you otherwise feel so helpless; fearing the loss of your children's love for you if they spend too much time with your ex; and having to manage your own loneliness when your children are away from you.

In the UK there is no automatic legal assumption that a father will have access, including overnight stays, unless there are overriding reasons why he should not. A father whose ex makes it impossible for him to see his children will have little power to change this until he gets to the First Directions hearing. A father who is not married to his children's mother has few automatic rights to see his children or to have a say in their upbringing. This can put men whose partners refuse to let them see their children for whatever combination of reasons – good or bad – in a terrible Catch-22. If he doesn't fight for his children, will he be seen by his children and by the courts as uncaring – and therefore undeserving of access? But if he does fight desperately, will he be seen as aggressive and therefore not safe for the children to be with?

In the last awful dog-days before his marriage fell apart, Jim had been furious and had hit out at everything – the walls and his wife, Lou, and had yelled frighteningly at his kids. After she kicked him out, Lou wouldn't let him spend more than the odd hour with his kids. He was so angry with her, he took some pleasure in turning up late, or bringing them back later than he'd promised. She was furious when he returned and would threaten him with not letting him see the children at all. When Jim found a place that was nowhere near as nice as his old home – but the best he could do in the circumstances – Lou wouldn't let them come overnight.

Jim fought in the courts and won a right to have the kids overnight. Lou refused to comply. Jim in desperation – and in a furious wish to punish Lou – applied for full custody. Lou was so locked into her conviction that she would not let her kids spend time with their Dad that she was seen by the courts as intransigent and bad. They awarded custody to Jim.

At which point Lou, in her desperate anxiety that Jim – in his fury at her – would hurt the children, went into hiding for several years.

It can be nearly impossible then to unravel how realistic or not Lou's fears might have been. Was Jim's anger so destructive that the only recourse was to keep him away from his children? How much was her perception of his dangerousness swollen by her attacks on him – and her dread of his retaliation? And how could the courts in this situation have done anything other than *side* with one or the other? Lou had 'won' in that she had protected her children from the man she feared would harm them, but her children had grown up in fear and secrecy. They had no view of their father as someone who may have difficulty managing his anger but might also have anything positive; instead he was only a *monster*.

As in financial issues, so in disputes over children, British law continues to insist on the *differences* between divorcing families rather than focusing on the similarities – which might lead to firm, clear guidelines.

There is evidence from an Early Interventions project that has been running successfully in Florida that clear legal guidelines can help regarding access to children.[4] There, the father is automatically entitled to have access to his children unless there is a legal decision that he should not. Divorcing parents have to attend classes on the destructive impact of ongoing battle on their children; they have to attend mediation sessions to help find ways to cooperate in parenting their children.

In the UK where this has been tried out, sadly the key features have been watered down. Fathers still have no automatic right to see their children after break-up, and attendance at parenting classes and mediation is voluntary. The take-up of these services is low and – not surprisingly – they are not seen as particularly useful.[5]

The lawyer

Lawyers differ in their legal skills, their taste for compromise, and in their capacity to be firm and clear with you. You can ask for recommendations for a good lawyer but you still need to make your own judgement – with few facts to base it on. Just because a lawyer seems sure of his (or her) view does not mean they are right or that they can negotiate well, or think clearly under the pressure of court. There are no league tables to help you assess a solicitor's claim that what you should be seeking is reasonable or over-optimistic. It would be so helpful to know information such as:

- Does this lawyer have a track record of losing cases because she claims too much?
- Does that lawyer compromise too early and leave his client feeling let down?

Divorce lawyers may genuinely believe that *getting the most* for you financially is in your best interests. They may not understand the stress of the legal battle; nor of the importance for you to find a settlement that offers a basis for a future peace (unless they have been through a similar experience themselves). Lawyers may not consider the emotional cost – but you need to.

We can all be reluctant to believe the solicitor who tells us, however sympathetically, that there is only so much to share out: that – however hurt and angry we are – we won't get it all our own way. By choosing to go to the lawyers who tempt us to expect more, we teach lawyers to avoid reminding us of these painful truths.

There are professional pressures on lawyers, which can make them opt for legal contest: it is more exciting, challenging and profitable than the dreary accountancy that a quiet, sad settlement entails. A reputation within the profession as a tough fighter can tempt lawyers to go for the highest possible claim – though the likelihood of a settlement out of court for you is reduced.

The judge

The judge brings his (or her) idiosyncrasies and prejudices – and lawyers are able to make a fair guess at how the case will go only when they find out which judge has been assigned to the case.

The legal process

It looks like the legal process should be straightforward – but in practice it is often less so. There are various websites, such as that of Resolution, formerly the Family Divorce Law Association, which describe clearly the legal process.

Both you and your partner fill out a lengthy document of your income and assets – savings, pension and so on (*form E*). Valuations are made on the house (minus the mortgage), business or other major possessions.

In addition, you are generally asked to fill out a form of your living expenses in great detail. Not only are you asked what are your mortgage, your overdraft, your utility bills and possibly school bills – but also you may be asked to factor in the cost of replacing curtains or having the carpet cleaned. (This seems a time-wasting and potentially provocative exercise since – unless you have a particularly high level of assets and income – it is not a question of what standard of living you had, or hope to maintain, but *how your limited income can fairly be shared between the two of you*: your standard of living will inevitably drop – unless one or both of you have a new partner who is reasonably wealthy.) These sworn testaments are presented at the First Appointment – a generally administrative court procedure, but one which can sometimes be used to achieve a settlement.

Based on the financial disclosure and your separate estimates of living expenses, you each make two claims: the first – in a *Calderbank* letter – is a lower offer of what you will accept if the two of you can settle before coming to court (and which the judge does not see); the second is an *open*, higher claim.

The hope is that with the threat of financial costs of a court hearing, you will negotiate well. But in reality, with time taken for letters to go to and fro, there is often little time before receiving your ex's Calderbank offer and the looming deadline of the court hearing. Having complaints made of you in formal legal language can feel infuriating, pompous and one-sided and can leave you less likely to compromise than more so. You can feel caught up in a fast-moving and unfamiliar current, with little time to think and the pressure of legal costs inexorably ticking.

If you cannot agree, the next step is the Financial Dispute Resolution (FDR) hearing – a preliminary, advisory court. Each side's representatives – a solicitor or a barrister – present your case. The judge offers what their likely view would be if the case were to be presented to him (or her) in full court: it is not a legal judgment. The hope is to knock heads together.

There is no official record of the judicial advice to which you both can refer. Instead, each of your solicitors produce their own summary – which leaves scope for different interpretations. If the judge's advice is not absolutely specific, you may both believe that your position has been endorsed. If your solicitor disagrees with the advice of the judge, you may not know whether to follow their advice and keep on fighting – or not. If you can't find a way to settle the battle now, the next stage is a full hearing – and the costs keep mounting.

The financial cost of battle

Compared to the financial calculations of a weekly budget and whether or not you can afford to buy a new fridge, or even a new car, the spiralling costs of legal fees can be truly breath-taking. It all starts to feel like Monopoly money when the figures add up at such a mad rate – and that is dangerous, because the money is real and someone is going to have to pay it. And you may not necessarily end up with more than you would have had in a tough negotiated settlement.

When you feel aware of so many losses and are full of fury, you may not care if vast amounts of money are spent as long as it leaves less for your ex: anything that deprives them can feel worth it – even if it deprives you too. If you have great wealth, then spending a great deal on lawyers may not matter. If you are on legal aid the bill does not come to you – unless you have a house, when you pay the legal costs on selling. For all the rest of us, between these extremes of wealth and poverty, fighting through the courts is a poor financial risk.

The emotional cost of battle

Whatever the financial arguments, when you fight there is a hefty and unexpected emotional price to pay. Fighting a court battle can consume and terrify you in a way that it's hard to imagine. Solicitors' letters can be adversarial – smug, quietly misleading and with a spin which can seem deliberately inflammatory. It can leave the recipient – whether you or your partner – waking in the night raging and planning a counterattack.

> Jane's solicitor reported to her with glee the letter she had written to Jane's soon-to-be-ex: he should be furious. She expected Jane to be delighted too – and Jane was, in part. But she wondered fleetingly how much it was in her best interests that her ex should be so inflamed.

Fighting court battles offers entertainment of a perverse kind, but the emotional cost, right now – when you have so much else to manage – may be a price you can't afford. You need your energy to slowly digest what feels like poison, to help your kids, to look across the gulf to the future, and begin to make at least short-term plans.

Even if you get a court judgment, the higher the level of bitter feuding, the more room for your ex to avoid complying. There are all-too many cases, and despite the CSA's best efforts, where fathers don't pay court-ordered child support – and cause all kinds of grief and rage in the process. Despite a court ruling that a father should have access to his children, there are many examples of mothers who make it impossible for fathers to do so.

You need to remember that this is not a final battle: there is a future peace to win. If your long-term goal is to avoid chronic, endless feuds you need – however resentfully – to find a deal in which your ex is not grossly deprived.

When the law (expensively) helps

Although it is expensive and brutal, a court case can sometimes be a relatively efficient way of resolving the battle if one or both of you won't compromise sufficiently.

> Brian's wife left. They fought furiously about who was at fault in the break-up and the battle extended into how they should share their (very limited) assets. Brian felt that his ex was demanding outrageously much and he too dug in his heels and would not offer any compromise. He was sure the court would vindicate him.
>
> The judge at the Financial Dispute Resolution (FDR) – unsurprisingly – suggested a compromise. Only then did both – furiously – agree.
>
> Had Brian offered a compromise earlier he would not have had to pay the FDR court costs – but neither he nor his ex could climb down off their high horses. In order to pay his share of the court costs Brian had to sell his flat, which he otherwise might – just – have managed to keep.

Maybe it was only by fighting this far in the courts, and facing the reality of the judge's advice, that each could accept the need to compromise.

What helped them agree, however furiously, was that the judge had provided clear advice and both sets of lawyers were prepared to bang heads together to get a settlement, rather than encouraging further battle.

It is possible though that if their solicitors had been firmer and more realistic with each of them earlier, Brian and his ex-wife might have been able to reach agreement without a need for the FDR, its financial cost, and the emotional turmoil.

When the law makes things worse – a cautionary tale

When lawyers are not clear, realistic and firm, before and during an FDR, both partners may find themselves – however reluctantly – continuing the battle.

> Dave and Ally had hoped their lawyers would help them organise a fair settlement prior to the FDR. Between them, they had already agreed much. But each side's lawyer argued that they were giving away too much, and with lawyers' letters which infuriated them, they ended up further apart. Having been told to expect a round-table discussion prior to an FDR, they were told the differences between their positions were now too great and they found themselves reluctantly in the preliminary court.

They were worse off than they would have been without their solicitors' 'help'.

It was not *only* the solicitors' fault. Ally *knew* the claim put in on her behalf seemed large: she had questioned it – but allowed herself to be lulled by her solicitor. Dave had knowingly *forgotten* a bit of his income: he stood to gain a minor advantage – but at the cost of losing Ally's trust.

> When Ally's barrister, before the FDR, saw the claim advised by the solicitor, she thought it was too high and submitted a new, lower, position.

Had the solicitor made the lower claim earlier, they might have been able to compromise prior to the FDR. It was bad advice from the solicitor, which Ally had queried, but she had taken a passive position assuming the lawyer *knew best* – and that was dangerous.

> The barrister told Ally the new position was not one for negotiation but that she should expect the full amount – which included staying in their family house. In court, the judge advised that the family house would have to be sold. Back in the discussion room (where Ally withdrew with her barrister and solicitor) her barrister aggressively told her she must give up her plan to remain in the family house – but Ally had not prepared herself to consider this possibility. From previously being overly reassured, Ally felt suddenly threatened and intimidated – and was less able to think clearly.

Of course Ally's barrister should have prepared her to be flexible and consider all possibilities – even if she still hoped to get all that she was arguing for. Had Ally known how daunting the whole experience would be, she would have brought a clear-headed friend or relative to court: they would not have been able to come into the court room itself, but they would have been there to support her in the discussion room, to reduce her anxiety and help her think clearly in the discussion with her lawyers.

> Possibly because it was a Friday afternoon, her team did not stay as she had been led to expect, to discuss with her, and her ex's team, until they had brokered a solution. And they made no arrangements to do so. Ally was dumb-founded.

A clear-headed friend would have been able to argue for continuing longer – even if after a break for a cigarette, a cup of coffee or a scotch. A friend would not have let the meeting finish so inconclusively, without arrangements for a further meeting. Ally had assumed that her solicitor would have taken this role for her – but she did not.

The judge had made a general ruling – that the house would need to be given up – but not a specific one about what a fair division of assets was.

That evening, Dave argued that he had been completely vindicated. Ally thought it was much less clear than that – but there was no official court record to rely on. After waiting over a week, at her wits' end and with no response to her enquiries, Ally wrote her solicitor a frustrated letter. At which point her solicitor replied that since Ally had lost confidence in her, she was not willing to act for her further.

Ally expected her solicitor to be able to tolerate and respond to a frustrated letter of complaint – and was astonished and horrified that she did not.

Unlike the medical profession, who would be considered negligent if they withdraw in the middle of an urgent case, lawyers it seems can do so. Though solicitors are advised by their professional society to take complaints seriously, without feeling personally attacked, if they do not, there is no comeback for the client – unless the client wants to risk further money by making a claim of negligence.

Finally, with a new team, almost a year later, Ally found herself, reluctantly, in full court. Because Dave's company had not been valued jointly, but there were contested valuations, the hearing went on for three days. Final costs were little short of £100,000.

The settlement reached was – unsurprisingly – somewhere between their two original positions.

If Ally and Dave had managed to agree, as they had originally intended, they would have had to give up claiming all they felt they were entitled to. They had each 'won' a little from their original fight – but at the cost of paying huge court fees. The extra money had gone on paying their lawyers, rather than being available to reduce the mortgages on their new homes.

For Ally, far greater than the enormous legal cost was the cost of the immense time and energy that had been taken up in the maddening battle and which she had needed for herself and her kids. Dave too had been so consumed with the battle that he had all but lost his company.

The surprising disadvantages of winning

You might reluctantly recognise the disadvantages of fighting – but what if you *win?* What about the tempting prize of being judged *right*, being *the good guy!* Maybe it's worth the risk for that?

Even then, if you are found *right* and your ex *wrong*, it's not the end game. If you get an unfairly good settlement you may feel judicially endorsed in being the *wounded party*. To justify yourself you need to stay bitter – because if you don't, you could begin to feel uneasy.

Linda was a beautiful, rather indulged woman. Her husband Jonathan was besotted with their three children. He had never expected to stray; he had not taken advantages of opportunities for affairs for years – until he fell for a woman he worked with, and she became pregnant.

Of course Linda was devastated and enraged. Jonathan felt terribly guilty and was willing to give up a lot so that his family could stay in their former home. Possibly in part because of her appealing beauty, the judge awarded Linda the house plus a large part of Jonathan's income.

You might have expected it to simmer down from there – but it didn't.

Linda was not able to help her children understand or forgive their father in any way. Five years on their now-adolescent children refuse to see their father, who has so much to offer them in the way of concern and care. They speak to him only when they want more money from him. They have lost the benefits of a devoted father. Linda has the gratification of feeling vindicated in her view of how unforgivably bad Jonathan is. But she is still caught up in it – and is not internally free to move on.

ALTERNATIVES TO ADVERSARIAL LEGAL BATTLE

Direct negotiations

There are possible advantages of negotiating directly. Once solicitors take over negotiations between a divorcing couple, much flexibility is lost. An accusation made face to face can be instantly rebutted, misunderstandings can be clarified. When negotiating stances are made in writing by a solicitor, tempers often rise and any wish to find a compromise can become lost.

On the other hand, face to face there is also the risk of tempers fraying and outrage and provocation taking over. Negotiating without a solicitor's help can leave you exposed to pressures to concede in an unfair way.

To the degree that you can stop rising to the bait and provoking each other, agreements which you do make will save time and money with the lawyers. It depends on trust rather than bullying or evading: as soon as you do that your chance of compromising will get lost. You don't have to have solved *everything*; there may still be areas left to resolve, but it is likely that these agreements you make together are likely to last better than when you have been dragged screaming to the courts and at least one of you is bitterly disappointed with the results.

Mediation

Mediation is now considered a better way for a fair resolution, but it depends just as much on the skills and weaknesses of the negotiator. It is a tough task to stay firmly anchored between a couple, both of whom are determined to be in the right and have it all. The conciliator can feel under pressure to concede to the one who exerts most charm, persuasiveness or threat: he (or she) may be no less vulnerable than a judge to pressure or to personal whim.

Sharon's marriage broke up when he started an affair. They agreed to mediation. Her experience was that her ex was charming, persuasive – and hiding assets. She felt, bitterly, that the woman mediator had been taken in by him. She was furious with the final settlement, which felt so unfair. She wished she had fought in court.

(In fact she could still have chosen to go on to the courts at this stage had she wished.)

Counselling

Some family divorce lawyers are now responding to defects in the system and are initiating new procedures. One of these is the recognition that legal advice is not always what is needed, but sometimes that of a counsellor:

> Because Caro felt so guilty for leaving her husband – and despite her solicitor's strenuous advice – she gave up a large part of her claim to a share of the family house; she felt she did not deserve it.
> Some years later she felt that she had been foolish and wished that she had fought for her equal share.

If Caro had been given counselling to manage her immense guilt at leaving her family, she might have felt more able to claim her fair share.

Sometimes a legal mediator is present, plus another with counselling qualifications. Another relatively new initiative is to have both of the divorcing couple with their respective lawyers in the room (or sometimes, if necessary, in adjoining rooms) – and the negotiation takes place over a series of meetings, rather than through written claim and counter-claim, which is so time consuming and so inflaming.

Thoughts to keep in mind

- Be clear what you want to achieve in the medium term.
- Be clear with your lawyer. Don't send mixed messages – and expect him (or her) to know which one you *really* mean.

- Be straight with your ex – the pleasure of *getting one over* on him (or her) risks losing their trust – which you will need for the future.
- Your lawyer won't do a better job for you or succeed in getting you a better deal if you keep on about your ex's misdeeds. It just increases your legal bill.
- If you need to offload on someone it's cheaper to go to a group for divorcing people – such as Relate sometimes runs, a web chat page or a professional counsellor.
- Painful as it all is, furious and hurt as you feel, there is no better alternative to negotiation.

Sometimes waiting to allow some of the heat of hurt and shock of the loss to die down, makes it easier to compromise.

Kate and her ex had waited for well over a year after they had parted to begin the financial negotiations – by which stage they each felt sadder, and could believe that the other was not out only to cheat and take revenge.

Kate resisted her solicitor's advice to fight hard. She managed to agree a settlement which she felt was fair enough, despite her solicitor's strenuous advice not to. Five years later she continues to feel this was the right thing to have done. She remains on good terms with her ex.

Having sufficient resources can make it easier to compromise: it is hard to feel generous when there is so little to go around. But generosity is often based less on comparative financial well-being – for many extremely wealthy couples fight no less bitterly – than on a sense of emotional resources.

Compromise offers many future advantages:

Jim had a long on-off affair with a colleague when his children were very young. He finally, painfully, left his family to be with this partner. His new partner earned well and they had sufficient for a good life.

Because he felt so sad and guilty, he decided not to ask his wife and children to move from the family house – and gave up his claim on it.

Even though, when looking back, he thought he had probably given away too much, he felt that making it possible for his family to settle more easily was worth it. His relationship with his children is very good and he remains on reasonable terms with his first wife.

Refusing to budge and keeping on battling in the courts can look admirably tough – but actually is brittle and self-defeating. Compromise can feel weak and defeatist – but is about accepting the reality that your marriage is over and has to be given up. Wishing to punish your ex, mutual distrust and financial self-interest can push you both towards the more exciting but expensive option of legal battle. Add to this the commercial interest of lawyers and the brew can be heady.

But as on cigarette packets, a warning needs to be given to all who plan to embark on a legal battle:

HANDLE WITH EXTREME CARE.

Notes

1 Kathryn Peat, personal communication (January 2001).
2 Hetherington, E.M. and Kelly, J. (2002) *For Better or for Worse: Divorce reconsidered.* London: Norton.
3 Johnston, J.R. and Campbell, L.E.G. (1988) *Impasses of Divorce: The dynamics and resolution of family conflict.* New York: Free Press.
4 Roberts, Yvonne (2004) Listen to the children, Mrs Hodges. *Observer*, 30 May.
5 Trinder, Jo, Kellett, Joanne, Connolly, Jo and Notley, Caitlin (2006) *Evaluation of the Family Resolutions Pilot Project.* London: Department for Education and Skills.

8

Refusing to *mind*

He who feels the pain but will not suffer it . . . fails to
'suffer' pleasure.

Psychoanalyst, Wilfred Bion[1]

Letting go of the lure of hatred and blame allows the
possibility of a truce – but it creates another problem. The
excitement of warfare distracts you from noticing other
unwelcome feelings, such as loss, sadness and self-doubt –
which you now may face once more. When you feel so
threatened and fragile, following break-up it can be difficult
to allow yourself to know of such troubling feelings.

Another protection against emotional pain is by *not
minding*, or being *only* excited and relieved, by having *no
baggage*. This is like the child who feels hurt or rejected,
and claims defiantly, *'I don't care anyway!'* The hope is that
if you can just believe it fervently enough, this will make it
true: there will be no wound.

The thought of mourning a marriage that has gone
wrong may seem ridiculous – even shameful. Sadness is
alarming. Being 'sad' in teen argot is equivalent to being
pathetic – the last thing you want to be. Surely only someone weak, a loser, would allow themselves to feel sad?
Sadness can be frightening: *if you let yourself feel sad, will
you be stuck forever?*

If you were the one to leave, and have any moment of
sadness, you may dread this means you made the wrong
decision – and you will want to do your best to keep doubt

at bay. Recognising that there *are* real losses makes leaving more painful and it can feel preferable to stifle awareness of loss, to protect yourself.

- Surely it's ridiculous to feel grief at the ending of a partnership when it was your decision to leave!
- How can that make sense?

If you *didn't* want the partnership to end, mourning may make you feel even more of a fool. You might feel able to mourn the loss of what you wanted and expected of Life, but how can you grieve the loss of a partner who no longer wants to be with you?

- Doesn't that just make you pathetic?
- Why should you give him (or her) the satisfaction of seeing you sad at their loss?
- Much better to tough it out and not give a damn!

Not minding

Not minding looks admirable. It has many apparent advantages: you are tough; in control: it looks like the obvious way to move on quickly. It is the generally accepted policy: *Don't think about it! Put it behind you!* But – as with other quick fixes – there is a downside.

Shutting down and refusing to care is grey and drab. If you empty yourself of feelings you would rather not have, you are likely to be left feeling depleted. If you cut any link between knowing what you feel – you may find yourself swayed by moods which no longer make sense. Rather than thinking, you can't concentrate. Rather than holding onto any competence and preparedness to take risk, you withdraw and avoid. Instead of desire comes indifference.

In the place of anger – which can be expressed and dealt with – you feel aggrieved; a sullen sense of being deprived and unwanted. You lose access to your active aggression – which may be destructive, but which is also an important source of drive and determination. Instead you are helpless.

There is a further problem: the attempt to *not think* actually often has the reverse effect – as if you have to constantly remind yourself what it is, which you need to avoid remembering.[2] So for example if you *try* to not think about the colour *yellow* – it is in fact much more likely to come to mind.

Treating the loss as if it is *nothing*, in order to short-circuit emotional pain, leaves you potentially blank and emptied: it is the equivalent of cutting out the face of the offending figure in all the family photos. It might seem to remove the painful memory – but at the cost of unreality and of unaccounted mental gaps. If you refuse to mourn, if you want to believe that there is nothing in your partnership to miss, then you can have no good memories from the years you were together. You have a wasted, blasted space inside, instead of a rich and complex, shared history – now past.

You may notice symptoms of distress, such as irritability and sleep difficulties but – since any link with feelings has been cut – your symptoms have no meaning: there is no room for them to be thought about or digested.

However much of a relief the ending of your marriage and the loss of your partner may be, that loss needs to be mourned. If you avoid mourning by shutting down your awareness of feelings, it results in a restricted capacity for experiencing any feelings – good as well as bad:

Bill had not expected to leave his marriage. It had all been going well enough: he was getting on well at work – though not *quite* as well as he hoped. He and Chrissie were settled in a lovely house, with great kids. He should have felt great . . . but he felt dreary, bored and restless.

He would come home tired and his kids would desperately want his time; Chrissie would want him to take over parenting duties – he just had no time for himself. What had happened to all those excited hopes he'd had at 22? Is this all there was? Would it just be downhill from here?

Having a beer after work with colleagues, including a newly single woman, Helen, they wound up grumbling about partners. Bill surprised himself by saying some harsh things about Chrissie. He felt ashamed, but angry and defiant too. He hadn't really talked about it with Chrissie – but then she was either too busy, or had all the right logical answers or . . .

Several months later Bill left. He felt miserable and ashamed – but also very excited. He was finally being true to himself. He hoped that the increasingly close friendship with Helen would blossom.

One year on much of the excitement had died down: the good excitement as well as the desperate sort. It was OK with Helen, but there were things about her that irritated him – and she could get irritable with him. She wanted children – and though his heart sank, he thought he'd lose her if he said 'No'. Bill saw his kids regularly and it gutted him how pleased they were to see him and how quiet they became as it grew time for him to leave. He wondered how much impact his leaving had on them.

Sometimes Bill remembered the good times and wondered whether he had made a stupid mistake. Sometimes he felt bloody miserable – and then he would become more angry and unpleasant. He didn't really know what he wanted from life – but maybe that was a stupid question anyway. He buried himself in work.

Rather than getting on blindly and hoping his life would sort itself out, if Bill could face what he had lost and mourn, he might still find that leaving was the best thing to do – but he would do so, knowing all that he had sacrificed. He could be clearer about what was intolerable: whether it was family life that was hard for him; Chrissie, whom he simply no longer wanted to be with; or something to do with his own unrecognised feelings – possibly including the blow to his self-esteem at not being quite as successful at work as he wished.

This would be undoubtedly painful but – since he was no longer shutting down parts of his memory and mind – Bill would have more mental resources in understanding what was driving him, he would feel more in control of his life. He would feel sadder and more guilty at the pain he had caused – but he would be at less risk of being stuck in this dreary, shut down, depressed state.

Only if Bill can face some of his sadness at the loss of his children, and his guilt at the impact his decision had (and has) on them, will it be possible for him to be emotionally available for them – and for a new partner.

The need to mourn loss

Only if he can tolerate the pining, the more or less conscious searching, the seemingly endless examination of how and why the loss occurred, and anger at anyone who might have been responsible, not sparing even the dead person, can he come gradually to recognise and accept that loss is in truth permanent and that his life must be shaped anew.[3]

Losses need to be acknowledged and mourned. If they are not, there are problems: several studies followed up those mourning the death of a partner. Some mourners were able to let go, grieve – and finally move on.

Others did not mourn, but rather shut down: in the short term, they became brittle and irritable, suffering troubled sleep and other psychosomatic expressions of distress. In the longer term, they complained that life was uninteresting, and that their relationships felt thin and unsatisfying. Some became clinically depressed and could not understand why this should be so. Clinically what helped them get over their depression was to make the link with the loss of their partner – and mourn.

It was harder to mourn the death of a partner when the relationship had been more hostile: angry memories stirred up painful feelings of guilt, and anxiety that the death was in some way a punishment for their hostile feelings.[4] Those whose self-esteem was higher found it easier to let themselves mourn.

Just as a death needs to be mourned, so does a failed marriage and the same factors that make mourning the death of a spouse harder – hostility and low self-esteem – are present when a partnership breaks.

A marriage which breaks up is almost inevitably hostile. Few couples breaking up will express any appreciation of what their partner once offered them, or acknowledge that there is anything about them which will be missed. The choice then can be that of having an alive memory of a former partner – but one who is a critical and hostile – or of barring him (or her) from memory.

You may want to argue that there was *never anything good*. But is this true? For – even if short-lived or naive in retrospect – weren't there moments of pleasure, of feeling loved and loving? Didn't you once have hopes for the future? If you can't bear to grieve for the loss of those good memories and excited hopes, they are lost to you as a source of pleasure and esteem.

Dealing with the loss of your former partner and your life together by making it *not matter* means that becoming close to anyone new is risky since it might expose you to further loss. In shutting down your feelings, you lose the emotional tools to be close – your capacity to be open to your own feelings and to empathise with those of others – and you are more at risk of feeling isolated.

Refusing to acknowledge your need for anyone means that you can't reach out, appreciate anyone or feel any warmth or gratitude. If you can't really let anyone close, you increase the likelihood of a further break-up. You may have saved yourself from agonising sadness or guilt – but instead you feel bleak and empty.

Refusing to accept the reality of loss

Another way of protecting yourself from the pain of loss is by holding on to the *idea* of love, and refusing to face the loss – despite all the other evidence.

'But I still love her', Mike said of his wife, Maria, smiling. He seemed to feel this was proof of his virtue. Even though his wife had asked him to leave two years before,

Mike had not made any financial arrangements with her that would enable him to afford a decent place to live.

He could not get on with the divorce proceedings. He continued to go and cut the grass at the house where he no longer lived.

An apparent idealisation of your lost partner can cover a refusal to let go. For what sort of love is this, if it is for someone who is no longer interested in you? For Mike, is it really Maria he loved; or his *idea* of her; or of Maria – *if only she would change a bit*? If Mike is really so selflessly loving of her, then he needs to let her go as she, apparently, wishes.

Mike may well be frightened and at a loss at finding himself alone – but he mislabels it as being *still in love*. Only if he can notice and sympathise with his *fear and uncertainty* can he think of how he might attend to his own needs in ways that will allow him to develop a new life and move on.

Mike's difficulty in letting go of *love* may also cover an angry refusal to budge. Despite being so *good*, those who met Mike felt exasperated by him: it is possible that Mike has difficulty acknowledging feelings of rage directly – and then acts in a subtly irritating way which provokes others to feel the anger instead of him. In this case, it would help Mike to finally separate – and take his share of the family assets – if he can find a way to acknowledge his anger.

Wonderful

If you don't want to notice that anything valuable has been lost which leaves you feeling empty, you will want to fill yourself up with activity and liveliness: with sexual conquests, with pleasure, fun, partying, enthusiasm, shopping, food, drink or drugs. But it is exhausting keeping up this frenetic pace to keep on proving how *unbothered* you are. Stopping or slowing down is dangerous since you might face painful thoughts and feelings: like a car with an over-revving engine you can feel that you have no choice but to go on and on.

In this state, drugs and alcohol can be particularly appealing in their offer of continuing excitement and energy – though the pharmacological low that follows only increases the emotional low which you are trying to keep at bay.

And if you do finally collapse in exhaustion, you then feel all hope is lost; that you are failure and worthless – and plunge into depression.

If the lost relationship wasn't all bad but had some good in it too, and if the responsibility for the loss isn't only your partner's – then the other threatening possibility is that some fault might be *yours*. If you continue to stay in the black and white, all good/all bad state of mind then this exposes you to your withering, condemnation:

It was all your fault – and you are bad and useless.

In the face of these horrifying possible beliefs, one way is to force yourself back into brightness, determination and activity.

Determination and activity are enormously helpful – up to a point. Emotional defences protect you as you slowly take in the magnitude of the disturbance. Sometimes false courage helps you get on and try new things. You may find yourself oscillating between these positions of enthusiasm and energy, and other moments of collapse and despair.

But if you can't bear to have any feelings of sadness or of guilt, then you will have to keep such feelings out with an increasingly sense of shrill excitement: a positive thinking that must be held onto relentlessly:

It's all for the best . . . Only a relief . . . Wonderful . . .

Notes

1 Bion, W.R. (1984) *Attention and Interpretation*. London: Karnac, p. 9.
2 Herbert, Claudia and Wetmore, Ann (1999) *Overcoming Traumatic Stress: A self-help guide using cognitive behavioural techniques*. London: Robinson.

3 Bowlby, John (1998) *Loss: Sadness and depression.* Volume 3 of
   Attachment and Loss. London: Pimlico, p. 93.
4 Freud, S. (1917) Mourning and melancholia. *The Standard
   Edition of the Complete Psychological Works of Sigmund Freud,*
   Volume XIV (1914–1916). On the History of the Psycho-Analytic
   Movement, Papers on Metapsychology and Other Works,
   237–258. See also Bowlby, *Loss.*

9

Depression

> Depression is flat, hollow, and unendurable. It is also tiresome. People cannot abide being around when you are depressed. They might think that they ought to, they might even try, but they know and you know that you are tedious beyond belief: you're irritable and paranoid and humourless and lifeless and critical and demanding and no reassurance is ever enough.
>
> Psychiatrist, Kay Jamison describing her depression[1]

When a marriage breaks down, it stirs up our deepest fears that we are unloved and unlovable.

If you have an affair or leave, it is almost always in response to feeling insufficiently loved: by leaving, you can hope to replace that feeling by being the one who rejects. But this presents you with one equally unbearable: that of guilt – of being *selfish*, of hurting your family, of being *unforgivably bad*.

If you are *left*, you are shown – and probably told – that you are unwanted.

It is an unenviable choice: either you are unloved – probably because of your faults and failings – or you are unacceptably *selfish and bad*. No surprise that everyone whose partnership breaks down struggles to find a way out of worthlessness and depression.

Depression is not about sadness, though the term can also be used to describe a low mood – which can lead to considerable confusion between the two.

Sadness, grief and regret are lively feelings. When mourning a loss, painful feelings – sadness, grief, despair, hopelessness and self-hatred – can all be experienced. If the reality of the blow can be faced and mourned, in time psychic energy can become available for new things in life.

But in depression these feelings become muffled and deadened. You are stuck. You feel empty of energy or interest in anything or anyone: or anxious, agitated and unable to concentrate – but not really knowing why. You may turn the same cruel scrutiny – the similar black and white state of mind of rage and blame, which you previously had turned on your ex – on to yourself: if you are not completely *good* then you are *rubbish*.

You lie awake anxiously rehearsing your failings: you feel increasingly exhausted and do less and less. You torment yourself with guilt, listing all your wrongs. You don't deserve to pay any attention to your own needs. The chaos which builds around you is further evidence of how useless you are.

No one else – you tell yourself – *is as pathetic and hopeless as you. No wonder your partner stopped loving you as much as you wished: who wouldn't, worthless as you are?*

This vicious self-hatred in depression is different from the painful despair of disappointment and loss: of facing what went wrong and your part in it.

Depression is set in motion by loss:

> the loss of the [other's] love . . . all those situations of being slighted, neglected, disappointed . . . a betrothed girl who has been jilted.
>
> (Freud)[2]

And if a broken engagement is very painful to bear – how much harder is the wound of a broken marriage?

What makes depression different from mourning a death is that

> In mourning it is the world which has become empty: in melancholia [depression] it is the ego itself.[3]

in other words, as well as having to adjust to the loss of the other, because you lose their love for you – and so you also lose your feelings of self-worth.

When depressed, it is as though you take sides with the one who is rejecting you: as if by agreeing with him (or her) – that you really are unwanted, unlovable and bad – you can somehow hold on to them and not have to let them go. Indeed he (or she) is still present in your mind – attacking you.

Freud pointed out how in depression feelings of anger become distorted: instead of using anger to push away your ex, you express it indirectly – by attacking yourself and inviting him (or her) to feel guilt for how badly they have hurt you.

Vulnerability to depression

Some people are more vulnerable to depression than others. Babies and children – and adults – have a series of disillusionments and losses to face: weaning, the arrival of other babies, not being the *one and only* or always *the best*. They – we – can respond with painful feelings of frustration, hatred and envy.

Those who are fortunate enough to have parents who can respond sensitively to their moods as babies and young children can learn that feelings can be understood, and their feelings of frustration are less. If our parents can sympathise with this struggle between our hateful, envious feelings and our loving, grateful ones it is immensely helpful. Learning that resentment and rage are a normal part of life, but that we are not always going to get our own way, is a blow – but a relief too: we have not destroyed everything.

We can learn that some feelings may be less approved of, but that are nevertheless thinkable – not *terrible* and worthy of only being pushed quickly out of sight. We are given emotional tools with which to notice and express feelings rather than shut them down.

Others have an experience which is much less good. External pressures – such as significant money worries, work pressure, unemployment or an abusive relationship –

mean that parents are less able to be responsive to their children. So will internal pressures – such as if a parent is caught up in mourning a loss, or in depression. Their babies and growing children will have more feelings of deprivation and frustration to face – and less help with managing them.

(I discuss these ideas further in later chapters in Part 5 – A wider focus.)

Whatever the emotional resources a child has built up, if they face an external stress that is beyond their capacity to cope, they will feel overwhelmed and are likely to face depression.

Children who were sick and frightened in hospital during the 1950s, in an era before parents were allowed to stay overnight, were filmed by analysts James and Joyce Robertson.[4] Initially the children protested and then, over a period of days, they withdrew more and more into a state of dejection and hopelessness, which often persisted when they returned home.[5]

Someone who has experienced the long-term absence or death of their mother in childhood is more vulnerable to depression in adulthood.[6] They are more likely to deal with subsequent losses as though they must be endured passively rather than actively faced and mourned. And of course in losing their mother early they have lost someone most likely to find words and ideas to help them think about their experience in an active way.

The more you have been helped in the past to face inevitable losses and disillusionment – and the resultant frustration and rage – with some sympathy so it is easier to face now. It is easier to bear that you are not perfect, without feeling that this makes you completely *worthless*. The more your frustration and hatred have to be hidden from view, as unacceptable, the more it remains as a source of anxiety and dread.

Loss, hatred and guilt

A loss – whether through death or through the loss of love – stirs up all kinds of feelings of deprivation and hatred, resentment and wishes for revenge. A sense of unfairness that others do not have to face the same loss; the pain of being helpless to change the situation – and a dread of being punished for such unacceptable, resentful feelings.

The withering, unhelpful, treadmill of self-attack in depression is illustrated in the following example:

> Julia was anxious, depressed and obsessionally concerned that harm would come to her young daughters – and that it would be her fault. Medication did not help.
>
> Julia's father had died young – just as she was about to leave home. She wondered whether her father's death wasn't somehow a sort of punishment for her excitement at leaving home. As well as her immense sadness at losing him, she hated her father for leaving her – and leaving her feeling responsible for her anxious, demanding mother.
>
> Julia was horrified at having such feelings. If she could have acknowledged them at the time, with inevitable shame and guilt, she might have felt freer to set limits on how much she should take care of her mother, and develop a life of her own – but she could not do this. Instead, to try to assuage her feelings of guilt, she became an anxiously dutiful daughter.
>
> The more Julia tried to be good, at such cost to her own life, the more resentful she felt – which provided further grounds for self-reproach. She felt critical of others who were more able to look after their own needs, whom she saw as 'selfish' – as well as envying their ability to do so. But she was not supposed to feel critical or envious – which gave her further reason to attack herself.

Most of us looking on would recognise how Julia might hate her father for dying – and know that this did not stop her also loving and missing him desperately. She might well hate the world, which had taken her father, and resent others who had not had to face her loss. We might feel enormous sympathy for her conflict; torn as she was between her concern for her mother and her wish to move out into a life of her own.

Julia hated and blamed herself – for not being a good enough daughter, mother or wife – but not for the real cause of her distress. She could not face that she was, necessarily, *selfish* – in that she had wishes and needs that were different from her mother's. Ignoring her own, *selfish* needs made Julia feel resentful and angry. Until she could face up to the fact that – in having needs and wishes of her own – she may not be *perfect* but neither was she *unforgivably bad*, she felt internally stricken; on an endless treadmill of proving her *goodness*.

Her father would certainly have had much sympathy for Julia but, since her feelings for him included rage, she shut down her memories of him – including the many good ones. She then was not able to keep him in mind as a powerful, loving internal resource. Julia's mother too, though she had her own difficulties in letting her daughter go, would not have wanted her to feel so consumed with guilt.

Julia's parents had been strict. But, whatever their flaws and idiosyncrasies, the version of her parents which Julia kept in mind – her *internal parents* – was much more critical and demanding than the reality.

Only when Julia was able to acknowledge and express her inevitable feeling of resentment was there a possibility that she might look on at her dilemma without such self-condemnation, and even with sympathy. Memories of her parents as loving figures came more to the fore. When Julia no longer berated herself so ferociously for her unwanted feelings, she found that she felt stronger, more determined and efficient – no longer useless and helpless.

The advantages of depression

> Healing is a slow process. You grow attached to your injuries. There is even a certain status in being one of the world's walking wounded.
>
> Poet and writer, Al Alvarez[7]

Depression can display to the world your state of mind. If you are clearly in a dreadful way, looking haggard, not eating or sleeping, behaving as if you are becoming ill or mad, it will cause people concern, and many will rally round supporting you – *and, you may hope, heaping blame on your partner*. You may also hope that it will make your partner feel guilty – '*See what you've done to me!*' – or less angry with you – '*how can you be angry when I'm in such a state!*' You may succeed in making your partner feel guilty, though irritatingly, probably also relieved to be away from you: but it is at great cost to you.

Being left is humiliating and undermining of your self-worth – but keeping a chronic, sniping feud going is a self-inflicted wound:

> Sheryl just could not stand it that Tony, her ex, involved his new girlfriend with their young sons. It made her feel so painfully left out and alone, looking in on this new happy family which included her ex and her children – but not her. She couldn't stand it that her boys would get to know and maybe like this woman who, as she saw it, was the reason for the break-up.
>
> Sometimes she felt more buoyant and could take it in her stride; other times she felt lower – exhausted, sad and fearful for the future – and then she would become angry at Tony: a complaining, hectoring tone would creep into her attitude and her voice.
>
> Predictably, he would react defiantly or with fury – leaving Sheryl feeling worse than ever. She felt that he hated her even more and she hated herself too: she could hear – however much she justified herself – that she was sounding like a grizzling, unappealing toddler.
>
> But to do anything different was to let Tony win! He would feel smug; that things were working out and that he had done the right thing in leaving. She could not bear it: she would not give him that satisfaction.
>
> The more she despised herself and the worse she felt – the more she blamed him. He had done this to her!

But even if – for argument's sake – the marriage breaking up really had been *all his fault*, Sheryl's miserable state now wasn't.

If she were able to let go of her grievance with Tony, it probably would be a relief for him and make it easier. She would have to accept that – for a time at least – she did have *less than him* in that he had a new partnership and she did not. She would have to give up her belief that she had the power to *make him come back* or alternatively to *spoil his happiness*. Giving up her grievance probably would make Tony's future easier – and their boys' too. But it is also the only way Sheryl is likely to get more for herself in the future.

It may be some consolation to Sheryl to know that when she stops being the *bad one* against whom her ex and his girlfriend can excitedly unite, they will have to get on and sort out their own inevitable difficulties and tensions in their new relationship.

Keeping a certain excited agitation going is exhausting. Your marriage breaking is a very tough knock – but just treating it as if it *should not happen* doesn't get you far. Arguably, only you now have the power to reach out and remove that painful irritant – your hurt, fear and hatred – and let life begin to move on.

Comparing yourself negatively

It is easy, but self-destructive, to foster your grievance and misery by comparing your situation with a – probably biased – version of your ex's. You can take the view that your ex has all the advantages – no turmoil, no losses – and it is only you who are left with the pain and hurt.

This one-sided view is the painful joke in Posy Simmonds' cartoon, 'How the other half lives' (Figure 1).[8]

It is also easy, and withering of self-worth, to hold on to a – probably idealised – view of your ex's new partner in which, in your constant comparison and scrutiny, you are always the *also-ran*.

Sara's wealthy husband had left her for a pretty and successful, younger woman. In the divorce settlement Sara had done well enough financially to ensure her a comfortable life.

Figure 1

Sara was a strikingly beautiful woman, though no longer 25 years old. She was bright, adventurous, creative – but her confidence had been desperately undermined.

Every achievement she made, Sara compared to her ex's girlfriend – which left her feeling hopeless. She wanted to find some way to be better than her younger rival – but desperately trying to do so left her feeling exhausted, drained and old.

To take herself off this dispiriting treadmill, Sara would need to let go of her ex's life and his partnership – however wonderful or flawed it might be – and let herself find out who *she* is, regardless of how she compared to her fantasy rival.

Withdrawal

> I want to be alone.
>
> Greta Garbo

There are different feelings that lead you to want to withdraw – and if you can't distinguish between them it makes it harder to know what to do to help yourself best.

- There is the withdrawal which is necessary when you are dealing with a huge blow: when you need to digest what has happened, when you are so preoccupied with what is happening inside that it is virtually impossible to reach out in any real way. And when you just need some of the time, space and patience and waiting. When pushing yourself will only prove to yourself that you can't yet do it.
- There is the withdrawal which comes from fear and self-doubt – where you worry that you *can't do it*; that you will *look foolish*; will *make a mess*. And then there is no alternative but to slowly try things out, keeping your expectations of yourself low – and if you have moments of interest and pleasure – then that is a great bonus.
- These two are different from the withdrawal that comes from deprivation and hatred, where you furiously lash out at yourself and – indirectly – your ex.

You can spiral between these different withdrawals – and if you don't recognise which is which, you can end up making yourself feel worse.

If you treat your need to withdraw – when you are not in a state to reach out and engage with the world – as something you need to bully yourself out of, you are likely to make yourself feel worse. You won't be in a state to really reach out and engage with the world – and forcing yourself before you are ready is likely to seem proof that you are useless. And managing a break-up takes time – however much we might all wish we could get over it quick.

If you are anxious and you have lost your confidence then allowing yourself to withdraw is more likely to make you worse than better: and encouragement might be more useful than bullying.

If you suspect that some of your withdrawal is of the last kind and more to do with feelings of grievance, you can't just rely on friends to pull this reluctant, resentful *you* out from under the – literal or emotional – bedclothes, because it is boring for them long term and they may stop looking for you: in which case you might then tell yourself that

You knew they would go because they are rubbish friends and anyway how could anyone really like you.

Only if you decide to get that fearful, stubborn, furious *toddler / teenager-you* moving, will you have much chance of success. You don't have to bully or terrify yourself: it's not that you'll be *rubbish* if you don't – but it is an enormous *waste* of your life. And really – what do you have to lose?

There are no guarantees for anyone – but you can be pretty sure that the outcome is likely to be better if you put some real heart into it than if you do so reluctantly and resentfully.

Guilt – and inhibition of pleasure

If you whip yourself up to a state of complete worthlessness (which you may know at some level is an exaggeration), then you don't have to look too closely at the smaller but specific and damaging things you – and we all – can get up to.

You don't necessarily have to be conscious of guilt feelings – indeed you may be busy telling yourself all the reasons you have no need to feel guilty – but it can still have an impact on you, acting as a chronic break, slowing you down. It is as if you believe in some part of your mind that by living your life in a constant state of atonement, you will keep some worse punishment at bay.

Hamlet is a good example of this: he is depressed, miserable, passive and self-pitying following the death of his father and the extremely rapid remarriage of his mother to Claudius, his uncle, who has taken the throne (and who, it subsequently transpires, has murdered his brother, the king, to do so). Hamlet describes how

> the earth seems to me a sterile promontory . . . it appears
> no other thing to me than a foul and pestilential
> congregation of vapours. What a piece of work is man!
> How noble in reason! . . . And yet to me, what is this
> quintessence of dust? Man delights not me: no, nor
> woman neither.[9]

Hamlet seems unable to take any useful action. He does not challenge his mother's wish to remarry so soon – but complains bitterly once she has done so. Even more odd is the unspoken puzzle of why, on his father's death, Hamlet has not claimed the throne for himself. Sometimes Hamlet is played as a raw adolescent but – in the grave-digger scene – Shakespeare goes out of his way to let us know that he is 30 years old: the age by which Shakespeare had been married eleven years and written at least eight plays.[10]

Consciously Hamlet is full of rage – at his mother, at women in general, at his own passivity and later at Claudius. If turning away from unacceptable hostile impulses leads to passivity and depression, what might Hamlet be covering over? Possibly feelings of frustration at being still a student at his age and of having any wishes – however mixed – that his father might die, so that he could inherit the kingdom. If such feelings seem so utterly shameful they can only be pushed out of mind, then it will be harder for Hamlet to have the internal strength to claim the throne for himself.

Equally, if Hamlet has any wish to have his loving mother to himself, and which he has to push away out of guilt, he will have fewer internal resources to effectively challenge her plans to remarry.

Instead Hamlet's aggressive feelings come out indirectly and destructively: he kills Polonius – mistakenly, but without any remorse. It seems not to occur to Hamlet that in killing Ophelia's father, he has done to her just what has been so cruelly done to him.

He professes to love Ophelia but in fact he shows no concern for her. Instead he taunts and curses her:

If thou dost marry, I'll give thee this to plague thy dowry, – be thou as chaste as ice, as pure as snow, thou shalt not escape calumny.[11]

Ophelia, maddened, kills herself. At this point Hamlet refuses to accept any responsibility for her death, but blames it all on his madness:

If Hamlet from himself be ta'en away,
And when he's not himself does wrong . . .
Then Hamlet does it not.[12]

Hamlet's state of impotent misery, self-hatred and excited preoccupation with ideas of avenging wounds – and his claim that *It's not my fault*, or *I didn't mean to* – may be familiar to those in the aftermath of a break-up.

The painful advantages of self-awareness

The mind veers away, reluctant to reveal the awesome pettiness, the huge egoism that often sparks mild depression, the bloated baby that screams in all of us and blackens our horizons with its bawling for attention. Once the baby is discovered, though, the blackness lifts.
Jill Tweedie[13]

Break-up stirs up the terrifying likelihood that the loss of our partner's love is a result of real imperfections which we half recognise – but dread knowing about and therefore keep out of sight. Noticing the ways in which we may have harmed our marriage can feel so distressing that it is tempting to ease that pain by becoming a victim instead – passive, helpless, hopeless – and hoping to find reassurance and nurture from others.

> David had an overly close relationship with his mother when he was growing up, and a rivalrous one with his father – who was quick to find fault, or ridicule him. David found this unbearable: since he could not stand up to his father directly, he got some revenge by being quietly critical and contemptuous of him. He continued to be very sensitive to any criticism.
>
> In his marriage he wanted everything to be perfect, and when it wasn't, he could get anxious and critical – in some ways not so unlike his father. He got furious if his wife, Bella, pointed out any way in which he might be at fault. When she left, taking their young children, he was distraught. It felt such proof that he was 'bad' – something which was intolerable for him.
>
> In time he married again and had other children. Even ten years on, he would not acknowledge that Bella could have had any reason to leave. There was one unforgivably bad person – her. Sometimes he could get very depressed – and he could not understand why.

If David could painfully face his part in the difficulties with Bella, he might recognise that he was not inexplicably mistreated – but that in certain ways he had contributed to the rejection which caused him such hurt and rage. He was not as perfect as he so wanted to be. He might have more sympathy with Bella, and maybe too with the younger *him* – rather than looking only to blame. If he could do so, he might learn valuable lessons to enrich his second marriage.

Misdirected hostility:

> (Depression) . . . becomes a habit, an unfailing excuse for behaving badly.
>
> Poet and writer, Al Alvarez[14]

If you can't acknowledge hostile feelings because these seem so shameful and unacceptable, then you lose out on the constructive use of your aggression. Your anger does not disappear but changes into resentment, passivity and sometimes misdirected hostility.

Noticing your increased tendency to be resentful, envious or self-absorbed can increase your self-hatred – but if you don't notice, you risk 'innocently' creating more damage – which gives you even more grounds to attack yourself:

> Harriet's husband had left her for another woman two years previously. Harriet hoped one day she might meet a good man. At a friend's party she met a lovely – and married – man. She had a fantasy that his wife would die and that she and the man would become a couple. She wanted the reassurance of being desired, of touch, of sex – which she felt so in need of, and that she felt she deserved.
>
> But Harriet half-recognised that this fantasy was a sanitised version of one that was more unsafe to think about: that she and he might have an affair. In her loneliness and anger, she didn't care if it hurt the man's wife – because this had been done to her. She had suffered – why shouldn't this other woman too!
>
> But Harriet hated the woman who had 'taken' her husband – and she hated knowing that she had it in her the potential to do just the same thing. Because she was half able to recognise these thoughts and wishes – and to face her shame and self-disgust – it was less likely that she would 'innocently' act on them.
>
> She felt terrible – but not so bad as she would have done if she had set out to seduce the man and had 'succeeded'. Or if she had attempted to do so – and had been rejected.

Should you take medication?

People have different experiences and different views about the use of antidepressant medication. Some prefer not to take any, even if they have moments of overwhelming misery. They may be anxious about possible side-effects or about the difficulties of withdrawing from the drugs. They may find other ways – such as those described in the following four chapters – which make them feel they have sufficient resources to get by.

Some find they have become so low they have no choice but to turn to medication, to help them through the toughest time. Others still may not be quite so desperate but nevertheless find that antidepressant medication makes them more able to face the emotional work, which then helps them move on.

It is not a contest to the most virtuous or the toughest. Nor a case of either/or. But if you just rely on medication and decide you can skip the other emotional work, it is likely to leave you simmering inside – just pharmacologically suppressed.

There are real difficulties for all of us in accepting reality – that we are human, flawed and not as *worthy* as we would like to believe. Recognising that these more hateful feelings can exist, the pain of breaking up can feel like a punishment that we deserve. But it can be better to face your internal demons than keep them lurking, threatening, in the shadows.

Living a life is a work in progress. Conflicts are inevitable between our own wishes and needs – and attending to those we love. However sadly, we have to let go of our expectation of being *perfect* – and of being *perfectly loved*. We have to let go too of the expectation that life should be without knocks and pain – for breaks and losses are an inevitable part of a life well lived.

Just like the child sitting on his parent's lap after a shock, in time you need to climb down from the lap of your family and friends, so that you can get on with the task of exploring your newly single world.

How to do that is the topic of Part 3.

Notes

1 Jamison Kay (1997) *An Unquiet Mind: A memoir of moods and madness*. London: Picador. p. 218.
2 Freud, S. (1917) Mourning and melancholia. *The Standard*

Edition of the Complete Psychological Works of Sigmund Freud, Volume XIV (1914–1916), pp. 251, 245.

3 Freud, Mourning and melancholia, p. 246.
4 Bowlby, John, Robertson, James and Rosenbluth, Dina (1952) A two-year-old goes to hospital. *Psycho-Analytic Study of the Child* 7: 82–94.
5 It was as a result of these studies that parents are now encouraged to stay with their child if he or she is admitted to hospital.
6 Brown, G. and Harris, T. (1978) *The Social Origins of Depression*. London: Tavistock.
7 Alvarez, Al (1981) *Life after Marriage: Love in an age of divorce*. New York: Simon & Schuster, p. 59.
8 Simmonds, Posy (1982) How the other half lives: A divorced woman rings her ex-spouse. In *Pick of Posy*. London: Jonathan Cape.
9 Shakespeare, *Hamlet*, II. ii.
10 The eight plays were *Henry IV*, Parts I and II, *Richard III*, *Titus Andronicus*, *Two Gentlemen of Verona*, *Taming of the Shrew*, *Comedy of Errors* and *Love's Labour Lost*.
11 *Hamlet*, III. i.
12 *Hamlet*, V. ii.
13 Tweedie, Jill (1982) The mind veers away. *Guardian*, 12 April.
14 Alvarez, *Life after Marriage*, p. 59.

PART 3

Toolkits

It's all very well to tell you what you should or shouldn't do for the best. And much harder to put it into practice. In Part 3 I offer a variety of tools which may help, both practical and emotional.

10

Emergency toolkit

> I attend to my body, something I once thought far too suburban a thing to do. My soul is in upheaval and you talk of a tonic or Vitamin C? Cold showers? Walk around the block? Would anyone have dared to suggest such cures to Byron?
>
> Jill Tweedie[1]

All good toolkits need a variety of practical gadgets for use in unforeseen difficulties. They don't need to be shiny, new or complicated: sometimes the old, simple tools, used with care and ingenuity, are the best of all. Like any good toolkit Part 3 contains a whole array of useful tools and it can be worth rummaging through to find what is available should you need it. You may use many of these mental tools when you are functioning well but now you are almost certainly more vulnerable and impulsive – and so I remind you:

- Take care of yourself.
- Take time to calm down.
- Don't rush into action.
- Don't burn your bridges.
- Prioritise – some things need to be done. Others don't.
- Look for company when you need it.
- Take time alone.

Protect yourself

- In your panic it is so easy to make things worse. You are erratic and vulnerable: you can easily explode in rage.
- Revenge and sabotage have heavy costs – financially and emotionally.
- You can inadvertently do considerable damage. Beware.
- Be careful when you drive.

Eating

- You may have lost your appetite and be pleased with the opportunity to lose weight so easily – but not eating deprives you of energy.
- You don't have to eat a lot – but make it nourishing.
- Stuffing food down as a way of stuffing down pain does not work – it just makes you feel bloated.

Sleeping

- Sleeping badly and then feeling exhausted make it more difficult to cope.
- Some people use medication to help them sleep. Others find herbal remedies leave them feeling less exhausted.
- Exercise can make it easier to sleep: you are running off your furies.
- So can finding words to express your feelings – whether talking to a friend or getting it out into a journal. (This is to get it out: not for posterity. You can burn it later if you want. Or you might be interested later on to see this record of your emotional journey.)
- If you wake in the night with your mind racing, write down your thoughts; make lists of what you want to do – and then let it go till morning.

Drinking, smoking, soft drugs

It is tempting to manage your mood with a combination of alcohol, nicotine, caffeine or – depending on the circles you move in – marijuana and cocaine. But in doing so you are just getting by, rather than attending to the problem. The point is to be in a position to think as clearly as you are able.

- Alcohol can calm you down temporarily so that you can get to sleep – but you can find yourself awake later in the night, agonising and worrying.
- Too much caffeine can leave you feeling even more agitated and stressed than you already are.
- Hard drugs have too many costs.

Medication

- Some people find prescribed antidepressants or tranquillisers help them cope when otherwise they are overwhelmed.
- There can be side-effects including, with drugs of the Prozac family, loss of libido.
- The herbal remedy, St John's Wort, operates in a similar way to Prozac, but the fact that it is herbal does not mean that it necessarily has fewer side-effects.
- People can suffer withdrawal difficulties.
- Medication can be useful if you use it to help you do the emotional work – rather than just to blot out painful feelings.

Sex

- You can want sex when your hunger is more for physical touch, and reassurance that you are wanted and lovable.
- But a dreary sexual encounter – or even a great one with little emotional contact – can leave you feeling more alienated and alone than reassured.
- Don't get into physically vulnerable situations.
- Don't kid yourself that sex with a friend's partner might be a good idea.
- Use a condom.

Shopping

- Getting a new hair-cut, some new clothes or a decent holiday can cheer you up – provided you can afford them.
- When you feel hurt and want to feel better, quick, you can feel you *deserve* treats. But it is not cost free – you are the one who will pay the bills.
- Getting into debt is frightening and self-destructive.

SELF-CALMING

Relaxed breathing

- When you panic, you hold the muscles in your chest and belly tight which means you can't breathe out properly: your breathing becomes shallow and rapid and you can start to feel faint.
- It can feel as if you can't breathe in – but in fact it's because you aren't allowing yourself to breathe out.
- Relaxed breathing is not over-breathing – which can leave you dizzy. It's gentle breathing – a bit like that of a sleeping child.
- The reason cigarettes are calming, though a chemical stimulant, is that you are inhaling and letting go – slowly and deeply.

> Let go of the breath you are holding. Slowly breathe in, letting your lungs fill – and then let go again.
>
> Breathe in for the count of five, hold for five, let go for five. Don't force it. As you breathe out, along with stale air, let go all the tension, the grief and stress . . .
>
> As you breathe in, along with the fresh oxygen, breathe in energy, pleasure, warmth . . .

Relaxation

- This involves becoming more aware of how you are holding yourself tense and tight – and letting go:

Lie somewhere comfortable. Focus your attention on your fingers and hand: as you breathe in, squeeze the muscles in your fingers and hand tight; and as you breathe out let go of any tightness in all those muscles – letting go, more and more. Breathe in and out two or three times, each time letting go more, as you breathe out.

Move your attention from your hands to your wrist, forearm, elbow, up your upper arms . . . round the back of your neck, up the top of your spine . . . over your ears, your brow, over your eyes, slowly down over your nose, mouth, jaw, down your neck. Let your shoulders drop.

Bring your attention down over your chest, the muscles down your back, your belly, your groin, pelvic floor; down your thighs, knees, shins, ankle, feet, toes . . . bringing your attention to any tightness across your body and as you breathe in and out, slowly and deeply – letting go of tension, more and more.

- When you have done this a few times, you don't need to do the tightening first – unless you choose to.

  Focus in turn on different parts of your body – where is it tight? As you let go of each breath let go of tightness in your body – gradually more and more. Think of the oxygen and energy easing all the tight parts of your body.

Guided imagery/meditation techniques

In association with deep breathing and letting go of tightness in your muscles –

- With each in-breath think of breathing in energy, life, hope. With each out-breath let go of pain and distress.
- Think of all the people who value you – now and in the past – they are your internal cheer-leaders. See them in your mind's eye: feel their warm gaze on you; the sound of their voice soothing, encouraging you – cheering you on.

- Hold words or phrases in your mind: such as *'peace'* or *'calm'*.
- Think of your life as a river: at this moment you are in a turbulent part: move down-river, noting dangers but steering round them and out into steadier waters. Look at the view around, smell the air; hear the water, the birds . . . When you find that you can bring yourself safely to calmer waters, it is easier to feel more confident in the turbulent times.

Touch

- Touch is deeply soothing – like a baby in a panic who is helped by touch, rocking and a lulling voice.
- There are many physical therapies which unblock tensions and leave you feeling nurtured and with more resources, more energy: Shiatsu, cranio-sacral therapy, reflexology, Indian head massage, acupuncture, a facial . . . all have their devoted fans and overlapping theories of how they work. One benefit is the sheer pleasure of having your body tended by capable, non-intrusive hands – just as when you were a baby.
- If such treats are outside your budget, you might be able to swap massages with a friend – or find a class that teaches massage. Giving a massage can be nearly as pleasurable as receiving one.

GETTING IT OUT – SAFELY

Exercise

- Exercise burns off adrenalin that otherwise can make you feel like a car with an over-revving engine. It raises your endorphin level. It makes you fitter. It is one area of life in which you can feel some control.
- Try something you enjoy – swimming, running, yoga, ballet, football, circuit-training, line-dancing, kick-boxing . . .
- Thinking through your problems, at the same time as doing something rhythmical and enjoyable, leaves you

feeling more in control than obsessing about those same difficulties when hunched, tense and miserable.

- Being out in nature can be soothing and can make you feel part of a much bigger universe: your current distress can feel smaller in comparison.

Express it – non-destructively

Attempting to push feelings out of mind can just make you feel worse. Getting it out in some way or another can be a relief – and can be fun.

- Find words to express your terror and fury. Write it down – complain, moan, it's for you – but safely in a private notebook, where it won't inflame things further with your ex.
- Smear paint across a canvas, slashes of colour. Play powerful music, sing as loudly as you can. Stomp. Dance.
- Get it out.

SELF-PARENTING

Parent yourself

Just as a baby in a panic needs parenting, so you need to find your internal resources to parent yourself.

- A capacity to soothe and comfort yourself – like a mother, who is attentive but not over-anxious.
- Plus a sort of *fathering* function: where you can challenge and push yourself that bit more – while not demanding too much.
- Mothering and fathering are aspects of parenting that men and women alike can offer to others – and to themselves.

What you tell yourself

- It is easy to make yourself feel worse with terrifying thoughts – like *I can't bear it! This should not happen! I will die!* Don't.

- Being falsely positive can be initially encouraging, but has the risk of being exhausting, setting up false hopes – and likely disappointment.
- Acknowledging the difficulty while reminding yourself of your strengths – some of which you may not yet know about – can be a great help.

For example:

- This is really hard – but the pain will slowly pass.
- I am not completely helpless.

Goal setting

- Make short-term goals. Make them manageable.
- Give yourself credit for what you have accomplished. You don't have to achieve all your tasks instantly or perfectly.

Company

- It is a great relief to be able to tell a friend of your feelings of panic, rage, sadness or discouragement. You are not alone: you are heard.
- Do something fun with friends. You – and they – need a break from going round in the same old mental circles.
- Sometimes groups are run for people who are still caught up in breaking up: it can be a relief to find you are not the only one.

Take time alone

- Filling up all your time with activity and company can be a way of avoiding thinking – and you need to do that too.
- You need time alone to digest what is happening.
- You may need time to let go and feel weak, frightened and very sorry for yourself, to sit and weep – but remember that this isn't the whole story.

- Being alone can be strange and alarming if you have been used to having someone around, or in the background, much of the time.
- It is startling but useful to be able to be alone and find out what emerges: it offers the chance to re-evaluate your life and what you want from it.

Stay in the moment

> Pain is what it took me to pay attention. In times of pain, when the future is too terrifying to contemplate and the past too painful to remember, I have learned to pay attention to right now. The precise moment I was in was always the only safe place for me. Each moment, taken alone, was always bearable. In the exact now, we are all, always, all right.
>
> Author and creative writing teacher, Julia Cameron[2]

Doing the emotional work

The tools offered over the following three chapters aim to help you do some of the necessary emotional work; to understand and help yourself best. And when such emotional work has been done, mediation or court settlements are much more likely to stick.[3]

Notes

1 Tweedie, Jill (1982) The mind veers away. *Guardian*, 12 April.
2 Cameron, Julia (1994) *The Artist's Way: A spiritual path to higher creativity*. London: Souvenir, p. 54.
3 Walker, J., McCarthy, P., Stark, C. and Laing, K. (2004) *Picking up the Pieces: Marriage and divorce – Two years after information provision*. London: Department of Constitutional Affairs.

11

Letting go of hatred

Martin Amis wrote of his father, Kingsley Amis, finally coming to terms with the breakdown of his second marriage:

> What mattered to me most at the time was that it announced a surrender of intransigence. I had hoped for this, as ardently as you hope for the cessation of an infant's crying-fit, of a child's marathon sulk, of a lover's disaffection. [His book] *The Old Devils* marked the end of his willed solitude. He backed off, he climbed down.
>
> My father emerged with a novel about forgiveness. He hadn't forgiven Jane, and never would, but he had forgiven women, he had forgiven love: he had returned to the supreme value . . . He came out of the room he had sent himself to.[1]

Many of us will recognise, ruefully, how we can send ourselves to that room of *willed solitude* and *intransigence*. In the state of mind of this *room*, our belief is that, if only we hold on for long enough, scream loud enough, hold our breath long enough, make enough of a mess, someone will come and make it all better – as our parents may once have done when we were in a panic as a child. The hidden demand is that we should be the central character in the drama of our lives and the job of others is to fit in around us: that we should never, quite, have to let go of our claim to have everything our own way and to be endlessly *entitled* to love.

Leaving the *room* of the *marathon sulk* and self-righteousness is a humiliating climbdown. It means accepting that this fierce version of the world – that we are *only* wounded and innocent – may not be the *whole truth*. It means noticing that our *sulk* may make us powerful – but the power is only destructive: sulks may work in coercing others to go along with us some of the time – but it doesn't help when reality just doesn't fit with our wishes.

If you can look at yourself from the viewpoint of a sympathetic but firm outsider you might be able to see that you are in a tantrum; that you do feel awful – but that you have some power to emerge. A certain wry humour might help. It is not only the fact of the break-up, or the crimes of your ex that subject you to your pain, but also that you are contributing to the pain by continuing to *shut yourself in the room*. And you are wasting part of your life in the process.

Letting go of grievance

It is in your interest to let go of grievance. Not to be saintly, or honourable, or mature. Not even for the sake of the children's well-being – though if your children are unhappy, it is hard to feel settled yourself. The most important reason is you: your peace of mind.

If you are no longer together as a couple – with each of your particular sensitivities, hurts and angers – it may seem that (with the important exception of the well-being of children) the interests of you and your ex no longer coincide. It may seem you will do better by attempting to control, manipulate or cheat – or to build as high a wall as possible to protect yourself against attack.

But in fact you *do* have a mutual interest – in a life that is not consumed by the relationship now past. It is in your joint interest to maintain a just peace – not one that is perfect, but is hopefully good enough. It helps if you can begin to find ways to establish the beginnings of trust, find ways of negotiating and of having some flexibility – as well as having a fall-back position if truces are broken.

Having a marriage break down is devastating. It can take a long time and heartbreak and emotional work to get through. Not everyone manages. At the same time it is not of the same order as living in a country suffering systematic terror, facing starvation or being in a war zone. It is not the same as losing a child to murder, accident or fate.

Breaking up is a huge blow, but it can be managed and overcome. Fury and hatred at your partner who failed you – as well as you them – can be let go of. Acceptance, understanding and – who knows – even forgiveness can make a big difference.

The work of the Truth and Reconciliation Commission (TRC) in South Africa and Rwanda was not some limp turning the other cheek: it was muscular and pragmatic. The TRC argued that what was more important for a country pulling itself together after years of bitter internecine war was for the participants to face up to what they had committed: not with a view to jailing the perpetrator or condemning them with retributive justice, but because understanding the other is an important factor in *cleansing hatred*, and facing responsibility is essential to healing. This sort of justice is *restorative* and allows a moving forward.

Most of us would be put to shame by the extraordinary forgiveness and magnanimity reached by one young woman, who had had her legs blown off in a terrorist bombing, and who said that:

> through the trauma of it all, I honestly feel richer. I think it's been a really enriching experience for me and a growing curve, and I think it's given me the ability to relate to other people who may be going through trauma.[2]

It wasn't that she was glad that her legs were blown off, that it wasn't a desperate loss that didn't matter: she was saying there were also gains – through her attitude and acceptance of the disaster that had befallen her.

Can you let go without an apology?

You may wish that your ex would acknowledge and apologise for his (or her) part in what went wrong. But

frankly, if you insist on there being only one person at fault
– your ex – you are unlikely to get any expression of regret,
acknowledgement of blame, and guilt.

Some victims of crimes much worse than the loss of love
have found that it helped them to let go of hatred. Others
manage to move on after horrific brutality and warfare: it
can be helpful to look at how.

Eva Moses Kor, a twin survivor of Mengele's deadly
laboratory experiments in Auschwitz, commented:

> I discovered I had the power to forgive, and it was a
> tremendously empowering and interesting feeling . . .
> forgiveness has nothing to do with the perpetrator [but]
> with the victim taking back their life. I don't have to deal
> with the whole issue of who did what to me and how on
> earth I am going to punish them and make them pay for
> it. I am free of all that baggage.[3]

Bishop Desmond Tutu, who was the Chair of the South
African Truth and Reconciliation Commission, and advised
– among others – the Rwandans on managing the aftermath of that country's savage tribal genocide, wrote:

> If the victim could forgive only when the culprit
> confessed, then the victim would be locked into the
> culprit's whim, locked into victim-hood, whatever her
> own attitude or interest.[4]

Compared to the crimes that occurred in those countries,
falling out of love and behaving poorly on the way out of
a marriage is arguably not so unforgivable. Even so, when a
marriage ends, the hurt and guilt are great. How you face
that pain will affect your chance of gaining from it: of
making it enriching – or not.

> (Forgiveness) does not mean condoning what has been
> done. It means taking what has happened seriously and
> not minimising it: drawing the sting in the memory that
> threatens to poison our entire existence. It involves

trying to understand the perpetrators and so have empathy, to try to stand in their shoes, and to appreciate the sort of pressures and influences that might have brought them to do what they did.[5]

Even when one partner seems more clearly *at fault* in a marriage breakdown, *trying to stand in their shoes* can be helpful – in understanding the past, and in cooperating as well as possible in relation to children:

> Jenny left Dan in outrage and contempt. He had been violent to her a number of times – but now he was beginning to threaten and hit their son. And he was refusing to pay child support. She was incensed. What a complete useless bastard!

If Jenny could find a way to put herself in Dan's shoes she might not forgive him, but she is likely to feel more understanding – and that would make it easier for her to deal with him with less uncomprehending contempt:

> Dan's father had had an exceptionally tough life. He was explosive and frightening. Sometimes he lashed out physically. He was demanding and critical with his eldest son, who felt he could do nothing right. Dan managed by staying away from the family and being quietly defiant.
>
> He felt looked after by Jenny, a warm, sympathetic girl in school, and married her. He wanted to do it so differently from his father. He wanted to show Jenny how much he could achieve but he didn't have as much confidence as her and he felt jealous seeing how much easier it seemed to be for her, than him. He would have been mortified to tell her his doubts.
>
> If Jenny was ever angry with him, he couldn't bear it: it felt that she, like his father, thought he was completely useless – and then he wanted to blank her out or thump her.
>
> When their baby son arrived, Dan was so pleased and proud – but he couldn't bear how much pleasure Jenny had in the new baby. He felt that now she only wanted

him as a provider for her and the baby. She got so tired and she had less patience for him.

Dan started to hate his son. It felt so unfair that his son was getting all this love, which he, as a child, had not had. Dan would yell at his son and at times lashed out – harder than he'd meant to.

This made him hate himself even more: was his father right? Would he never amount to anything good? Dan could not bear the look of horror in Jenny's eyes: he really wanted to smash her up then.

When Jenny left with their young son, it felt such proof that he was worthless. Dan felt desperate – and then defiant. He would show them! He would give them nothing! He would not care!

If Jenny were able to treat Dan less like a vicious dog that should be put down, he might be able to calm down a bit, and need to protect himself less ferociously from her contempt. If she could support him in finding safe ways to spend time with their son, rather than trying to push him away, he might feel less threatened and enraged.

If Dan did not condemn himself quite so ferociously, he might have less need to pretend defiantly that his outbursts were not important. He doesn't need to make excuses for himself, but to see how vulnerable he can feel and how hypersensitive to criticism. If he could acknowledge his rage – rather than push it out of sight in disgust – he might have more chance of learning to have some control of it.

Were Jenny to remember the good things she had once seen in Dan – even if she had not understood the depths of his vulnerability – she might have some sympathy for her wish to make a good relationship with him; she might berate herself less for having been so stupid to get together with him in the first place; and feel that it was an honourable effort and sad for them both that it failed.

Letting go of blame

We all prefer to blame the other when things go wrong – and a failed marriage is no exception. But the more we look

in a wider way at the pressures and influences we bring to
a partnership, the question of who is *at fault* becomes
increasingly less clear.

Take the following case study.

Al's side

Jane was fun and a real partner for a long period of their
early marriage. She was gorgeous – energetic, warm and
resourceful. When they had two children, one rapidly
following on the other, she loved mothering. Al felt that
he had lost his lover. He felt unbearably left out, as if he
were looking on at her love affair with their new baby. He
resented that she had little energy left for him and he felt
burdened, being, for a while, the sole bread-winner.

Al knew he was being irritable and unreasonable but
he still felt it. If Jane tried to reason with him, he felt
treated like a naughty child. If she was angry, he felt hurt
and misunderstood. If she was anything less than competent he felt anxious. He began staying later at the office
and was reassured by the interest of a younger colleague.

Jane's side

Al was charming, interesting, lively. He was fiercely ambi-
tious and hardworking. He was good at being centre-
stage – but less good at sharing with Jane and in being
responsive to her needs. Somehow he was so busy that he
could never share in household responsibilities, which left
it all to her, though she had a job of her own and young
children.

For long periods she did cope, knowing as she did
how important work was to him, and how exhausted he
was. They made sure they had times away when they
reconnected but as soon as they got back Al dived into
work again.

Jane felt increasingly unloved, tired and resentful. She
turned away from expecting much from Al and found her
pleasures instead through her children, her work, her
friends. She hoped that Al would miss her and come
looking for her. Instead he became sullen and started an
affair with a younger colleague.

It is possible to take a wider view of these two; their earlier experiences and the assumptions and anxieties they brought to the marriage:

Al's mother was overwhelmed with the demands of looking after a large family; his father coped by being out of the house, working and being a pillar of the community. The family would all wait for the lively exciting father to return (often late) to eat.

Al wanted to find a woman who would not become overwhelmed like his mother. He learned to be an effective fighter, with his many siblings, for the attention that was available. He wanted Jane to be happy but he also felt she was a rival – like his brothers and sisters had been – for what felt like scarce resources. He wanted to be reassured that he was *specially* wanted and waited for – not 'only' a desired part of the family.

Al wanted someone resourceful, independent and happy – but if Jane was, he could feel left out and resentful. He wanted Jane to reassure him of her need for him – but when she was more vulnerable, he became anxious that she was too like his mother.

Jane's mother too had been depressed, isolated and busy with moves during Jane's early years. By the time her mother had settled and found friends, she had had another baby who took up her time, and she needed Jane to be a 'big girl'. Jane learned to get on and manage on her own. She felt dismissive of mothers and of dependence. She could manage on her own.

Jane admired Al's independence and ambition – but felt left out and resentful at his success. She wanted someone who could nurture her – but when Al did, she felt uneasily that she might be too like her mother – and she would push Al away and prove she could do it on her own.

Al and Jane came to their partnership with particular anxieties, and defences against them – which created inevitable tensions. These stemmed from their own experiences in their family of origin, in their unconscious assumptions of themselves, each other and the world.

So which one of them is *really* to blame? Did they both have some share of blame? Or was it the fault of their mothers who, for their own reasons, were unavailable? Or was it the fault of their fathers who were unable to provide more support? What about their parents' experience of being parented? Where do you draw the line, going back through the generations?

Acknowledging responsibility in the failure of a partnership is very painful. Avoiding responsibility and guilt by denial and blame is all-too tempting – but such self-protective strategies make it impossible to learn from experience. It is only when anxieties can be consciously faced that there is any real possibility for change.

> If Jane can't acknowledge her tendency to withdraw and her anxiety about dependence, she may avoid finding a new partner. If she does, she may find one with whom she can repeat the same pattern: a relationship in which she can be independent and in control – but secretly deprived and resentful.
>
> If Al can't acknowledge how his frequent absence due to work allows him to avoid his anxiety about closeness, and his fear of being left out and deprived, he risks repeating the same difficulties in his next partnership.

Accepting a truce

Self-fulfilment when outside of a marriage, as well as within it, may not come from grabbing it all but may be more to do with recognising and appreciating others and feeling appreciated in turn.

To be able to accept a truce and find a way to a peace settlement, you might have to accept *good enough* rather than *triumph*. But there are surprising benefits:

> Steph's marriage broke up after her husband, John, had an affair, married his new partner and had a second

family. Although John earned more than Steph did, he complained about even paying his half to contribute to their children – even though the children of his second family went to private school and those of his first went to the local state school.

It is easy to feel inflamed at this account. *How outrageous! Should Steph not fight for more!*

Steph decided to accept it: it wasn't 'fair' – but she could live with it. She knew too she had an 'unfair' pleasure in that her boys continued to live with her – though they saw a fair bit of their father. There were disadvantages to her acceptance: she might have ended up with more cash if she'd fought harder – but there were advantages too. Her kids' state school was, in fact, a good one – she didn't feel they were deprived not going to a private school. And when she was in difficulty – intruders had broken her front door – John was the one she phoned and who came round and helped.

Being helpful to your ex can have unexpected advantages for you too:

Nick phoned Jo in a panic from the airport: he needed confirmation from her that she agreed to his taking their children out of the country to see his family. She knew she could have made it difficult and that it might 'serve him right' – but she didn't. Mostly she didn't want to spoil the kids' holiday. She put everything else on hold and arranged to fax off her consent.
    She expected to feel virtuous and a bit smug. What took her by surprise was how cheerful she felt afterwards. She felt lighter: inadvertently she found she had 'cleansed' herself of several notches of hatred.

If you're looking for a model for managing the disaster of your marriage breaking up, then the Asian Tsunami (of December 2004) might be more helpful than one of revenge and warfare. In the Tsunami, many thousands faced terrible loss and heartbreak – but there was no perpetrator to blame, so violent action had less of an outlet. Helplessness in the face of natural disaster had to be faced, and people were able to work together to clear up some of the wreckage and enable life to continue anew.

If you can let go of your tight grip on the idea of the cruel perpetrator and the innocent victim, the break-up of a marriage – which has its own subterranean pressures; its own conflicting, shifting tectonic plates – might look much more like the sad scene of devastation following those overwhelming waves.

Notes

1 Amis, Martin (2000) *Experience*. London: Jonathan Cape, p. 258.
2 Tutu, Bishop Desmond (1999) *No Future without Forgiveness*. London: Rider, p. 113.
3 Eva Moses Kor, quoted in Lawrence Rees (2005) *Auschwitz: The Nazis and the Final Solution*. London: BBC Books. Also in *Observer*, 9 January 2005.
4 Tutu, *No Future without Forgiveness*, p. 220.
5 Tutu, *No Future without Forgiveness*, p. 219.

12

Facing your part

Taking responsibility

> the world breaks everyone and afterward many are
> strong at the broken places.
>
> Ernest Hemingway[1]

If you hope, over time, to become strong at your broken places it takes courage. But what is the kind of strength you want to achieve? Is it the tough, brittle *'I don't care!'* kind of strength? Or would you rather find a certain resilience; a capacity to acknowledge failure and so learn from experience; a capacity to take emotional risks in the future and trust in others – because you know that you can feel, but survive, loss and pain?

We may think of it as wrestling a marlin at sea, as Hemingway loved to do – but the powerful, thrashing, wild creature we have to bring in to land is as much inside us as outside. We reel in this barely known creature not by brute strength and determination but by respect for this foe and careful thought. So what is this creature?

Seeing things differently

The political philosopher, John Rawls[2], suggested a way to get a just society. In his model you can create a society any way you wish – but you do so under a *veil of ignorance*. In this just society you propose, you can choose to have extremes of wealth, privilege and power – but you don't know where your place in it will be: whether you will be black or white; Muslim, Hindu, Christian or Jew; Catholic or Protestant; landed gentry sending your child to Eton or unemployed and sending them to an inner-city school.

Suddenly, under this *veil of ignorance*, you have to let go of the familiar arguments you make to justify your position. You have to pay more than passing attention to the experience of the other – you have to do this utterly seriously.

You can look at your marriage and it's ending like this. Not out of fairness to your ex – which may be the last thing you are interested in – but because, for all of us, living with ourselves fully means facing up to reality – good and bad.

Dealing with the disappointment of a failed partnership by pushing it out of mind – as if it is only repugnant – does not leave you at ease. It is like swimming in water where you can't see the bottom and you know that somewhere, something nasty is lurking. You can tell yourself that it is not there – or if it is it won't hurt you. You can live a life where you avoid swimming. Or – if you want to have as full a life as possible – you can, with reluctance and in small doses, take the risk of *seeing things differently*, of confronting the monster.

The monster that is kept barely submerged includes hatred as well as love; envy as well as generosity; selfishness as well as concern. It may also include resentment and a wish for vengeance towards the partner you are breaking apart from. If you know – however fleetingly – of such feelings, then you must assume that your ex harbours similar, if not worse, feelings towards you. Your terror of being discovered as unlovable has come to pass – and you doubt that you can ever be loved again – by yourself, let alone by anybody else.

The particular agony, the *monster in the depths* that needs so painfully to be faced, is that when the marriage breaks – you played some part in its going wrong.

Truth

If one part of restorative justice practised by the Truth and Reconciliation Commission in South Africa was about the capacity to put yourself in the other's shoes, the other part is to face up to your own part in what goes wrong.

Facing truth heals. It is healing for the person who can acknowledge what they have done and – if they do so aloud – for the one who hears their acknowledgement.

> Let us have a public meeting and . . . for you to stand up and say there are things that went wrong, there are things that went wrong and I don't know why they went wrong . . .
>
> There are people out there who want to embrace you. I still embrace you because I love you and I love you very deeply. There are many out there who would have wanted to do so if you were able to bring yourself to say something went wrong . . . and say, 'I am sorry. I am sorry for my part in what went wrong'.[3]

Bishop Desmond Tutu gave this moving speech to Winnie Mandela, during the TRC hearings, hoping – and indeed achieving – some acknowledgement of her involvement in the necklace burnings carried out under her instructions by her 'football team' and the death of 14-year-old Stompei Moeketsi.

Tutu argues that even when blame is unequal it is important for each side to acknowledge their part. Winnie Mandela had had immense provocation to commit the actions she had: the years of apartheid discrimination; the long imprisonment of her husband; her own banishment to tribal homelands. But, despite such huge provocation, she was responsible and if she could face up to her personal part it would help the healing of her countrymen – and herself.

In the ups and downs of your marriage, you may have had severe provocation too – though almost certainly nothing like as extreme as Winnie Mandela's.

Facing your internal Truth and Reconciliation Commission can also be healing. As in the South African TRC, the internal judge you need is not the cruel, condemnatory one of a criminal court – whom you need to use your wiles to outwit. Instead you need the sort of internal judgement provided by restorative justice: one who *wants to embrace* you – not because you are without fault, but *when you can acknowledge it.*

We all want to cling on to the belief that we are perfect and good and it is painful facing up to the fact that our loving feelings can coexist with other, darker, more shameful ones. Pushing these feelings aside does not make them go away, we continue to act under their influence, but – because we do not acknowledge them – they cannot be ameliorated by other feelings of love and or concern.

Slowly unpicking your part in the break-up might cause you *anguish* – but you might then feel less oppressed by hidden threats and feel freer to move robustly on.

Stephen was horrified when his wife said she wanted to end their marriage. He had thought it had all been going pretty well, though he knew she found his long hours working, his irritability and the demands of looking after their young children trying. It was an immense blow for him and the loss of his children was devastating. To highlight his good intentions, he was financially generous with his ex.

Underneath he was seething. He would not understand her position: she had hurt him and was therefore unforgivable. Though externally his life moved on, this core of bitterness and grievance continued to gnaw away at him – and left him feeling drained and miserable.

If Stephen were able to understand what some of his part had been in the difficulties, he might have not seen his former wife as only a *complete bitch* who had done something inexplicable to him. He might notice that though she could be utterly exasperating, he too could be impatient, critical – and not always easy to live with. If he could notice this without subjecting himself only to unremitting, withering judgement, he might be able to learn for himself and his future relationships.

They would both of them have contributed to the difficulties: possibly they were not a good match in the first place; maybe the demands on them had just been too much; maybe both. It was very sad their marriage had ended – for them and for their children – but not a cause for such draining, ongoing grievance.

Managing feelings of responsibility and guilt by blaming only your ex will make you feel more virtuous – but less in control: since if you were so perfect and the marriage went wrong anyway, you have no reason to hope that a future relationship will have any better chance of success than the last.

Maria's husband left. It was an aching, miserable blow. A part of her wanted to stay stuck and miserable, two years later, since moving on would 'let him off the hook'. She hoped it would somehow stop him getting on and having a good life. She did not want to face that she might have had any part in the marriage breaking down.

Maria told herself that if he had stayed, everything would have been great – but she had an uneasy feeling this was not completely true: she knew that there was some restlessness and dissatisfaction that she had brought with her into the marriage – which probably contributed to the strain on it.

If Maria could let herself begin to recognise that she was not easy to live with – and her prickly refusal to accept any fault was a part of that difficulty, she would feel less resentful – but more crushed and concerned by her part in the break-up. If she could let herself really, sadly, notice this, she might begin to do some of the emotional work that would help her in future relationships.

Facing failure

> Success is going from failure to failure without loss of enthusiasm.
>
> Abraham Lincoln

The *enthusiasm* described above is not due to a glossing over of the fact of failure: it is accepted as a – painful – part of life that can be learned from.

We all fail in certain ways, and did so in the marriage now lost. If circumstances had been less hard, you might have managed to keep your relationship alive – or you might not. Your partner will have contributed his (or her) share, but almost certainly you had some part in it too. By facing your contribution to failure, however hard it is to do so, you put yourself in a position to learn and to move on. Real *enthusiasm* is more likely to come from facing those facts rather than evading them.

In the studies, couples who broke up had experienced more external stresses than others who remained together, which had triggered break-up.[4] In that sense your break-up really is *unfair* and *not all your fault*. At the same time some couples managed to survive the external stresses they faced, if they had tended their partnership well.[5]

A particular agony in managing the break-up of a marriage, which needs so painfully to be faced, is that – however inadvertently – you played some part in its going wrong. Noticing ways in which you contributed to the break-up is not to say that it is *all* your fault: that you are the *completely* bad one – only to realise that you had *some part*. You may not have done these things more than other couples, who nevertheless managed to remain together – but your contribution played its part. By carefully disentangling the various pieces, you can learn from your part in what went wrong for the future.

Of course however hard you work at a relationship, however noticing and confronting of difficulty, you cannot keep it alive on your own. In which case did you put up with too much rather than face the worry of leaving? There may be a strength in doggedly going on – but there may be a risk too of staying, fearfully, with the status quo.

A part of the dismay at noticing what we can all get up to is that many of our deeds are not grand, operatic or often even interestingly *wicked*. They can be more like a chronic petty swindling than grand larceny: more the inadvertent result of being careless, or reluctant to take emotional risks. It is the cumulative impact, which can have such unexpected and destructive results.

Look at the ideas that hit you in the middle of the night and make you squirm. Did you really never do things that were nasty, thoughtless, self-centred or mean – in any way? If you quickly answer 'No!' then consider: is it possible that you are blinkered and quick to self-righteousness? If so, this doesn't make you an easy person to live with.

Put yourself in your ex's shoes for a moment, or those of an impartial observer, looking on at your partnership over the years. Have you always been so blameless? What if:

- You were selfish – and sometimes grabbed more than your fair share?
- You wanted too much – and raged, sulked or withdrew if you didn't get it?
- You expected your partner to understand your point of view – but weren't really too interested in understanding his (or hers)?
- You could have been more emotionally generous with them – and weren't?
- You did things that hurt your partner: sometimes inadvertently – but other times deliberately?

(I say more about this later in Chapter 18 on conflicts of intimacy.)

Guiltiness versus guilt

> People love guilt because they feel if they suffer enough guilt, they'll make up for what they've done, whereas in fact, they're just sitting in a puddle and splashing.
> Sister Wendy Beckett[6]

There are two sorts of guilt and it can be easy to confuse the two. One is the inflated, exaggerated, self-lacerating guiltiness, which does not end with a painful acceptance of reality, but goes endlessly around. Staying burdened with this *splashing* form of guiltiness, after a partnership has failed, does not help:

> When Suzie left her husband, she wanted him to take some of the blame for the marriage ending – she knew there were many ways in which he had made it impossible to stay. But he would not accept any responsibility and clung on to his resentment. Because Suzie liked to feel approved of, she found this unbearable and she struggled with huge guilt and depression.
>
> Suzie knew that she hadn't fought as hard as she might have done for herself, and the well-being of the partnership. It wasn't until too late that she realised quite how furious and resentful this made her feel.
>
> She berated herself cruelly for not knowing this earlier: maybe if she had, the marriage would not have collapsed. She told herself that the pain everyone faced was all her fault.

Whatever our best efforts, life – and relationships – don't always go the way we might wish. Noticing specific, shameful things that we all can get up to may seem particularly unappealing when your self-esteem is already so low. But if the excessive plaints of your *utter worthlessness* are a cover for impulses you feel uneasily ashamed about, then facing such *worst fears* is relieving and liberating – since you no longer need to put energy into keeping shameful feelings out of sight.

Compared to her splashing, condemning *guiltiness*, Suzie might be helped by facing terribly painful, but more limited, *guilt*:

> If Suzie could let go of the endlessly bullying, critical internal figure she might be able to acknowledge that she had made mistakes: if she had fought harder, it might well have helped her marriage – though not necessarily

enough for her to have wanted to stay. Suzie would need to face that just looking after others' needs so selflessly was not good for her, or for a partnership – and that she needed to pay more attention to her own needs. She might accept that she wasn't perfect and give up the fruitless attempt to be so – and put her energy more productively into the present.

If Suzie could accept and forgive her less-than-perfect self, she might be more able to let go of the need for her ex's forgiveness. It is possible too that if she minded less about her ex's goading resentment, there would be less pleasure for him in continuing it.

The pain of real guilt

Sister Wendy Beckett contrasted the *splashing* type of guilt (which I describe as *guiltiness*) with *contrition*. She says:

> I don't think being truly human has any place for guilt . . . contrition, yes, but guilt no. Contrition means you tell God you are sorry and you are not going to do it again and you start off afresh. All the damage you've done to yourself [is] put right.[7]

But in my view, even this thoughtful writer slips away from the full anguish of guilt – of facing the extent of the damage – because the fact is that *all the damage **can't** be put right*.

When a marriage breaks there is damage which you *have* contributed to and which can't be *put right*: damage not only to yourself, but also to the one you once loved and in particular – if you have any – to your children.

You can't *put right* the fact that your partnership has foundered, in part, because of your contribution. You can only live with it.

Damage to your children may be ameliorated – but not *put right*. What you have done has an inevitable long-term impact on them. As Martin Amis concludes:

> In filling out the pain schedule 'the hardest items of all have to do with love' . . . I, in leaving home, did what [I]

did 'for love'. But how does it look, the love ledger, by the time you're done? Because you are also the enemy of love and – for your children – its despoiler. 'I hate love' said my son Louis at the age of five or six . . . He didn't mean that, but he could now say, 'I no longer trust it'.[8]

To *fail* is an inevitable part of a life that reaches out to growth and change. Learning anything even moderately worthwhile consists of a constant succession of *failures*. Inevitably you will sometimes fail – as we all do, when we face something challenging, and which takes real effort and perseverance. None of us learns to walk, speak a foreign language, play an instrument, or a skilled sports manoeuvre without trying again – over and over.

The likelihood of *failure* depends on how high you've set your target for *success* – and if you set it too high you demotivate yourself, just as you might with an overly critical teacher who fails to acknowledge successes, and only finds fault. Learning complex tasks is a succession of approximations – and the tasks of a good partnership, good parenting and a good life are dauntingly complex.

Failure is painful – but there is much to be learned from it.

It is harder to notice your faults and failures, and learn from them, if you are moralistic and bullying. It is true that your faults may well be shameful, humiliating, petty, nasty – but if you can find the courage to face your part in failure – and face real guilt, rather than the *splashing* kind – then you can learn from your experience and find once again your *enthusiasm*.

It helps having someone on the sidelines cheering you on. And if there is no such person conveniently present, then you need to find that encouraging figure within you. You need to find a capacity to provide yourself with a warm, but not too anxious, *mothering*: to have sympathy for the difficulty you are in, notice and applaud the efforts you make, and not to make a *disaster* out of a fall on a banana skin.

You also need to find a firm, challenging *fathering* capacity in yourself so that you don't give up after the first

bruise or scraped knee: that encourages you and can differ-
entiate between when you have had enough and need a
break – and when you are making a fuss and will feel
better if you push on.

When a marriage breaks it is a failure: you and your
partner *have* failed in certain ways – though not necessarily more than those who continue to stay together out of
fear, or those who never took the risk of committing themselves in the first place. The biggest *failure* of all is to use
fear as a reason to avoid the challenge – and the opportunity to learn from the experience.

You become stronger – not by being brittle and protecting yourself against failure and pain – but by finding
that you can, in time, survive disaster; that you have more
resources than you might have previously known about;
that risks are necessary in an engaged, involved life; that
hurt and failure are part of a life well lived – and not
necessarily the end of the world.

With hindsight we might all of us have done better, and
that is cause for regret and learning – but not for endless
self-flagellation.

Reparation

If – painfully – you are able to consider your contribution
to the stresses in the partnership and the unexpected and
devastating consequences of it, you can attempt to repair
the damage as much as possible – by looking for a just
peace.

You can work to have the best possible relationship
with your children. You can help your children understand
that love withers without feeding; that it is a risk really
loving another – but one that is worth taking.

Reparation includes recognising and accepting your
former partner's difficulties and anxieties; accepting that
they are not a perfect Hollywood superhero (or heroine),
scripted and airbrushed – but then neither are you.

It means acknowledging the efforts your former partner
makes. A father who accepts his role in providing for
his family financially makes a sacrifice. It may be legally

expected of him but he is nevertheless being honourable when he holds to it – and many do not. If a father continues to make efforts to be close and helpful to his children, he is doing something immensely valuable. If he makes efforts not to spoil their relationship with their mother, he offers her and them a gift. A mother who can recognise these as acts of generosity, will feel more forgiving.

A father who can recognise what his former partner does in looking after the children as best she can, however imperfectly; if he can appreciate when she does not get in the way of – and particularly if she actively helps – his ongoing relationship with their children, he may notice that she continues to offer him something special.

Such ongoing acts of reparation are a much more important use of apology than any form of words.

Notes

1 Hemingway, Ernest (2004) *A Farewell to Arms*. London: Arrow, p. 222.
2 Rawls, John (1971) *A Theory of Justice*. Cambridge, MA: Harvard University Press.
3 Tutu, Bishop Desmond (1999) *No Future without Forgiveness*. London: Rider, p. 135.
4 Wallerstein, J.S. and Kelly, J.B. (2004) *Surviving the Breakup*. New York: Basic Books.
5 Wallerstein, J.S. and Blakeslee, S. (1995) *The Good Marriage: How and why love lasts*. London: Bantam.
6 Beckett, Sister Wendy (2006) *Sister Wendy on Prayer*. London: Continuum.
7 Beckett, *Sister Wendy on Prayer*.
8 Amis, Martin (2000) *Experience*. London: Jonathan Cape, p. 256.

13

Acceptance – and mourning

I long ago abandoned the notion of a life without storms, or a world without dry and killing seasons. Life is too complicated, too constantly changing, to be anything other than what it is . . . there will always be propelling, disturbing elements . . . at the end of the day, the individual moments of restlessness, of bleakness, of strong persuasions and maddened enthusiasms, that inform one's life, change the nature and direction of one's work, and give final meaning and colour to one's loves and friendships.

Psychiatrist, Kay Jamison[1]

Mourning

Grief is like rain: you have to put your head down and walk right through it.

Martin Amis[2]

We must each of us find our own way through grief. Most of us do it reluctantly – and only if we decide there is no other way. It is easy to become fearful of experiencing emotional pain but by constantly shutting it out, you lose the experience that pain can be survived – and indeed that things of value can come from it.

The courage that is needed is not to do with *being strong* and doing your best to *not care*. Rather it is to do with finding the internal strength to face the facts of life you would much rather avoid. Mourning is about facing the reality of the loss – and the pain and sorrow that goes with that.

Mourning takes its own time. It doesn't help to be pushed into it. You can't do it to order. It is not a race to get through as fast as possible. You have to be gentle to yourself in this time: you are an emotional invalid. The pain will, slowly, slowly, ease. Use medication, alcohol in moderation if you need to – but if you blot out all pain, you inhibit grief and may stay stuck.

Much of this task you have to do alone – though it helps to have friends or family to check in with along the route. No one can make everything all right. Nothing will be all right in quite the same old way again – but you can survive, and you can grow. If you feel you are getting too stuck on your own, there is always the possibility of therapeutic help.

Mourning is a bit like digestion. All that you brought into your partnership – all that occurred in the time you were together; and in the time of breaking up – all needs to be turned round and round, tasted, chewed over, taken in, bathed in acids to break it into bits – and given time to absorb.

It is possible to keep your suffering and loss as just a constipated, meaningless lump – smelly and harbouring germs: better just to flush it away. Emotional constipation leaves you a passive, outraged victim: but you are a victim not only of your ex's deeds, but also of your own attacks on your capacity to think, feel and to know yourself. And how can you hope for good relationships in the future if you can't bear to confront your own feelings – let alone face anyone else's?

Mourning is a bit like childbirth. In labour it is possible to suffer horrific pains but, because of worry and tension, the labour does not advance. Birth coaches encourage women in labour to *ride the pain, like a surfer riding a wave*: in other words, not to fight it, but to go with it. It can be huge and dangerous. It is terrifying. But there can also be a curious pleasure and exhilaration in experiencing and riding this overwhelming human experience.

Like a woman in labour, you have something inside that kicks, puts pressure on you – and is life-threatening if it stays stuck. You need to open yourself up to allow this unknown thing out. It may be the birth of something creative and alive, or it may be stillborn. Either way it's better to let it out, than have it fester inside.

> Ideas come to us as the substitutes for griefs, and griefs, at the moment when they change into ideas, lose some part of their power to injure our heart; the transformation itself, even, for an instant, releases suddenly a little joy.[3]
>
> Marcel Proust[4]

When you can allow yourself to have words to think and know what you feel, rather than facing a confused blur of misery, there may be unexpected pleasures: it can be a relief – and one which *releases . . . a little joy.*

Take time alone – look at photos, listen to music, walk along beaches, stay in bed, whatever you feel like doing – and find out what comes. Weep, scream, sing . . . self-rock, run, dance . . . paint, write – but find some way to get feelings, impulses, words out.

Protect yourself. Reassure yourself with thoughts that there *are* those who love you. Think of them. Stay in touch. Remind yourself of the other things you like about yourself – now and in the past.

There are two losses to mourn.

The loss of feeling *perfect* and justified

As you pull back from your fierce assumption that any flaws and failings are all outside you, in someone else, such as your ex, you face – we all of us face – that we are flawed: selfish, careless, sometimes deliberately hurtful, self-protective, withholding, bullying. That is not to say that there are not other desirable aspects to us – that we can be loving, courageous, forgiving, doing our best – some of the time.

The downside is that life and relationships are more precarious, if we are not just *entitled* to love.

But there are some advantages too: if you don't just *deserve* to be loved then what you are offered – by friends, family, community and maybe a partner – is more of a gift, something to enjoy, value and be grateful for.

The other advantage of being able to bear noticing imperfections is that it is possible to know yourself more, good and bad, rather than having to so carefully keep aspects of you out of sight, lurking and threatening in dark corners of your mind.

The loss of the partnership

The partnership you have to grieve for is not only the increasingly troubled relationship of the years leading up to the break. You have lost the passion and sexual excitement of the early partnership; of the sharing of hopes; of your youth. You have to mourn all that. You have to mourn the years in between; of many difficulties that were overcome, many good experiences shared.

You have to grieve for the time when your partner held you in a cherished place in their mind: he (or she) may have looked at you with passion, tenderness, humour, admiration. Then they were your *companion and (your) familiar friend*. While they may have looked at you also with exasperation and seen your flaws, they still felt you were special and had wanted to remain linked to you. That profound reassurance is now lost. You lose your unquestioning belief that fundamentally you are *lovable* – and that is a sore blow.

You also have to grieve for the loss of your love for your partner, or its enfeeblement: that once you may have felt excited, loving, giving, open, generous – and then you stopped. As a couple you failed to keep those loving feelings sufficiently alive. You got bored. You took each other for granted. You both failed – in countless ways – your original hope and dreams for the two of you.

Your future is different from what you had assumed. If you don't have a new partner currently, you can't know whether you will in the future, or not.

If you are in a new partnership, it may be fresh and exciting – but it is also less safe and known. It may, or may not, work out. It doesn't yet have much shared history. Despite the pleasure and hope of a new relationship, it is a loss in its own way: your new partner will never know that younger *you*. That shared history of your younger years is lost – along with the partner with whom you shared it.

You may want to argue that there were no good memories – but are you sure? If so, why did you stay together at all? Did you keep hoping that things would get better? In which case there is the disappointment of all those hopes and wishes – however unrealistic they may seem with hindsight.

If you really believe the whole partnership was a waste, then the anger you will face is not only with your partner – who was not the person you imagined they were – but also with yourself: for committing to the relationship unadvisedly; or for being too hesitant to take action earlier. What you then have to grieve is the time lost, opportunities lost, when you were too fearful or uncertain to leave.

If you feel too sad – remember to widen your focus: when compared with the suffering that others have to endure, many face worse. That is not to say your suffering is little: it is not, it can feel horrific. But it isn't – it really isn't – the worst in the world.

In remembering the good things in your partnership that are now lost, you may well feel overwhelmed with sadness, and you may need to remind yourself that all was not good: there were times which were hurtful, infuriating – or just plain dreary.

If you feel depressed and low, don't automatically assume it is a result of the break-up. Were you never low when you were together? If you were with your ex now – not only in one of the best moments but also as it was more recently – would you really be feeling so much better?

Living with someone who is no longer loving, and is not sufficiently interested in becoming more so, is not a good long-term solution – or even a short-term one. Many in the follow-up studies – including those who did not end up with a permanent partner, and after the shock had died down – felt that it was a relief to be away from the silent draining of a relationship where resentment had crowded out interest and affection. Their emotional and physical well-being was better than those who had stayed in an unhappy marriage.[5]

Watch out too for idealising your friends' marriages as a way of feeling sadder, lonelier and sorrier for yourself. Yes, they are lucky if they have someone who can share with them, put their arms round them, be reassured by, have a good sexual time with – but all marriages have their difficulties, struggles and compromises.

> Mourning [a death] never ends: only with time it erupts less frequently.
>
> John Bowlby[6]

Similarly for those whose partnership fails, moments of sadness or regret may likewise never completely end – and if you think about it, it would be unrealistic to expect that a relationship that was once so important, would never again stir up such feelings. If the trajectory of recovering from loss is of feeling sadness less frequently, and the intensity of distress slowly diminishing – and provided there are new interests to satisfy your need for involvement in life – that is not so bad.

Having moments of sadness and regret doesn't mean that breaking up was the wrong thing to have done. Had you stayed in your partnership you may still have had memories of the past which would stir up sadness – since, together or not, those times are past. Staying together would not mean that you had no regrets – just different ones.

Robert Graves' poem on 'A Former Attachment' describes this slow diminishing of grief and hurt:[7]

And glad to find, on again looking at it,
It meant even less to me than I had thought –
You know the ship is moving when you see

The boxes on the quayside sliding away
And become smaller – and feel a calm delight
When the port's cleared and the coast out of sight,
And ships are few, each on its proper course,
With no occasion for approach or discourse.

And the dried remains of your ended marriage? You might want to store them on a high shelf – not as something that tugs at you day to day, but as a record of a once-important, and hopefully interesting, part of your journey in life. And – like old mementoes that you stuff carelessly in a cupboard and come upon unexpectedly – you can be pleased and touched to find old memories.

Notes

1 Jamison, Kay (1997) *An Unquiet Mind: A memoir of moods and madness*. London: Picador, p. 216.
2 Quoted in Cooke, Rachel (2006) The Amis papers. *Observer*, Review, 1 October.
3 Les idées sont les succédanées des chagrins; au moment où ceux-ci se changent en idées, ils perdent une partie de leur action nocive sur notre cur, et même, au premier instant, la transformation elle-même dégage subitement de la joie.
4 Proust, Marcel (2000) *In Search of Lost Time: Time regained*. London: Vintage, p. 268.
5 Hetherington, E.M. and Kelly, J. (2002) *For Better or for Worse: Divorce reconsidered*. London: Norton.
6 Bowlby, John (1998) *Loss: Sadness and depression*. Volume 3 of *Attachment and Loss*. London: Pimlico, p. 101.
7 Graves, Robert (2000) *Robert Graves' Complete Poems in One Volume*. Edited by Beryl Graves and Dunstan Ward. Manchester: Carcanet Press.

PART 4

Children

Figure 2

14

Noticing children's distress

It is hard to bear someone's sadness and distress when there is little you can do to make it better. It is worse when the one who is suffering is your child. And worse still when you are, in any way, the cause of that suffering. But if – to protect yourself from feeling guilty – you shut down awareness of your children's pain, then not only do they lose your physical presence, but also they lose a *you* who is able to parent them – to hear and think about them.

A child's anguish does not diminish because it is not acknowledged. The message that he (or she) will receive is that the disruption of his world should be easy to bear and is no reason to make a fuss. Since your break-up is inevitably painfully distressing for him, then he has not only failed to keep you – his parents – together, but now he is *failing* to manage your separation as calmly as he should. He really is utterly alone.

Andrew was 8 when his parents were breaking up. He drew a vivid picture (see Figure 3). In it:

Everything is sucked into the air in a tornado – trees, umbrellas, chairs, books. An aeroplane seems to be heading straight for the centre of the storm. Some people are running or bicycling away. A figure on the far left seems not to notice. There is a signpost saying, uselessly, STOP.

Andrew was told by a loving family friend, 'You are the man of the family now. You have to look after your Mum'.

Figure 3

So Andrew was not supposed to feel overwhelmed and terri-fyingly little: he was expected somehow to take on adult functions and make everything all right for his mother. His little *STOP* sign was supposed to calm the tornado – and he worried that he was letting everyone down when it did not.

Andrew's father would come back to visit, artificially bright, and want to talk about school or football – but not about why he was not living there any longer. His mother was unreliable: she dropped him off for football on a bitterly cold day without a sweater and forgot to pick him up on time. Andrew waited ages, wondering whether she might forget about him altogether. It seemed the safest thing to do was to get used to the coldness and neglect all around and not expect anything.

It is hard to notice or respond to your children's reactions when you are in the middle of breaking up – whether you are parenting alone or involved in a new relationship. If you manage your own feelings by suppressing them, you will similarly want to shut out any awareness of your children's distress – but doing so leaves your children emotionally abandoned.

If your children are quiet and seem not to make a fuss it can seem easier to turn a blind eye and hope that everything is OK. You can tell yourself that:

Talking about it will only make it worse – or make you feel worse.

If they make a fuss it can be hard to know what to do to help:

You can't do anything to make it better anyway.
They'll get over it.

But time does not automatically heal. Ignoring your child's pain, loss, anger and guilt may make these feelings submerge, but it does not make them go away. Unhappy children – whose feelings are not acknowledged – become adults with scars, which make it harder for them to partner, and parent, well in their turn.

As a parent you can fear that if you acknowledge any guilt that you are less than perfect, then your children will lose their trust in you and will never forgive you.

In fact the reverse is so: if you don't acknowledge that the break-up has hurt him (or her), or you put all the blame on your ex, it means that your child is not given the freedom to express their feelings – including hate for you for not protecting them from hurt: they are given no opportunity to accept and forgive this less-than-perfect you: they can't move on.

Ben's father left when he was 5. Ben felt that his father had never really acknowledged or apologised for the impact this had had on him and his mother: if only his father had been able to, it would have helped him so much. As Ben's desperation at not being understood grew, so did his rage – which made it even harder for Ben's father to hear him.

Thirty years later Ben came for therapy because he was unhappy with his life and feared he might leave his young children, in the way that his father had left him. His anger, which had never been acknowledged by his father, continued in a chronic resentment and subtle punishment of his father – who despite his other faults remained involved with, and concerned for, Ben.

Ben got a certain pleasure from his own suffering: it showed his father how much he had hurt his son. He found it hard to acknowledge his anger directly, because he feared it made him unforgivably bad. Was that why his father had left? Was it all *his* fault? Ben would torment himself and his feelings of despair, and deprivation kept growing.

Ben's father may have worried that to acknowledge the hurt to his son would only make Ben's anger worse. But not acknowledging it did not make it go away: rather Ben's anger remained stuck and increasingly rancid. Had Ben's father been able to acknowledge the hurt that his leaving had caused his son, he would have offered him some real parenting: the experience that terribly distressing things can happen – but that they can be thought about, shared and borne, however painfully.

Ben felt too that he was protecting his mother, by continuing to keep going to war with his father: had she been able to let go of her own resentment she might have made it easier for Ben to let go of his and to find an accommodation with his father, however imperfect.

As a parent, you are much more able to do this if you have done some of your own emotional work. This then makes it possible for you to be able to recognise your children's feelings – with inevitable distress and guilt – but without being overwhelmed by it. If you can't bear to hear your children's distress, they are left with the options of suppressing their feelings, or of expressing them in actions – which may be temporarily relieving, but is less controllable because your kids are learning from you to shut down their capacity to feel and think.

The difficulty is often not so much that your children don't express their distress – but that it is so upsetting to notice when they do. After her father left home, Rosie, aged 10, wrote:

I feel like I'm in jail
and all alown.
I don't know what
To do I whant help as well
As need it. But I know
what tipe I need a gental
person a kind and loving
person funny as well as
one who goes away
to much

One is my Mum

The other is my Dad

and don't have much more to say
except I'm trapt, sad
and all alown.

Rosie's vivid writing – and her spelling which has gone awry – conveys her enormous distress and confusion: her father is one who *goes away too much* – with whom she feels angry, but he is also one who is *kind, loving, funny* – and whom she sadly misses. Rosie may also feel that her mother, caught up in her own immense distress, has *gone away* from her emotionally too.

When you are so caught up in the stress of breaking up you may risk overly burdening your children with your misery. But equally, by attempting to be overly cheerful, you can deny the reality of their loss.

> Annie, still devastated by the break-up of her marriage, tried to cheer herself, and her daughter Lily, up by saying, 'In the long run it may end up better for all of us'. Her daughter replied, 'It won't be for me'.

While this is painfully sad to think of, it is true: Lily's life would have been easier if her parents had been able to remain together. Annie meant well and was attempting to be cheerful for Lily – but in doing so she pushed aside Lily's agony that her world had fallen apart and her parents were in pieces.

When one parent stops loving the other, a child will dread that his (or her) parents' love for him is equally unreliable. One way to cope is by being very good, taking care of and reassuring his parent – who can be so in need of reassurance. A child may try and ensure love by being successful – but his striving is not for himself, for the pleasure of it, but is driven by a deep anxiety about the loss of love.

> Lily feared her father's leaving meant he did not love her as much as she had believed. For how could he love her and still leave? She was terrified of losing him completely.
>
> If her father could leave, maybe her mother could too? If she were angry with either of her parents they might stop coping altogether. Or the explosive rage she had observed between them might turn on her. She worked very hard to be good and to make them proud of her. Maybe then she would be safe.

Children can feel that there is no one left to be the parent –
and that they are the only one to fill the gap. Lily wrote in a
card to her mother:

> Don't worry we will take care of everything. I'm not
> joking. Ha ha.

The *ha ha* has a pretty hollow ring to it. Lily's world will
never feel quite the same again – a world in which she can
effortlessly take for granted that there are adults who will
take care of everything. However good the relationship she
might regain with each parent, she would still prefer they
had remained together, providing reassurance that love can
work, and not asking of her that she split her life and love
in two, in order to have time with both.

Lily's belief in the resilience of love was damaged in the
short term – but worryingly, maybe in the long term too
(see Figure 4):

> She illustrated the story of Rumpelstiltskin – but after a
> happy wedding picture and the promise of '. . . happily
> ever after', there was a last page – 'or maybe not' – where
> the couple are rowing furiously:
>
> > The wife says, 'I hate you your so mean and I am so so
> > so so glad were divorceing'. The husband yells back, 'your
> > so ugly I hate you as well and I wish you were dead you
> > ugly thing and if we werent divorceing I would be dead'

– a picture which many couples breaking up will recognise.

Robbie, aged 9, made a cartoon story (see Figure 5):

> A child is in bed and hears something howling. He goes to
> investigate in the graveyard. Something is happening – a
> man is changing into a werewolf.
>
> > 'The werewolf noticed. He pounced. Michael gave in
> > [in] a huge fight, but the wolf was a bit too strong'.

In the period leading up to his parents' acrimonious break-
up, Robbie is likely to have heard *howling* in the night – of

Figure 4

panic, hurt or rage: something terrifying and dangerous. It is impressive that in the story Robbie even has the courage to *investigate*.

If you consider – as an analyst or child psychotherapist might – that the *werewolf* expresses something of Robbie's experience then, like the *werewolf*, both his father and his mother are unexpectedly and fundamentally *changed*. If Robbie's mother and father can find their way to settle down slowly after the shock of separation, they may be able to

He ran over quickly and saw what was happening. A man was changing into a werewolf!

Figure 5

resume something like their old familiar *shape*, and their capacity to parent him. In which case, Robbie will be able to settle too, even if the safety of his *bed* – his previously safe ordered world – will never be quite the same again. But if his parents remain in their changed *werewolf* shape – whether embattled or collapsed – Robbie's world will remain disturbed.

Even when parents are able to recover their parenting capacity, a child can be left with anxieties which he may need help to notice. For the *werewolf* may also represent a part of Robbie – raging and biting in panic and distress in response to the family disruption. If Robbie fears that his biting *werewolf* feelings will do too much damage to his parents, whom he also loves and desperately depends on, he may be inhibited in approaching them for comfort. If Robbie believes that his *werewolf* feelings will not be recognised with any sympathy, he will miss out on the experience of opening up and gaining comfort – and in the future he may be less able to risk reaching out in any future intimate relationship. It may seem safer to retreat back to *bed*, to hopelessness and silent depression, and shut down his capacity to *notice* and *investigate*. If he retreats in this way, time alone may not be enough to make him feel better.

> Three years on Robbie, now age 12, could not remember life before his parents' break-up.

Without help from his parents, another adult or professional help, Robbie risks remaining withdrawn.

> Lizzie's mother left her father when she was 5, taking her back to her family home in a European city. Her mother told her what fun this was and why there was no reason to miss her father. This was confusing for Lizzie, who was fond of her father and did miss him and her previous safe life before – unlike now when she often waited anxiously for her mother to come home from work. To say this, even to think it, would have felt like a terrible betrayal – and so Lizzie did not think it.
>
> As an adult she had an underlying constant sense of panic; that she had to make everything all right: it left her little room to express her pent-up feelings, which sometimes burst out in incomprehensible ways.

A child whose sadness and anger are not recognised may express his feelings in varying ways. He may attack others, hoping to make them feel little and intimidated, instead of himself. He may attack himself by actions such as cutting or starving himself. He may try to prove that he is not little or intimidated, but the opposite – fearless and strong – by dangerous risk-taking. He can deny feelings of dependence, or wish for closeness, by withdrawal and contempt of anything tender. He may attempt to deaden his feelings by stuffing food compulsively, heavy drinking or drug-taking.

Adam was 13 when his mother left his father. He stayed with his father, partly because his father was devastated and angry – as he was too.

Gradually, as his mother settled with her new partner, Adam visited and slowly accepted her having left. But his father felt Adam's renewed relationship with his mother as a terrible betrayal: as if he were taking her side.

Adam felt that he had lost his father's love. He could not risk talking to his father about it because his father got too angry. He worried about expressing any anger with his mother in case it overwhelmed her with guilt. He found that drinking helped him feel less anguished.

Boys such as Andrew, Robbie and Adam can feel that they should be strong and that any other feelings – of fear, need, deprivation or anger – should be denied. If they cannot accept care for themselves, they will end up empty and may have trouble finding the emotional resources to care for a future partner.

Girls such as Lily and Lizzie are at risk of building their sense of self-worth by mothering their mother or their father – but in doing so miss having their own needs met. They may have difficulties leaving home – partly out of guilt at leaving their mother, but also because they have missed out on the emotional nourishment they need to be fully separate.

If you can stay open to your children's anger, you help them learn that angry feelings can be expressed and can be heard: they don't have to be kept inside like the monstrous *were-wolf* feelings of Robbie's cartoon. If you can listen to your children's distress, you help them discover that, though painful, feelings can be expressed; that thinking – *investigating what is happening in the graveyard* – can help sort out reality from the dread when these feelings remain unexamined. It doesn't remove the source of the pain – but it makes the distressed feelings *thinkable*.

You may well have to be first to raise the subject: to show your children that painful feelings can be addressed, even if doing so stirs up your – and their – grief and anger.

Sometimes feelings can be eased by sharing them, rather than by blocking them out.

> Annie was holidaying with her son, James, and family friends. Seeing the close – but not perfect – marriage of her friends she felt sad that her own imperfect marriage had ended. She noticed that James was moody and wondered whether he might not feel the same.
> She asked whether it was hard for him seeing his friends with their Dad, when his own Dad no longer lived with them. He agreed it was hard – and seemed relieved. Subsequently James warmed to the other Dad, even enjoying teasing him and learning from him.

Painful things happen and – however good a parent you want to be – you can't protect your children from that. Sometimes, as in a break-up, that painful experience is the result of your (and your partner's) actions and inactions. If you listen to your children's anger without collapsing into endless self-berating guilt, or by retaliating, you are doing a good job. Some of their anger may be unfair – and that can be discussed. Some of it will be painfully accurate.

Your children have a real complaint. Your break-up is almost certainly the worst thing in their world. Having parents living apart is a real, ongoing blow. Their lives may settle, their relationship with each of you may survive and grow, but it is a tremendous blow for them – and it helps them if you can face that fact. It is not a cause for endless self-abasement and appeasement – not least because feeling endlessly guilty doesn't help you to parent your children well.

You are not perfect – but if you can forgive yourself sufficiently to acknowledge this to your children, then you make it possible for them to face up to this reality too. They can then know that you are neither an ideal nor a monster, but human, have been foolish, have made mistakes – which gives them the option to face reality and, with however mixed feelings, continue to love this imperfect you.

Life is not always easy or fair – and we all have to come to terms with that fact. You can't make things magically better. Acknowledging the impact on your children is one thing you *can* offer. They may not like it – because they too want it made *all better*. They may rage at you for failing at the marriage, for letting them down – and you won't like that. But if you can tolerate all these feelings without pushing them aside or retaliating, you are doing one of your most important jobs of parenting.

15

Evidence of the impact on children

The examples in Chapter 14 are single case studies and, it could be argued, may not be relevant for all children of divorce. But those children are on the *fortunate* end of the spectrum in that they did not come from overly disturbed families; the fathers stayed in their children's lives and contributed financially. The difficulties the parents faced were *normal* in that they were not to do with managing particular poverty or violence, but with the feelings of hurt, guilt, resentment and despair associated with breaking up. The impact on the children of their parents' break-up was *normal*.

Follow-up studies

Long-term studies of many families after divorce also highlight the risk to children, compared to those whose parents have stayed together, despite equal levels of marital dissatisfaction. Such evidence is alarming and unwelcome – and it's tempting to turn the page – but at least knowing about the potential risks puts you in a better position to recognise them and avoid them as best you can.

There are several large, wide-scale surveys carried out in the United States and the UK which document the increased risk of difficulty children of divorced parents face – independent of separate factors such as loss of income; or personality factors in one or both parents which might make them more likely to break up.[1] The impact is not only to do with short-term stress, but also one which persists over time – and indeed some problems reveal themselves more later when those children of divorce face the tasks of adulthood such as managing a relationship, work and a family.

In addition two teams led by clinicians – psychoanalyst Judith Wallerstein and her team in California and psychologist Mavis Hetherington in Virginia – followed adults and children of divorce in great detail over many years.[2] They looked at how adults managed post-divorce and their capacity to parent – and how this affected their growing children.

When the studies began in the early 1970s, both teams were relatively optimistic of the capacity of adults and children to adapt – but as the years passed, they became more concerned. Based on their continuing work with families after divorce, both teams argue that – though divorce is now much more frequent, and less stigmatised than in the 1970s; while fewer fathers completely withdraw from the family than previously; and while women have more work skills – the impact on children has not changed. It has to do with our all-too-human ways of managing painful hurt, guilt and loss.

> Many people, adults and children alike, are in fact not better off. We have created new kinds of families in which relationships are fragile and unreliable. Children today receive far less nurturance, protection and parenting than was their lot a few years ago.[3]

Parenting

Researchers have documented how in the short term parents were preoccupied by their own massive internal disruption. They could be depressed, exhausted, overwhelmed or frantic. They might rush out socially to keep depression at bay, or sink into torpor. Many occupied themselves with bitter fights over access to the children and over money, which seemed to the researchers a desperate attempt to maintain self-esteem. One in four children witnessed physical violence as the marriage was breaking up.

Parents faced external demands that took their time and energy. One, if not both, partners needed to move; arrangements needed to be made about money; both partners faced loss of available income; mothers who had not worked, or worked part-time, all of a sudden had to work longer hours. The parents often felt in need of looking after themselves.

In this initial period of intense distress, both partners could show extremes of volatility and hostility. Many attributed their partner's disturbance to personality factors they just had never previously noticed, rather than to the short-term impact of the disruption. As a result each could have anxieties about the other's suitability to parent responsibly and could attempt to exclude him (or her) – which exacerbated the tension between them.[4] A father who felt shut out in this way might resort to force and bullying to get access to his children, rather than attempting to reassure the mother that he could be responsible and responsive to their children.

Children complained of being given virtually no information by either parent about what was happening, or how to make sense of it. Few children had other adults who talked to them in a calm way about the break-up, but when one did – an involved grandparent or family member – it was enormously helpful. Children often lost touch with their grandparents on the non-resident parent's side.

A parent who was in a new partnership would invest much hope that this new person would make life good again. In relation to this, many children felt an also-ran.

What was particularly detrimental to parenting well was when or if the following happened:

- Parents continued to fight bitterly – often in the courts.
- One parent tried to enlist the child's support in their battle with the other parent.
- A parent was not coping well and – rather than looking outside for support – relied on his (or her) child to parent them: to keep them company and provide reassurance of their worth.
- A parent did not provide consistent, firm, but flexible boundaries.

Mothers

What was most important for children's well-being was how well the resident parent managed – in the vast majority of cases when children were young, their mother.

Post-divorce, many mothers had less time to attend to the needs of their children, not only because they were preoccupied with their own shock and need to adjust but also because they needed to work longer hours to bring in an income. This need was compounded if fathers did not pay their full contribution, regularly – and more than half did not. Women who could find a way to be tactful with the father and could help them remain involved with their children's lives, rather than get drawn into battle, were more likely to get the father's financial support.[5]

A mother who could not bring herself to adjust to the inevitable drop in her standard of living would also need to work longer hours. A decision – for example, to hold on to the family home when it was a struggle to afford it, or to keep children in fee-paying schools rather than moving to the area of a good state school – which might look courageous at first glance also had its downside: to fund this former lifestyle the mother needed to be absent and exhaust herself working and as a result had less time and energy available for her children – and herself.

A mother's extended absence was a particular problem for pre-school children:

The loss of the mother pervades and forever changes the way a child, especially a young child, experiences the world.[6]

If they began a new relationship, many women found themselves torn between the competing demands of her children, her job and her new partner. Children often felt excluded by their mother's involvement with her new relationship, and the biggest reason for new partnerships foundering was difficulties between the children and her new partner.

Fathers

Many fathers underestimate the impact on them of the loss of their children. They lose their role as a parent; many fear that they will lose touch with their children and that their former partner will turn the children against them.

For a father who generally has his children for a shorter time, he has to manage the strains of an intermittent relationship with his children: no sooner has he and his children slowly begun to adjust to each other, than they have to let go until next time. It is harder for him to set limits on his children when their stay is short. It is particularly difficult when the children's visit does not include an overnight stay: one father commented,

> It's hard for me; having her but not really having her. It's to the point where I've begun dreading visiting days. I know I'll only be with her for the day and then I'll have to give her back.[7]

Fathers are more at risk of managing their pain and distress by withdrawal than absent mothers. Researchers were startled by the degree to which many fathers, even ones who had been devoted before the break-up, became emotionally blunted towards their children.[8] Twice as many teenagers reported that they had a poor relationship with their father than in intact families – though few fathers acknowledged the difficulty.[9]

Within an intact marriage, a father is helped by his partner to understand what is going on with their children – and he loses her help in this as he struggles to maintain his relationship with his kids, post-divorce.

Some fathers withdrew completely from their children's lives: not so much out of lack of interest, but as a result of rage at their ex-partners; their feelings of powerlessness; difficulties bearing feelings of loss and guilt; and the struggle to maintain only an intermittent contact with his children, who could be suspicious, mistrustful or angry. Younger men in particular had difficulty in having any faith that their children needed them – especially if the mother had found a new partner.

But it is a terrible blow for a child if the father withdraws. Wallerstein describes one sad example was of:

> a father who kept up his financial commitments to his family, but did not involve himself with his children, who lived not far away, saying *I doubt that they miss me*. His son meanwhile was going through all kinds of adolescent delinquency. When asked by the researcher how much he was seeing his father, the boy sobbed for 35 minutes.[10]

In addition to many such tragic accounts, there were other times when fathers, who had not necessarily been involved before the break-up, became more engaged with their children as a result of the divorce.[11]

What helped a father remain involved with his children was if they could stay overnight, and if the father shared legal responsibility. In this case the father was less likely to withdraw from his children's lives and he was more likely to provide the legally expected financial support.

Many men found it difficult to accept that the separation meant that their former partners had significant control over access to their children – and if they refused to accept this fact, they could attempt to use power and bullying to gain control – in a vicious spiral which ended in making their ex more suspicious and hostile.[12] Many women were then reluctant to share legal custody with a former partner who was feared and resented.

Ten years after break-up, half the parents got by by parenting *in parallel* to each other: they did not interfere with their ex's relationship with their children, but they could not discuss together their children's problems or agree consistent ways of responding to them. Their children had to manage very separate lives in the two households, and felt they had to protect one parent by keeping their life with the other parent hidden.

A quarter of the parents had not found a way of letting go of ongoing battle and resentment: they continued to undermine or disparage the other parent. Some refused to be flexible about times of visits to fit in with the children's needs, but rather insisted their children fit in with theirs. They could not negotiate with each other but would return to the courts to resolve disputes – and often when a solution had been imposed on them by the courts with which they did not concur, many would not abide by it.[13]

Only a quarter of the parents had found a way to parent cooperatively: where they could be sufficiently flexible to fit in with the needs of their children; had found a way to talk together about the children, when necessary, without overwhelming distress or rage; and were able to discuss and agree limits.

When parents *could* manage to cooperate in this way, it helped their children. Not only did the children feel less responsible for keeping warring parents apart. They also gained the experience that, whatever their parents' private battles, the battles did not take priority over their love, and concern for the best interests, of their children. The divorce may have demolished much – but it had not broken their parents' commitment to them.

Children

The Wallerstein team observed what the children, whose parents were breaking up, expressed in their play. They described in detail one young boy's struggle in the face of his parents' break-up.[14]

Noah was three when his mother left suddenly: his mother was described as chaotic and she needed Noah to parent her.

In his play with small dolls, three year old Noah persistently searched for good care for a baby doll. But each time, the mother doll replied 'I'm too busy now. I'll do it later'. Or 'I can't stand to hear about it right now'.

A year later, aged four, Noah's play was wild and chaotic. There was no sense of any parent who might be a possible source of comfort. In Noah's play: a flying, aeroplane father was falling and a baby was looking for a place to hide away.

At one moment Noah held a bullet near the doll father's head. Later the father doll was walking backwards, away from the babies. Noah commented sadly of the father doll, 'he does not know that he is walking backwards'.

Noah's perception of his father's retreat was accurate: shortly afterwards his father lost contact with him for six years.

Age six, Noah's play centred on running away from parental figures, with no safe place to hide.

Noah's father, following the failure of several marriages, suffered a lengthy depression. He regained contact with his son when Noah was in adolescence. Noah accepted his father and recognised his father's limitations, saying 'he's good at organising and being practical, but I would like to be closer to him than I am.' In his father's eyes the resumed relationship *was* a close one: the father seemed more concerned to reassure himself, than to recognise the difficulties and look at what he might do to be closer to his son.

Noah was comparatively lucky. At 18 he seemed to be doing surprisingly well. The researchers felt he had been able to receive good parenting in the first three years of his life, which helped him. There was also, importantly, a stable, resilient aunt–uncle couple who were reliably there for him – and this is unusual. He was an imaginative child who had been able to make use of the adults who were around – including the researchers. Noah was hopeful about future relationships but he had not yet faced the complexities and anxieties of an intimate relationship – which is often when difficulties become more apparent.

One note of concern might be the degree to which Noah feels able to acknowledge anger to his father and to his mother. At 4 years old, the father-doll walks off after Noah holds the bullet by the father-doll's head. It is possible that Noah's father could not bear to know about his son's hurt and anger, however hidden – and this contributed to his withdrawal. Certainly if that is what Noah believes, he is likely to have difficulty expressing anger – which might create problems for him in a future intimate relationship.

Adolescence

Ten years after break-up, only half of the mothers and a quarter of fathers were seen to be providing *nurturant* parenting – responsive, attentive, warm and firm – to their now-teenage children. A third of the teenagers were described as *essentially unparented . . . abandoned physically and emotionally* – often those children of parents who were continuing to fight bitterly.[15]

Many mothers were busy working and by the end of the day had little time or energy to attend sufficiently to their teenage children, or to provide consistent limits for them.[16] The less a mother was available to her children, the more they were likely to be aggressive and rivalrous with each other. Mothers had more difficulty managing adolescent boys, who tended to be more challenging, oppositional and physical than girls. One adolescent commented how

> the worst thing about the divorce was that Mom wasn't home. There was no discussion, no rules – just an empty feeling. That's how I got into drugs and sex.[17]

It is hard for a mother to set limits when she feels in need of support herself, and particularly if she is without the support of a partner. But if she can't find a way of negotiating firm limits with her teenage children, their behaviour is likely to become more challenging – which is even more exhausting for her, and unsafe for them.

Many teenagers described being *scarred* by the impact of their parents' divorce.[18] They showed more signs of difficulty, compared to peers from families who had remained together despite similar levels of marital dissatisfaction.

Some responded with depression, anxiety and withdrawal; others were aggressive and insecure. Adolescent boys in particular were more likely to get into delinquent behaviour – heavy drinking and drug-taking; serious risk-taking; and violent behaviour. Teenagers from divorced families had sex earlier, were more promiscuous, and sex was often separated from affection for a partner – it feeling safer not to risk trusting another person in an intimate relationship. If parents went through the disruption of further broken partnerships, the impact on their children was more severe.[19]

Fewer teenagers from divorced families attempted college and more dropped out. Fewer fathers helped their children financially through college, even though they had the money – and even when sometimes they supported the children of their current partner to do so.[20]

Those who had more resources – who were attractive, bright and responsive – did well. Others who were physically or emotionally more vulnerable were at particular risk.[21] Some from large families were more likely to lose out – when an absent parent might be able to maintain a bond with one or two children, but often not all when the family was larger.[22]

There was some concern that some teenagers who seemed to be doing well might be doing almost *too well*; they were charming – but were felt by the researchers to be rather manipulative and inauthentic.[23] Girls were particularly likely to have taken on the role of parenting an unhappy parent, and they could continue being *good* and providing caring for the needy parent, and others, at the expense of their own needs. Hetherington and Kelly point out that there are potential advantages – in that some learn a resourcefulness and resilience that distinguishes them from peers from intact families.

Elizabeth Marquardt, herself a successful *child* of parents who had a *good* divorce (in that they did not fight) and who studied grown up *children* of divorce argues that they can feel in *permanent inner conflict*: they compartmentalise themselves to manage their parents' split world; feel pulled in two directions; have to keep secrets to protect their parents; manage loneliness and missing their absent parent; and do not feel safely, taken-for-grantedly *at home* in either setting.[24]

She cites Rebecca Walker:

I remember coming and going, going and coming. That for me was home . . . I move through days, weeks, people, places, growing attached and then letting go, meeting people and then saying goodbye. Holding on makes it harder to be adaptable, harder to meet the demands of a new place. It is easier to forget, to wipe the slate clean, to watch the world go by like a film on a screen, without letting anything stick.[25]

Young adulthood

Divorce is a cumulative experience. Its impact increases over time and rises to a crescendo in adulthood. At each developmental stage, divorce is experienced anew in different ways. In adulthood it affects personality, the ability to trust, expectations about relationships, and the ability to cope with children.[26]

In their work, many young adults had done well enough – and some extremely well – compared to their peer group. If the parents had managed their break-up without too great ongoing stress many had been able to rise to the challenge – though the researchers felt that their good performance had a certain fragility: that they anxiously needed to achieve and please to ensure love, which otherwise felt uncertain.

When the parents continued in bitter battle and had not been able, or willing, to provide warm and firm parenting, the challenge could be just too great for the now-adult child of break-up.

Socially, these young adults from divorced families had more difficulty than peers from intact families. They had poorer relationship skills: they had too high expectations of their partner; they were less able to trust or express affection; and less able to express differences – other than by explosive anger or by withdrawal.[27]

Young women had difficulties trusting in, and expressing anger towards, their partner. They tolerated – and sometimes deliberately chose – a partner who treated them poorly, arguing that it was better to put up with someone disappointing, because at least then they would not risk being left – or if they were, they hoped not to mind too much. Girls who had a good relation with their father or stepfather were more likely to choose relationships in which they could be valued.

The young women in the studies seemed more able to learn and mature. Some learned from the experience of a poor relationship; some from becoming a mother themselves; and some from seeking out therapy.

Young men seemed particularly vulnerable. Many avoided risking intimate relationships at all. As children and adolescents they had withdrawn silently from a relationship with their mother that, in the absence of their father, could feel overly-close – which left them deprived and reluctant to risk stirring up feelings of need which could feel too intense.

One young man was quoted as saying

I decided I had to be my own father and take control of my own life. I couldn't rely on anyone, I was the only one who was responsible for me.[28]

And while his courage and determination is impressive, we may well also be concerned for this young man, who has decided that relying on anyone is unsafe.

Because of their greater tendency to withdraw rather than reach out, the young men were more at risk of remaining apparently – but deceptively – self-sufficient and reliant on drink and drugs to control their mood.

There is evidence that the impact of divorce extends into the third generation: parents' decision to divorce has a small but significant impact on their grandchildren, who are less educated, have more marital difficulty and weaker ties with their own parents.[29]

These facts are alarming and I am pointing them out not to terrify you, but to let you know that making a mess after break-up does not only hurt your ex, which is what you may hope; nor only you, which you may not care about; but also can damage the confidence, resourcefulness and capacity to trust of your children as they go through their lives.

What helped children

> It requires parents to stand apart from their raw, hurt,
> jealous, competitive feelings and take an objective,
> compassionate look at what life will be like for the child.[30]

These studies provide evidence of more vulnerability in
children after break-up than is generally acknowledged –
but they also provide evidence of what helps. What helped
most was:

- Parents not fighting.
- Having a stable, close relation with their mother: if she
  could settle after the break-up, and regain her resources
  to provide attentive, responsive, firm parenting – this
  was most important for the children.
- The father's relation with his children was also important: more important than the absolute amount of time
  he spent with them, was their sense that he valued the
  time which he had with them.
- A good new relationship for one or both parents also
  provided a helpful model of managing a relationship
  positively.
- Stepfathers, grandparents, extended family and friends,
  and mentors were also helpful in supporting the family
  and in providing role-models – especially for boys as
  they approached adolescence.
- So too could the choice of schools – and a decision to
  move, if necessary, to the catchment area of a good
  school had a cumulative good effect.[31]

The need to avoid conflict – and more

The avoidance of ongoing conflict was very important – not
least because it allowed the parents each to settle and regain
some capacity to attend to the needs of their children. But
the evidence is that not fighting is not enough on its own to
protect now-adult *children* from future difficulties.

One of the 'star' girls, Lisa, visited the Wallerstein
team twenty years after her parents' divorce. During her

adolescence, she had seemed to be doing extremely well psychologically, socially and academically – partly, it seemed, because her parents had been able to cooperate in parenting and not actively fight each other.

The team were surprised and concerned to hear how Lisa was tolerating a difficult, disappointing relationship with a boyfriend from whom she felt unable to separate because she feared hurting him, in the same way that she perceived her father had hurt her mother. She could feel sexually aroused by a man whom she did not care for, but not by one for whom she did. It was not until she had had some psychotherapy that she could finally choose a partner who could value her properly and with whom she felt safe to express her needs.

While her parents did not actively fight there was enormous, barely concealed tension. Lisa reported that she

> knew every waking hour [that] my father and stepmother hated my mother and hoped she would disappear. My Mom was jealous of my stepmom and felt that their happiness was based on the *ruins of her life*. (my emphasis)[32]

What Lisa's mother, a successful professional in her own right, conveyed to her daughter – however inadvertently – was that divorce was an unmitigated disaster from which it was not possible to recover even after twenty years. If a parent's life is still *ruined* by an unhappy end to a marriage, how is it possible to risk trust in love? How can you stand up for yourself or express any feelings of anger, when the hurt you cause could be so catastrophic? Or when it could lead to a break-up which you will spend the rest of your life mourning?

Their parents' break-up is hard on children – not in a way that is once and then is over – but which continues to affect their future. How we manage break-up, and a relationship with our ex, can significantly help or hinder our children.

If as adults we can let go of resentment, and move on as well as possible after a break-up, we help our children learn that – although relationships have their difficulties and disappointments – these can ultimately be challenged and lived with, not just fearfully avoided. Our children can have some realistic hope, and skills to know themselves and to relate to others, as they move out into their own adult, independent lives.

Notes

1 Amato, Paul and Keith, Bruce (1991a) Parental divorce and adult well-being: A meta-analysis. *Journal of Marriage and the Family* 53(1): 43–58.
   Amato, Paul and Keith, Bruce (1991b) Parental divorce and the well-being of children: A meta-analysis. *Psychological Bulletin* 110(1): 26–46.
   Amato, Paul (2003) Reconciling divergent perspectives: Judith Wallerstein, quantitative family research, and children of divorce. *Family Relations* 52(4): 332–339.
   Cockett, M. and Tripp, J. (1994) *The Exeter Family Study: Social policy research findings*. York: Joseph Rowntree Foundation.
2 Wallerstein, J.S., Lewis, J.M. and Blakeslee, S. (2002) *The Unexpected Legacy of Divorce: A 25 year landmark study*. London: Fusion.
   Hetherington, E.M. and Kelly, J. (2002) *For Better or for Worse: Divorce reconsidered*. London: Norton.
3 Wallerstein, Lewis and Blakeslee, *The Unexpected Legacy of Divorce*, p. 233.
4 Johnston, J.R. and Campbell, L.E.G. (1988) *Impasses of Divorce: The dynamics and resolution of family conflict*. New York: Free Press.
5 Hetherington and Kelly, *For Better or for Worse*.
6 Wallerstein, Lewis and Blakeslee, *The Unexpected Legacy of Divorce*, p. 140.
7 Hetherington and Kelly, *For Better or for Worse*.
8 Hetherington and Kelly, *For Better or for Worse*.
9 Marquardt, Elizabeth (2006) *Between Two Worlds: The inner lives of children of divorce*. New York: Three Rivers Press.
10 Wallerstein, J.S. and Blakeslee, S. (2004) *Second Chances: Men, women and children a decade after divorce*. Boston, MA: Houghton Mifflin, pp. 220–230.
11 Hetherington and Kelly, *For Better or for Worse*.
12 Simpson, B., McCarthy, P. and Walker, J. (1995) *Being There: Fathers after divorce*. Newcastle upon Tyne: Relate Centre for Family Studies, University of Newcastle, p. 70.

13 Johnston, Janet (1994) High conflict divorce. *Children and Divorce* 4(1): 165–182.
14 Wallerstein, J.S. and Resnikoff, D. (1997) Parental divorce and developmental progression: An inquiry into their relationship. *International Journal of Psychoanalysis* 78: 135–154.
15 Wallerstein and Blakeslee, *Second Chances*, p. 299.
16 Hetherington and Kelly, *For Better or for Worse*, p. 120.
17 Wallerstein and Blakeslee, *Second Chances*, p. 169.
18 Hetherington and Kelly, *For Better or for Worse*, p. 7.
19 Fomby, P. and Cherlin, A. (2007) Family instability and child well-being. *American Sociological Review* 72(2): 181–204.
Hetherington and Kelly, *For Better or for Worse*.
20 Wallerstein and Blakeslee, *Second Chances*.
21 Wallerstein, J. and Lewis, J.M. (2006) Sibling outcomes after divorce. Presented Division 39, American Psychological Association, Philadelphia, PA.
Cockett, M. and Tripp, J. (1994) *The Exeter Family Study: Social policy research findings*. York: Joseph Rowntree Foundation.
Hetherington and Kelly, *For Better or for Worse*.
22 Wallerstein and Lewis, Sibling outcomes after divorce.
23 Hetherington and Kelly, *For Better or for Worse*.
24 Marquardt, *Between Two Worlds*.
25 Walker, Rebecca (2001) *Black, White and Jewish: Autobiography of a shifting self*. New York: Riverhead, pp. 3, 116–117. Quoted in Marquardt, *Between Two Worlds*.
26 Wallerstein, Lewis and Blakeslee, *The Unexpected Legacy of Divorce*, p. 233.
27 Hetherington and Kelly, *For Better or for Worse*.
Amato, Paul (1996) Explaining the intergenerational transmission of divorce. *Journal of Marriage and the Family* 58: 628–640.
28 Wallerstein, Lewis and Blakeslee, *The Unexpected Legacy of Divorce*, p. 103.
29 Amato, Paul and Cheadle, Jacob (2005) The long reach of divorce: divorce and child well-being across three generations. *Journal of Marriage and the Family* 67(1): 191–206.
30 Wallerstein, Lewis and Blakeslee, *The Unexpected Legacy of Divorce*, p. 173.
31 Hetherington and Kelly, *For Better or for Worse*.
32 Wallerstein, Lewis and Blakeslee, *The Unexpected Legacy of Divorce*, p. 221.

16

Parenting after break-up

Life isn't about fairy-tale endings that last forever. Disasters happen and the challenge for us all is to manage them as best we can. The break-up of their parents' marriage *is* a disaster for children. There may be many reasons for parents to separate. Because children will be significantly affected is not to argue that you must masochistically remain in a poor marriage – but you should be honest. This move is for you, not for them, and you owe it to your kids to do your best to help them with it.

Life in the future will be irrevocably changed but this does not mean changed only for the worse. That depends a lot on you: your capacity to manage the change for the best; attend sufficiently to the needs of your children; and find a way to cooperate with your ex in parenting, so that your children will survive with sufficient resources and skills to be able to risk marriage, and parent children well, in their turn.

What is lost when the parents break up

When it is good enough, long-term partnership provides a structure in which the couple help each other to parent as well as possible. The couple both contribute their part to the income and running of the family. Parents play an organising function, keep their children's needs in mind and monitor difficulties. Life for the child is relatively predictable and safe.

With two parents in the family, it is safer for a parent and child to be close without becoming enmeshed. The father's absence makes it less safe for the mother to express physical affection to her adolescent children – particularly a son. Both son and mother may have anxieties about being overly close, which make it more likely that he will pull away from her – and receive less warm affection than he otherwise might. Similarly a father in the absence of a new partner may feel awkward at expressing affection to his daughter.

If all goes well enough, parents who remain together support each other in setting limits on their kids. It is safer for adolescents to challenge and resent parents who are reasonably robust – as well as, with luck, also to love and learn from them. As children grow and move away from the safety of the early intense involvement with their mother, the father's presence can help his child – and the mother – from hurt or retaliation.

A father, in part because of his greater size, his physicality and by the model he provides, may make it safer for an adolescent boy to explore and manage his sexuality and his aggression. If a mother is single or more vulnerable, her adolescent son may have to inhibit his aggression, or act it out in a way which can feel dangerously without limits.[1]

When the father is in the household, the mother is available to help him to understand his children more; she can also support the teenager – and her partner – when he is challenged. Parents who remain in place make it safer for adolescents to be able to move away into independent activity – and to return, when they need, with less fear of becoming trapped.

Parents who no longer live together have to provide these containing functions for their children without the support of their partner – and it is a harder and lonelier job to do.

The immediate aftermath

- Reassure your kids as best you can.
- Keep their routines as stable as possible.

- Don't deny that you are upset – but protect them from the worst of your despair.
- Don't make them your therapist or your new best friend.
- Acknowledge that they are confused, terrified, hurt, angry . . . They don't have to be grown-up – if being 'grown-up' means hiding feelings.
- Support links with your children's grandparents, aunts, uncles and cousins from both sides: they need all the stability they can find.
- Help your family and friends not to bad-mouth your ex – particularly in front of your kids.

Needing the child to be the parent

If you are able to look after yourself and reach out for supportive relationships with others, you will need to rely less on your kids to provide you with support and companionship. Finding your own resources to re-engage with life means that your children don't have endlessly to reassure you how good you are. The more you have something good in your life, it makes it easier to bear your kids having a good relationship with their other parent, or enjoying time with their friends.

Your children do better if they don't have to feel too responsible for your well-being in addition to the other pressures on them. It makes them less tied to you out of anxiety and guilt: they become freer to challenge you – and to appreciate you.

Providing boundaries

Children do best with parenting that is authoritative: concerned, responsive, flexible but also firm.[2] To be able to provide those limits you need to have your own sources of nurture and valuing rather than relying on your children alone for support. If you need your child to reassure you that you are lovable, then it is difficult for you to establish boundaries. If you are fearful of your kids' resentment and challenge, you will find it harder to be firm or open to reasonable discussion: you will be more likely to back down – but if you do back down, you are likely to become more resentful and then you may feel even worse:

> Sally worried that if she was too firm with her boys they would get angry with her and stop loving her. They might want to go and live with their father. The only way she felt she could have some control was by going quiet and showing them how hurt she was by something they had done. For a while this worked, but her boys got fed up with being made to feel so guilty: they would explode and walk out.
>
> Sally swung between so hating them for being like this that she wished they would leave for good – and then feeling so guilty for these hateful feelings that she would vow again to be patient and long-suffering.
>
> It was only when Sally got some outside help that she began to stand up for herself more. She didn't collapse at the first sign of resistance from her boys and found – to her astonishment – that they were more responsive to her.

Fighting

> Maisie was 'a ready vessel for bitterness, a deep little porcelain cup in which biting acids could be mixed. They had wanted her not for any good they could do her, but for the harm they could, with her unconscious aid, do each other . . . More married than ever, inasmuch as what marriage had mainly suggested to them was the unbroken opportunity to quarrel.'
>
> Henry James[3]

When parents continue to fight, children have more difficulties adjusting. Between a quarter and a third of divorced couples kept on fighting and undermining the other even six or ten years after the break.[4] They could not negotiate, be flexible, nor cooperate with each other.

It may be that some of those parents who continued to row most explosively brought that same impulsive, explosive style to their marriage – and which contributed to the marriage's collapse. If so, when a chaotic marriage ended, it helped the children only if one of the parents was able to establish an emotionally settled base.

But the majority of those former couples who showed traits of explosive hostility after break-up had been able to function well enough when within their partnership: it was the wound of the break-up which had precipitated this extreme state of mind, and the couple had got locked into a vicious spiral of suspicion and attack, which neither could let go of without help.[5]

When faced with painful losses – and there are many when you break up – it is hard to separate your needs from those of your kids. The following example is of a father who was involved and caring – yet acted in a way which was destructive for his family – and probably himself too:

Robert thought he was happy enough living an idyllic country dream with Hannah and their two children – until he fell into an affair and in love, and left. He hadn't expected to miss his children as much as he did, but he felt tortured without them. It occurred to him to talk to his kids about what had happened, to say how sorry he was, but he didn't know what to say and worried that he might feel too sad and guilty. If his kids were silent or withdrawn when with him, Robert thought that Hannah must have turned them against him. He was terrified that his kids might stop wanting to visit at all.

Robert and his new partner had hoped to start a new family, but she did not conceive. It wasn't logical, but it felt like a punishment for being 'bad' and having left which made Robert feel guilty – and then deprived, angry and punitive. He stopped paying regular child support: it made him feel he had more power when otherwise he felt he had so little.

Robert saw how furious and desperate Hannah was, and convinced himself that she was not a good enough mother. He decided his children should come and live with him. He began a ten-year battle that ended with his younger daughter, Hattie, coming to live with him aged 12. He was triumphant. He had won!

Robert passionately believed that his fight for custody was in his children's best interests – but was it really, or was it more a way of dealing with his sadness at the loss of his children, a loss made even more poignant when he could not have a new family?

Almost certainly it would have been better for his children if Robert had provided regular financial support to his family, worked hard at his relationship with the children and done his best to support theirs with their mother. They would have had a less anxious mother, a more settled childhood – and they might voluntarily have come to live with him later on. His children would have had the invaluable experience of observing their parents cooperate in parenting, post-divorce, rather than seeing them caught in such relentless, draining fighting.

Fear of a parent's risk to children

Anxiety about the possibility of incest is greater when there is not a current partner around to make physical affection between a father and child – or a mother and child – safely boundaried. It can be greater when loneliness and need for reassurance and physical touch is so strong. You can worry about the state of mind of your partner to parent responsibly when they – as well as you – are more impulsive, explosive, violent, drinking more, depressed or withdrawn. Such concerns may grow when the hostility between parents is such that you may worry that your ex might retaliate at you indirectly by hurting your child.

It can be hard to sort out when your fears are realistic and when they are more to do with the fact that you can be pleased when your ex behaves badly – and may want to provoke him (or her) to prove what a useless parent they are.

You can't just ignore concerns about how your ex manages as a parent. At the same time there are strong disadvantages when one parent – most often the father – is excluded from contact and care for his child. A more useful question might then be not 'Should this father should be allowed to see his child?' but 'How might he do so in such a way which reassures the child, the mother (and sometimes a statutory agency) that it is safe to do so?'[6] There are organisations which support men spending time with their children, and help them learn parenting skills.[7]

Sexual abuse does sometimes happen – but in fact it occurs much more commonly between the mother's new partner and child, rather than the biological father. (And some paedophiles deliberately target single mothers.) It is possible that a mother is so busy protecting her children from perceived risk from the father, that she ignores the potential risk from a new partner. It may also be that a mother who has not done some of the emotional work after breaking up, and whose confidence is still very low, may feel unable to challenge an abusive partner – since to do so would risk being on her own again and she could not bear that.

Battles over access

Battles over access to, and responsibility for, children can be even more bitter than those over money. For what is at stake is not only the need to have sufficient contact time to keep a relationship going with the child but also that the excluded parent feels that he (or she) is being dismissed as a not capable parent. Generally – though not exclusively – it is the father who is excluded from the child's life.

Fears of the capacity of the excluded parent to parent well may – or may not – be well founded. But whatever the justification, the excluded parent is likely to react with outrage. This includes the sad number of devastated fathers who could play a helpful role in their children's lives, as well as others whose fight can seem more for their own *rights* than for the quality of the relationship they hope to build with their child.

The barely suppressed rage of these fathers may be the reason their ex-wives and judges are reluctant to allow them access to their children. But it is also true that men can be placed in a position of helpless fury by wives who want to punish them. And once the battle between the couple is fought through the courts, there is so much more room for polarised positions and outrage.

It is painfully difficult to disentangle – and even when courts come to a decision that a father should have access to his children, there is room for a mother not to comply (and the courts have little authority other than to imprison her).

Courts don't solve everything – and relying on them to do so can be unhelpful, if it leaves one feeling in the *right* and the other in the *wrong* – and furious and misunderstood. In two books written by the Fathers4Justice group, it seemed there were few happy endings from going through the courts.[8,9]

The *happy endings* in those books were examples where couples finally found their own way to compromise. The father faced that he needed to work to reassure his ex that he could look after their children well enough in his own way; and that just bullying her did not help. The mother faced that it could help her to have a break from the children; that it was good for the children; and that maybe it was not too much to ask, that she be flexible with her ex and help him do his part well.

Cooperation

Children do best when they have as good a relationship as possible with both parents. It may be hard to realise that your children need your ex still to be there, to love them. It can be hard to bear their having a loving relationship with your ex, when this leaves you painfully excluded. But these things are part of what makes your kids feel safer, happier and more confident – and the greater your children's well-being, the greater your peace of mind.

It is hard for a child to feel free to love their other parent – as well as feeling free to be angry with them and recognise their flaws – if you are denigrating of him (or her). Or if you spend a lifetime proving how wounded you are by them.

It is in the interests of your children for you to find an alliance with your ex. As in countries which, suspiciously, carefully, come together on certain shared strategic common interests, while keeping their own sovereignty on other issues, so parents, who no longer live together, can parent their children best by making a non-aggression pact and finding ways to cooperate.

It isn't vital that you get on well together, approve of your ex or even like him (or her) much – but you need to be able to bear continuing rivalries, such as the dread that your child may sometimes love their other parent more than you. It can be hard in any way to help your once-loved partner to be loved by your children. You can so much want to spoil it.

You can't *make* your ex co-parent with interest, but you can refrain from interfering with their capacity to do so. It is possible that by continuing to punish your partner or mock their efforts, you will undermine them as an effective, involved parent. But a parent who is inadequate, vengeful, or plain absent is not one that your children need.

There are even advantages of helping your ex to do the best job of parenting. You might consider offering your ex information or opinions that could help him (or her) understand your children more, as you may have done when you were together – as long as it isn't a hidden way to attempt to control them, and you don't expect that he (or she) will necessarily go along with your suggestions. It might also mean that they will offer suggestions back and – however infuriatingly – some of these might be useful.

If you can find a way to cooperate together as parents it offers the advantage that you are not completely alone in parenting as best you can: in that important task, you are accompanied and partnered.

Helping children make sense of what went wrong

If the version of your marriage that your children hear is that it was *bad from the start* then they have no model of a partnership entered into with love and hope – even if naive in retrospect. If the only version of reality you offer, is of one parent who was all good (though possibly a victim) and the other all bad, they learn that there are two dangerously different, black and white versions, and that the only thing to do is to keep such differences apart. They miss out on learning that for a partnership to work there are two points of view, both of which need to be kept in mind.

Your children can be helped to know that you managed some things well together – as well as what, with calmer reflection, went wrong. Your children need to learn from you, that for a relationship to keep on working, it needs attending to. They need to learn that their own needs are important and that they can expect a partner to pay attention to them – but that a partner's feelings are important too. They cannot just stamp their feet and expect to get their own way.

If children and adolescents have not learned from you about expressing feelings, listening to a partner's, negotiating and finding compromises they will have difficulty expressing their needs and differences, or have a capacity to put themselves into the other's shoes and make some sacrifices for the other's well-being.

The *father* in the mother's mind

Children and adolescents need a realistic view of their father – neither idealised nor demonised. It is not only the real external father, his strengths and weaknesses who is important – but also the version of the *father* who is held in the mother's mind.[10]

A boy who learns from his mother that *all men are bastards* without any redeeming qualities – or even that his particular father is one – isn't free to express and explore his own masculinity. He can't feel excited or proud of his gender and sexual identity. If *all men* are so bad, he may worry that if he is strong or assertive this will risk his mother's collapse or her condemnation. If the only way he feels free to express challenge and anger is by turning away from home – the adolescent boy loses the parental concern that helps him learn to take care of himself – and to have the emotional resources to care for others. If, as a man, he is bound to be *worthless* anyway, why bother to make any effort to be different, or expect anyone to love him?

And if men are only either *perfect* or *complete bastards*, how can a girl learn that a partner may be frustratingly imperfect and challenged, but still loved?

The version of the *mother* in the father's mind is also important. If his father continues to rage at the mother, it is harder for a boy to learn to trust and care for a woman, but also to be able to argue with her rather than retreating into his shell or into violence, in an attempt to get his needs met.

If her father finds her mother so hateful, it will be harder for a girl to feel that she can be valued as an individual and as a woman, and can expect to find a partner who can value her.

New partners

Given the other losses they have already had to face, children are likely to feel anxious at losing their special relation to that parent – and therefore feel resentful of a newcomer. A new partner coming into an already-established family can resent the child's suspicious presence, which intrudes on their wish for exclusive time with the child's parent. It isn't easy being cast in the role of wicked stepfather or stepmother.

But as a parent you may have some part to play too in difficulties that arise between your new partner and your child. Consciously you may want your new partner and your child to get on well and value each other but you too, with your losses, can feel particularly sensitised to being *left out* however momentarily and you can subtly act to sabotage any growing bond.

Karen had lived for many years alone with her daughter, Sissy, after her marriage ended. She had had boyfriends but Sissy had been desperately jealous – which may have contributed to those relationships going wrong.

Karen cautiously started a relationship with Peter, who hoped to have a good relationship with Sissy. Karen was fearful that Sissy's suspicion and hostility would drive Peter away – and so she kept him out of Sissy's way.

Consciously Karen was being very tactful – but she was not allowing Sissy the opportunity to find her own way to a relationship with Peter and to find that he might have been of some help to her as well as simply a threat.

But if Sissy and Peter had a good relationship, might she feel jealous? Karen's mother had been very jealous of her good relationship with her father and it is possible that Karen was repeating this pattern with her own daughter.

Parenting well after break-up is a hard task: the logistics of managing in two households are more complicated; the possibilities for miscommunication increased; and the anxieties and rivalries stirred up are more painful. It is easier if both parents accept that it is in their children's best interests to restrain from impulsive behaviour and to negotiate with each other. But even if one doesn't want to accept this, the other making efforts to do so is a good start.

A mother needs to restrain her impulse to push her children's father away; a father needs to restrain his impulse to punish and withdraw emotionally and financially – and yet they need to find a balance between this and not getting too friendly, which can make the task of letting go harder. If both parents are able to find a way to be tactful and respectful of their former partners, there are many advantages for their children and – surprisingly – for themselves.

Notes

1 Blundell, Suzanne (2001) Fatherless sons. In Judith Trowell and Alicia Etchegoyen (eds) *The Importance of Fathers*. New Library of Psychoanalysis. Hove: Brunner-Routledge.
2 Wallerstein, J.S., Lewis, J.M. and Blakeslee, S. (2002) *The Unexpected Legacy of Divorce: A 25 year landmark study*. London: Fusion.
Hetherington, E.M. and Kelly, J. (2002) *For Better or for Worse: Divorce reconsidered*. London: Norton.

3 James, Henry (1997) *What Maisie Knew*. London: Everyman, p. 14.
4 Wallerstein, Lewis and Blakeslee, *The Unexpected Legacy of Divorce*.
Hetherington and Kelly, *For Better or for Worse*.
5 Johnston, J.R. and Campbell, L.E.G. (1988) *Impasses of Divorce: The dynamics and resolution of family conflict*. New York: Free Press.
6 If there is concern about possible abuse, the family doctor, health visitor or the police are all in a position to help.
7 See Appendix B for details of Fathers Direct, National Association of Child Contact Centres, and Health Visitors.
8 O'Connor, Matt (2007) *Fathers 4 Justice: The inside story*. London: Weidenfeld & Nicolson.
9 Rayburn, Tina and Foster, Timothy (2007) *I Want to See my Kids! A guide for dads who want contact with their children after separation*. London: Fusion.
10 Davids, M. Fakhry (2001) Fathers in the internal world: From boy to man to father. In Trowell and Etchegoyen, *The Importance of Fathers*.

PART 5

A wider focus

Freedom of thought – and at best I think we still have a very limited freedom in that respect – means the freedom to know our own thoughts and that means knowing the unwelcome as well as the welcome, the anxious thoughts, those felt as 'bad' or 'mad', as well as constructive thoughts and those felt as 'good' or 'sane'.
Psychoanalyst, Hanna Segal.[1]

In this part of the book I shift the focus from that of the immediate difficulties after break-up – and take a wider look at how early experiences affect the assumptions we make and the ways in which we relate with others. The inevitable tensions in intimate relationships; the particular anxieties men and women can face and the defences we use to protect ourselves; and the various emotional pressures of dealing with each stage of life.

I hope that it will help you understand yourself more, see what went wrong in your previous partnership and learn lessons which may help you in a new one.

17

Roadmap of the unconscious

- How do you make sense of yourself in shock and panic?
- Or rage or jealousy? Hurt or grief?
- Why does putting something out of your mind not work?
- How can you know that what you feel is unreasonable – but still feel it?

There are many possible maps of human experience. Just as it is possible to make different maps of geographic landscape – some emphasising the contour lines and the streams, others the motorway exits and the rail links, and others still an A–Z of street names – so it is possible to have different models of the mind, which may overlap but whose different emphases can be more or less useful depending on the task.

The map I offer here is a psychoanalytic one – which underlies the thinking in the rest of the book. What it offers is a particular focus on our less conscious, less rational feelings. This can seem threatening: *what terrible and disturbing things might you find if you start looking?* In fact what is *unconscious* is mostly what we push out of mind and glimpse only in passing. It is not so much *unknown* as *shameful* and *unwanted*: that as well as more loving, appreciative feelings, we also have other ones such as those of envy, jealousy and rivalry – which can contribute to anxiety, shame and self-doubt.

Feelings that we don't acknowledge don't just disappear: they emerge in other, less controlled, ways which can leave us – and others – puzzled, enraged or wounded. It helps to have feelings in the open, where we can think about and live with them rather than hold onto them tightly inside, or act them out in ways that are outside our conscious awareness.

You don't have to *believe* in psychoanalytic theory but what it offers is a model in understanding our complex emotional lives. There are many clinicians who find the thinking gained from psychoanalysis immensely helpful in understanding what goes on in us all. There are many people who have had their own experience of psychoanalysis (or a less intensive psychoanalytic therapy) who felt deeply touched and helped. And studies show its usefulness.[2]

Analytic thinking sheds light on what otherwise lingers in dark corners of our mind: assumptions and expectations which often have their origin in our infancy, before we had words in which to think, many of which have a powerful, ongoing impact on our adult emotional life – often out of our conscious awareness. When all goes well enough, we operate at a more or less adult, rational way: when under stress we can react very much like that panicked baby we once were – and particularly so after a break-up, which stirs up so many early fears of abandonment and loss of love.[3]

I give a brief summary and, as I go along, look at how it helps to explain the impact of break-up.

A psychoanalytic view of the developing baby – and the infant part of the adult

The baby is not only a recipient of his mother's care, but also active – sucking, grabbing and biting; watching and registering experience – before he has words yet to *think* about his experience. His relationship with his mother is an intensely physical, passionate one: of his mouth and tongue to the breast (or the teat); the sensations of sucking and swallowing; being held in her arms; gazing at her face; and the pleasant fullness in his belly, or the pressure of pushing out faeces.

The baby needs his mother's milk to survive. He also needs her (and his father's) emotional nurturance to be able to come alive emotionally – her arms, eyes, voice and her empathy. When his mother notices the baby's distress and can respond to it, without becoming too alarmed or frustrated herself, the baby learns that his panicky feelings are manageable, thinkable and he is helped, or *contained*, by her. He is not all alone. He is not falling to bits. He is held and safe. This provision of satisfaction, physical and emotional, is felt as something immensely *good*. (Analyst, Melanie Klein, described it is as an experience of a *good breast*.)

However, the experience of the baby is not only the calm looking-out from his mother's arms, after he is fed and satisfied. Even in the best circumstances, he sometimes has to wait. He may develop strategies to satisfy himself, such as sucking his fingers, or soothing himself looking at patterns of light flickering on a wall – but he discovers that even if this works for a time, it doesn't work for long.

The baby then starts to feel deprived, which soon can turn to increasingly agitated protest and panic. For the young baby, who has not reliably grasped that the provision of satisfaction is something separate from himself, it may feel less that something helpful and good is missing – but that something hurtful and cruel is present. The baby tenses his body and lashes out at this hated, unwanted experience.

The baby's *bad* experience not only may then be a result of his accurate perceptions of something depriving or cruel but also that his reaction, inadvertently, may make the situation worse – as seen in the following example.

Rowan was 10 months old and was left, briefly, by his mother with a neighbour Gemma, herself a mother. After holding himself together for a while in his pram, Rowan became agitated. The stranger picked him up and his cries became louder. Rowan heard the cries echoing round the room and he became more panicked; his back arched and he struggled desperately.

Gemma's heart sank. He was in such a panic! She'd never settle him! It would just get worse and worse! When would his mother get back?

She took the flailing baby into the garden and started talking to him, walking him round and showing him the flowers; pointing at them. 'Look, isn't it lovely!' Rowan's cries did not echo so much in the garden and he was less frightened by the awful wailing. Seeing the roses calmed Gemma and this too was reflected in the tone of her voice.

Rowan's eyes followed her fingers to the brightly coloured petals. As his cries calmed, Gemma was encouraged: she talked more enthusiastically and risked looking and smiling at him – something she would not have been able to do earlier.

Rowan's panic and protest – his physiological arousal, his physical tension, the sound of his screams – all contributed to the terror of what he faced. His perception of reality had been exaggerated by his panic and rage. Only when Rowan could allow himself to be calmed could he realise that the situation might not be as bad as it had first seemed. Now if he looked at the woman holding him he might see someone who was not his mother – but possibly not a *terrifying monster*.

The baby's panic and rage in response to this *bad* experience may also have an impact on the quality of care he receives:

If Gemma had been unsuccessful in her attempts at calming Rowan, her impulse would have been either to turn away from him feeling either that she was 'no good', or that he was a 'bad' baby.

This is relevant now

- Perception – which operates in other, calmer, more rational states of mind – gets obliterated under stress.
- As an adult, under stress – such as in breaking up – it is easy to revert to this panicked *baby* state: that *extremely good or hatefully bad* state of mind, where you lose any sense of the other as a mixture of good and bad. (Analysts describe this as *splitting*.) Mostly it is your ex who becomes the *all bad* one: but sometimes you become the *worthless, hateful* one – which is depression.

- You can protest, and metaphorically arch your back and scream – and in doing so can make the situation feel even more awful than it is. If so, you make it more likely your ex will recoil or retaliate.
- It can then become very confusing: it seems all the hatred is *out there* – but actually the source of some of it is *in here*, making things worse.
- If, in this panicky, infantile state of mind, you can find some capacity to *mother* yourself – to reassure yourself and hold yourself together – then you might find that the situation you face, while very frightening and upsetting, is more manageable than you had at first thought.

The threat of separateness

The baby begins to realise that the source of his *good* experience is the same source as the *bad* ones – which he hates and attacks. He has a mother who is *good* – and is passionately loved. But she is also *bad* – and is equally passionately hated.

The baby may hate and rage at his mother when she deprives him and makes him wait. He can also hate it that she offers him such precious nurture and care – but that he can't possess it all for himself: his mother may *offer* him her love and attention but they are not *his*. The baby can then want to spoil what she has and he doesn't – which is *envy*. But if his mother and her provision of goodness is separate from him, it means that her love for him can be lost: lost because of his frustration and hatred of her when she is not satisfying, and also because of his envy of her when she is.

If the baby is lucky, his mother – with the support of her partner and others – has sufficient confidence in herself and will be able to sympathise with her baby's frustration and fury without feeling that she really is unforgivably *bad*. The baby gains the reassurance that his raging feelings have not destroyed her and her love for him:

> Yes, she has felt exhausted and used up. Yes, she desperately needed to get away. Yes, there were moments that

> she hated him – but here she is again, restored (more or less). Still here for him.

This reassurance makes it easier to bear the knowledge that the goodness is not all in him: that he needs love from his mother, his father – and subsequently others.

The baby who, even in his more hateful moments, feels understood or tolerated, will feel that he has worth. He is likely to be less demanding; he comes to trust that others are essentially helpful and he is more rewarding to be with – in a benign spiral. These repeated experiences of good loving figures, contribute to an internal sense of stability and a source of affirmation – to which he can turn, even when alone: this is described by some analysts as having a *good internal object*.

The analyst and paediatrician Donald Winnicott spoke of how the baby needs someone who is not perfect but who can be *good enough*.[4] Waiting, learning that the world is not at his command, that he shares his mother with others, is an important part of experience – if not too much, too soon.

The baby who has the experience of someone who can take in and reflect on his cues, who feels emotionally as well as physically held or *contained*, can gain relief that his anxiety may indeed be managed.[5] He can learn that there are words to describe his experience and which he can use to register protest or need, rather than only responding with reflex physical action: he will learn that feelings can be conveyed to another without too great a fear of mockery or blame. He learns that it is safe to be known. This is a vital tool in his developing relationship with others.

A baby – and developing child – who is less lucky, and whose parents are less able to understood and reassure him, will feel more deprived and his frustration, hatred and envy are likely to increase. He may dread that these feelings are what makes him unlovable in the first place and his guilt and self-doubt will grow.

A child who learns to expect that his needs will not be met, and is unable to meet them himself, may deal with his dependence by denial, and deciding that he can meet his own needs so much better alone. *He doesn't need anything or anyone else! He's all he needs!* And in this way he may turn away from what is – however imperfectly – on offer.

Others make attempts to please and enliven the mother so that she is more likely to pay him the attention he needs; or will cling and not let her go – but are unable to feel reassured by a reassurance that seems less freely given.

Relevance to adults

- As adults too, we continue to struggle with feelings of hatred and envy towards the ones we most love – because they have such value to us, and their loss would be so painful.
- The more worried we feel about the loss of love, the more we can be tempted either to deny any feelings of need; or to attempt to manipulate or please a partner, in order to ensure their love.
- The more we have difficulty in recognising and putting feelings into words, but only withdraw or explode, the more we make it hard for a partner to get close.

Not being the mother's one and only: jealousy

A further loss for the baby is the recognition that his central love figure – in most cases his mother – has a life of her own. She has pleasures without him, and relationships that exclude him – such as her hidden, exciting relationship with his father; her care and love of other babies and children; her interest in her own world, apart from him. And indeed that she *wants and needs* her other relationships to support and sustain her. He is very important to her but he is not omnipotent. He is not *the one and only*.

The young child faces a painful quandary. He wants to have his mother completely to himself – he may not want her all the time but he certainly doesn't want her to have anyone else – and this involves getting rid of his father. At the same time he also wants to have his father all to himself, and get rid of his mother. He loves, but is in deadly rivalry with, his mother. He loves, but is in deadly rivalry with, his father. Both at the same time. This is the *Oedipus complex*.

If the growing child can be helped, painfully, to let go of the wish to have it *all* – because what he has got is reasonably firm and good – he can discover that life, including the pleasures of his relationship with his father, offers many new consolations.

For a child whose parents cannot bear to disillusion him, but allow him to believe that his relationship with either of them is the *only* special one, it can be gratifying – but also a burden: he can become stuck, unable to find the propulsion of reality to help him move out into the world beyond them.

The arrival of a new baby can be a particular blow, leaving the child deprived of his position as *special baby*, and looking on with intense jealousy at his mother's pleasure with the newcomer. But the more he rages at his mother and father, the more anxious he will be that they will stop loving him.

A young child, who finds little reassurance and help from his parents, can attempt to kill off in his mind not only the new baby, but also his mother and father – as ones who were ever loved and wanted. And in doing so loses them – however less-than-perfect – as a source of sustenance:

> Mel was full of herself in a rather brittle way. Her confrontational, arrogant style had led to difficulties at work and in her marriage. She complained bitterly of her 'vulgar, hysterical' mother and her 'pompous, angry' father – and felt superior to them both. In the course of psychotherapy it became clear that as a young child, Mel had had a very close relationship with her mother – and in her mind, her father had been consigned to a peripheral place.
>
> Mel's view – of herself and her mother in a cosy, exclusive alliance – was shattered with the arrival of her brother when she was 5. She was overwhelmed with jealousy and reacted with rage, provocation and contempt.

She was delighted when she could provoke her parents into an outburst: it proved how powerful she was and how useless they were.

Sadly for them all, Mel's parents were unable to recognise her panic about being second best or possibly – given how full of rage and hatred she felt – not loved at all. As a result of therapy, she developed a much gentler relationship with her mother; she was able to retrieve much fonder memories of her now-dead father; and her work relationships improved – but it was too late to save her marriage.

- As adults we can still struggle between wishing to *have it all* at all costs, and concern for those we love.
- Unacceptable feelings such as envy, jealousy, rage, rivalry and greed continue to underlie our relationships – often out of conscious awareness – since we have done our best to cover over the traces.
- When we push such feelings out of the way they are not available for thinking, nor for direct action or communication – to our cost.

Security of attachment

Studies of infants and their parents demonstrate how experiences and expectations learned in infancy determine later development. They also show how parents' capacity to be responsive to their baby's expressions of distress determines his security, measured not only in infancy and childhood,[6] but also later on.[7]

When 18-month-old babies were left briefly by their mothers in a strange situation, on their mothers' return, the babies responded in characteristic ways. Most babies – those described as *securely attached* – went to their mother for reassurance, could be comforted, and then put down from her lap to explore once more.

However, some babies – the *anxiously attached* – clung desperately and angrily to their mothers on her return, but could not be consoled nor allow themselves to be put down from her lap again. Others still – the *detached* – did not seek comfort from their mothers but looked, disconsolately, away from her.

How securely attached these babies were, was directly linked to how much the mother (and the father) were able to pick up and respond to their baby's cues. And the parent's capacity to do this could be predicted even before the baby's birth, by how they described their own experience of having been parented in their own childhood. Not surprisingly, those who had a good experience of being parented found it easier to offer responsive parenting to their babies.

But those who had had a more difficult early experience were not automatically destined to be unable to offer emotionally attuned parenting to their child: what was important was the degree to which they had been able to face and emotionally digest this difficult early experience. Some who were able to talk clearly about the difficulties without too much distress – evidence that they had been able to think about and emotionally digest it – were able to be attuned to their babies.

Some talked about their childhood in an over-idealising way. They had managed their own distress by denial or doing their best to push it out of mind – and in turn they were likely to ignore, or to respond over-anxiously, to their baby's distress.

Others could acknowledge earlier difficulties but were still caught up in significant distress and anger – and then were less able to be open to their baby's cues. Since they still so resented their own parents, any expression of distress from *their* baby could feel like a terrible accusation of their failure.

Some parents tried too hard to be a good parent and make up for their own sense of neglect:

Twins arrived soon after Gill, and took much of her mother's attention. Gill never had quite as much special attention as she had hoped for when she was little – and probably would have got in different circumstances. She felt deprived, and resented her mother – which made her feel guilty. She assumed her – understandably – hostile feelings were why she was less loved.

In her teens and early adulthood Gill tried to camou-
flage her considerable anxiety about being unlovable by a
superficial confidence – which could be grating: this
proved to her again there was something wrong with her.

When her own children were born, Gill determined to
get it right for them in a way that she felt had not been
done for her. She wanted to make her boys wonderful
healthy meals, play lots of educational games with them,
and have intense interactions with them to reassure
herself what a good mother she was. Her husband worked
away from home a lot and when he returned was often
exhausted, stressed and irritable.

The trouble was it was all so exhausting. She could
not allow herself any time off. When one of her boys
wanted something she could not say a firm 'no' or 'later',
because he might feel deprived or be angry at her – which
would be terrible. She would find herself screaming at
them in exhausted frustration – and then would feel so
guilty that she redoubled her efforts to be good.

Her boys found her unpredictable and frightening.
But this was not because Gill did not care enough. Rather,
she was trying *so* desperately hard to be good and loving
that it left nothing over for her own needs.

In fact what might have been better for Gill would be to find
ways to look after her *own* needs as well as her children's.

The role of parents

If parents are struggling with many external stresses –
worries about money, the demands of many other children,
job insecurity or illness – it makes the task of being emotionally responsive much harder. A mother or father who is
bereaved or depressed may simply not be able to do so.[8]

The more isolated the mother is, the more vulnerable
she and her baby are. When she has the support – of a
partner, parent or friends – she has more to sustain her in
the task of responding to her baby.

Some fathers have particular difficulty in sharing their
partner with the baby. Some mothers too have difficulties

allowing her partner to share in the intense mother–baby couple. In this case the father is more likely to withdraw – and the mother, finding herself alone, is more likely to have difficulties and become postnatally depressed.[9]

Some parents enjoy their baby at one stage of development more than another. One mother may find her young baby's dependence on her very reassuring – but when he becomes a toddler can find it hard to let him become more independent of her. Another can find the demands of infancy hard to manage, but will enjoy and respond to her child more as he becomes more active and independent.[10]

Some feelings may be tolerated more or less well by different couples: in some families, sadness may be tolerated – but not anger; while in others, anger is seen as desirably *tough* – but sadness or vulnerability is unacceptable.

The baby

There are temperamental, physiological differences between babies, which make some easier to parent than others. Some babies from birth seem to find it harder to settle to sleep and rouse at the slightest disturbance. These babies hate having their nappy changed or being undressed to be bathed: they also startle more and tend to have poorer eye–hand coordination.

These temperamental differences may be genetic. It may be that a baby, whose mother is particularly stressed during pregnancy, is exposed to a different balance of neurochemicals in the womb. The baby may be exposed to other chemicals – such as nicotine or alcohol – which also have an impact.

It is not the baby's *fault* – but a baby who is more reactive is harder to parent – and this in turn has an effect on the mother (and father). Rather than being reassured that she is able to offer good things which help her baby, the mother may conclude that it is *her fault*: she is a *bad mother*. This can contribute to depression in the mother.[11] And if she then becomes less emotionally available to her baby, the difficulty is likely to spiral.

Other babies are calmer and seem to have more capacity to tolerate their mother's inevitable delays and imperfections. Parents of such a baby gain more reassurance that they are doing a *good enough* job.

Being able to recognise and express feelings without fear of ridicule or contempt makes it possible to know yourself, learn from experience and reach out to others – but not everyone has learned to do that.

Those who are fortunate enough to have had parents who were reasonably emotionally attuned to their infant and growing child – who were able to empathise and respond without excessive anxiety – are given mental tools to deal with their emotional world and notice feelings rather than shut them down. They have a blueprint not only for managing their own feelings – by thinking rather than by acting on impulse alone – but for reaching out to others too. Because they don't feel that their feelings are quite so shameful – even if not socially acceptable – they have less need to hide feelings away but can feel sufficiently safe to know about them.

A combination of factors – lack of emotional responsiveness in the parents, a particular temperamental reactivity in the child and other external stresses – can create a spiral of avoidance and increasing deprivation, resentment, self-hatred and lack of self-worth.

As adults we too can

- push aside awareness of distress or need – but feel secretly deprived and resentful
- attempt to be pleasing, or anxiously cling but are unable to feel really reassured
- protect ourselves against knowing of more vulnerable feelings towards our partner, and are less responsive to him (or her) than we might otherwise be.

As parents, if we push aside awareness of our own emotional difficulty, we will be less able to be open to cues of distress from our children.

214 A WIDER FOCUS

Notes

1 Segal, Hanna (1986) *The Work of Hanna Segal: A Kleinian approach to clinical practice*. New York: Free Association Books.
2 Leuzinger-Bohleber, Marianne and Target, Mary (2002) *Outcomes of Psychoanalytic Treatment*. London: Whurr.
3 I write on the assumption that the mother is the main carer in the baby's earliest days and that she is his first loved figure. The mother is helped in her task if the father is able – and available – to be supportive. Increasingly after this early time the baby develops his own relationship with his father, and other carers. The point is not so much about who offers care, but the psychological impact stirred up by the baby's relationship with his (or her) main carer – and the issues which dependency, deprivation and satisfaction stir up. For clarity I refer to the baby as a *he*.
4 Winnicott, D.W. (1991) *The Child, the Family and the Outside World*. Harmondsworth: Penguin.
5 Bion, W.R. (1962) A theory of thinking. In W.R. Bion, *Second Thoughts*. New York: Jacob Aronson.
6 Fraiberg, S., Adelson, E. and Shapiro, V. (1975) Ghosts in the nursery: A psychoanalytic approach to the problems of impaired infant–mother relationships. *Journal of the American Academy of Child Psychiatry* 14: 387–422.
7 Fonagy, P., Steele, M., Moran, G., Steele, H. and Higgitt, A. (1993) Measuring the ghost in the nursery: An empirical study of the relation between parents' mental representations of childhood experiences and their infants' security of attachment. *Journal of the American Psychoanalytic Association* 41: 957–989.
8 Murray, Lynne (1992) The impact of postnatal depression on infant development. *Journal of Child Psychology and Psychiatry* 33: 543–561.
9 Marks, Maureen (2001) Letting father in. In Judith Trowell and Alicia Etchegoyen (eds) *The Importance of Fathers*. New Library of Psychoanalysis. Hove: Brunner-Routledge.
10 Mahler, Margaret, Pines, Fred and Bergman, Anni (2000) *The Psychological Birth of the Human Infant: Symbiosis and Individuation*. New York: Basic Books.
11 Murray, L., Stanley, C., Hooper, R., King, F. and Fiori-Cowley, A. (1996) The role of infant factors in post-natal depression and mother–infant interactions. *Developmental Medicine and Child Neurology* 38(2): 109–119.

18

Conflicts of intimacy

Sharing of any sort is difficult. Even in a simple friendship – before expectations of love, exclusivity, sexual intimacy are involved – there are inevitable tensions. Take an afternoon shopping with a friend. Even if you both want to shop in the same store, you still feel irritated as they linger too long over something, or they want to pull you away frustratingly quickly from what interests you. All kinds of subtle give and take are needed. Sometimes we compromise. Sometimes one wins. Companionship is a great pleasure – but the cost is that we have to give up complete indulgence of our own wishes.

There are the inevitable differences to manage. What if our friend has more money to spend than us? Is taller, better-looking, has a more interesting job, a better relationship than ours? Or they have a relationship when we have none, or the joys of a single life when we feel caught up in one that is less than perfect.

If the two are joined by a third, the situation becomes more complicated. There is the danger that one will feel left out and jealous of the special friendship of the other two.

At work, when everyone is equal, we can get on well with colleagues – particularly if we side together against a boss who becomes the *outsider*. But if one gets a promotion and the other not, all kinds of familiar difficulties are stirred up such as 'Who is best? Who has most?'

In a business partnership there is no boss to be the *bad* one. Pressures of individual wishes run alongside mutual concern for the business and the partner. In the short term it can be exciting and the company of the partner reassuring.

But if the business goes well over the long term, tensions will inevitably grow. Do the partners take different roles? What if one has particular capacities and the other doesn't? If there are less pleasant functions to do in the organisation, how are these balanced out and managed? What if one is better socially and they take on the more extravert tasks and get more of the attention? What about jealousies, rivalries? Can they be acknowledged and managed, or are they just felt as unacceptable and a hidden source of grievance?

If these emotional difficulties underlie other simpler relationships – acknowledged or not – what about when a partnership includes sexual intimacy and the expectations of love?

The expectations of love

There is such a compelling pleasure in being 'in love' – its newness, discovery, its sexual tug. There is the thrill of being under an adoring lover's gaze: your lover finds you lovely, funny, fascinating, sexy . . . and under their gaze you bloom and become more of all these things. It recreates a past time (or even just a wish for such a time) of being an infant under a mother's (and father's) doting gaze: when you were adored just for being who you were, without having to do anything to earn it – except maybe gaze adoringly back.

Being in love can be irresistible – sometimes even when reason tells you that it is mad – because it taps into a time before speech, when the senses were paramount. Like the baby you once were, all your senses are aroused: you gaze at the crinkle in your loved one's ear; the way their hair springs from their head; the different expressions that flicker over their face. You are absorbed by the sound of their voice. You taste them; smell them. You delight in the sensation of their skin on your fingertips, and in their touch. They are fascinated by you – and you by them – just like the best moments as a baby.

Feelings of need, vulnerability and self-doubt seem gone for good. You are filled up, on top of the world. Any past disappointments – that left you feeling in any way deprived, ignored, misunderstood – are made up for by this current blissful state. *This is how it's meant to be! It should last forever!* Just like the baby, you hope the tasks and stresses of life will endlessly, magically be attended to: that love will conquer all – including the washing up.

But of course – like the washing up and the daily tasks of living a life – there are still emotional chores to attend to, and if you ignore them, the mess piles up.

Being fused

> Love means never having to say you are sorry.
>
> Novelist, Erich Segal[1]

This was the extraordinary claim made in a popular romantic novel and film of the 1970s, *Love Story*. It subsequently found its way onto countless cards with various cute cartoon characters. Clearly it is a message that has a strong appeal.

But there is a problem: the assumption underlying *never having to say sorry* is that you don't need to apologise because you are not really two separate individuals, with minds of your own, but one, fused. If so, your lover should automatically know what you feel – as should you, them. If you are selfish or thoughtless, he (or she) should understand and be endlessly forgiving, like a parent with apparently boundless resources. You shouldn't need to cope with the messy reality of a partner's different needs – or feel any guilt if you ignore them.

Otherwise *never saying sorry* is sustainable only if, as in *Love Story*, the lovers are going to be separated by a lingering, but beautiful, death – and the relationship can then be idealised in memory.

The advantage of being fused is that you don't have to face any of the pain, anxiety or outrage to do with being separate – when your partner has his (or her) own, unpredictable ideas that don't always mesh with yours. The downside is that you can also feel trapped and engulfed – and then you will need to get away.

Sometimes partners in a couple will oscillate between these two positions: one chases and the other flees – until the chaser gets fed up and withdraws, and the other turns round and chases in their turn. If this push-pull dynamic has some flexibility, and meets both partners' needs, it can be exciting; part of the zest of being a couple. If not, it may feel tantalising, frustrating – and ultimately unbearable.

Ben was a charming but angry man – a bit like his father. There was a provocative edge to his relation to others: he was rivalrous with peers; with superiors he showed an anxious wish for approval, with contempt just below the surface. He raged at his father and was contemptuous towards his mother. He had had considerable success in life, fuelled by his determination to beat various father-figures.

Now that he was becoming more successful, he was anxious about the bright young sparks just below him who, he feared, would outshine and humiliate him in turn.

He knew that his marriage was in difficulties. The relationship worked best for him when he angered his wife, Alex, enough to get her to push him away. Then he worked hard to woo her back – but as soon as she was close again, he could not bear it. Closeness was frightening: he felt too at risk of being exposed – and he dived once more into work and into occasional sexual encounters. Finally Alex could bear it no longer – and they divorced, acrimoniously.

Ben raged at Alex and her perceived faults. Only when he began to face up to his part in their marital difficulties and his terror of being vulnerable – could he hope that in the future he might have more chance of being able to be close to a partner.

Being separate

The hero of Angela Carter's *Nights at the Circus*[2] – who had not previously known fear despite all kinds of external dangers, had fallen in love – and suddenly experienced it:

Now he knew the meaning of fear as it defines itself in its most violent form, that is, the fear of the beloved, of the loss of the beloved, of the loss of love.

If you experience your partner as separate, the relationship is less engulfing – but it faces you with the same kind of dilemmas you had as an infant. The more you commit yourself to your partner and allow yourself to really want them and to hope they will continue to love you – the more you are vulnerable to hurt if they don't.

One way of protecting against fear of *the loss of the beloved* (or) *of the loss of love* is by subtly putting your partner down – as illustrated by this Marx Brothers' joke:

Boy! Is your wife ugly!
Yes, but she won't leave me.
Ugly women still leave their men.
Yes, but I wouldn't care!

Vulnerability to hurt

Protecting yourself from the risk of hurt may seem a sensible thing to do – but it has its costs:

Phil argued that having discreet affairs was good for his marriage: he felt more loving of his wife, Rosa, more generous, freer – it seemed to him win-win. But not so to Rosa. Phil was busy and successful at work and – she was pretty sure – with affairs too. She learned not to ask and to put up with not getting as much of him as she would like: they could be good mates but they didn't really feel like lovers. She had odd affairs too – which were fun in a way but left her lonelier.

Phil sometimes wondered what would happen if he really fell in love with someone else: he knew he relied on Rosa's stability. He also worried that Rosa might fall in love with someone new – and what would he do then?

'Envy

Paradoxically, it is when you feel your beloved is *so* wonderful, that it can be hardest to really love. Maybe not in that first, excited *in love* moment, when you feel that you too are perfect and adored – but when you begin to settle and hope your loved one will stay long term. The realisation of your love and need for him (or her) can leave you feeling smaller – and you may fear that you are less worthy of their love as a result.

When your lover has so much that is admirable and lovable – and their *riches* are swelled by your love too – you may feel pangs of painful envy and want to grab, or spoil them: something that is easy to see happening uninhibitedly in the nursery playground.

Recognising feelings of resentment or envy of what your partner has, may make you fear that they could never love this nastier you. Pushing these feelings out of sight does not make them go away: they still operate – but out of sight.

Unacknowledged feelings of envy and rivalry can undermine a partnership – whether or not it formally ends:

John resented his mother's pleasure in the babies who came after him. He wanted to be his mother's best, only baby!

When he married, he wanted his wife to do well. He was proud of her. He loved her. But he also knew momentarily – before he quickly pushed it out of sight – that he resented her when she started to do well. She seemed to have it so easy! It wasn't fair! He was supposed to be the best beloved! He felt torn and ashamed and pushed his envious feelings out of his conscious mind – but they still continued to have an impact: he just didn't notice – until too late.

Jealousy

As well as envy, for what your partner has which you love and admire, you can also feel jealous of him (or her) – for their pleasure in relationships which exclude you.

You might know that *you* need the world outside your partnership – work, interests, friends, space to think – and know rationally that of course your partner needs these too.

At the same time, at a less rational, more infantile, level you may resent being on the outside, looking on at your partner's pleasure – and fear that his (or her) interests in the outside world, or in your children, could take away from your partner's love for you.

One of the most poignant examples of being left out of a threesome, apart from a partner having an affair, is when a first baby arrives with all the possibilities for a passionate love between the baby and your partner – and your feelings which may be a mixture of pleasure and fear of being *left out*.

Disillusionment

Just as over time you begin to notice that the one you love is not entirely perfect, so you can start to worry that they will begin to notice that neither are you: that perception of a more flawed *you* in your partner's eyes is a painful loss from that blissful period of being *perfectly loved*. Not surprisingly, 80 per cent of marriage breakdown occurs in the first nine years – under the disillusionment of both partners' dreams of ongoing gratification – often in addition to the demands of the early years of child-rearing.

Some of the disillusionment with your partner may be that you know him (or her) better and have a less idealised view of them – but it may also be the result of a subtle undermining of your partner, which makes it easier to love them if they are not quite so enviably *wonderful*.

Incompatible hopes of a partner

Tensions in the relationship are inevitable since you have conflicting feelings: for example you want to indulge in your own wishes – as well as wanting the best for your partner; you have feelings of hatred – and of love. What you want is inconsistent and impossible to fulfil.

You may want your lover to:

- not need anyone in their life but you – but they should also recognise your need for space and not smother you

- feel you are perfect – but they should see the *real you*, not some dream in their head
- express their needs – but their needs should fit in with yours; they should not inconvenience you
- be successful or they will shame you – but not too successful or you might feel rivalrous or inadequate
- make everything all right: be a combination of a nurturing mother and a capable father – the household managed; the family organised; the money made
- provide this because they love you: therefore gratitude or reciprocity is not necessary and if they get depleted or resentful, they are boring.

The capacity to nurture and be nurtured

To the degree that each of us can tolerate the disillusionment of reality: that the other is not a complete answer to our infantile dreams – the *One* who will make everything, endlessly, all right – then we can begin to negotiate real tasks of intimacy.

Being loved and having our needs met is the easy bit. We usually have more difficulty in loving and responding to the needs of our partner – especially when their needs and wishes conflict with our own. But if we can't nurture our partner then, sooner or later, they will become depleted or angry, and look for care elsewhere.

Men often want to get away with doing less domestically – which is a source of many battles between couples.[3] As Kureishi's autobiographical hero observes:

> There is no doubt that I have an aversion to shopping, housework, washing. Somehow I expect them to be done without my having thought about it.[4]

The trouble is if you don't *think about it* to avoid noticing feelings of need and dependence, it means that you also won't notice feel appreciation or gratitude to the one who provides this care – leaving them depleted.

Women may have their own double standards about money and take for granted what their partner provides financially. This can be seen when women feel that it is *fair* that their partner has more earning power or independent wealth, which should be shared in divorce as well as in marriage – but not if it is the other way round.

Generosity

One of the elements that most distinguishes extremely happy couples is their capacity to be generous towards each other – and to do this not out of duty, but because they recognise that caring for their partner and the partnership is in their best interests.

As one man, who had been learning about the 'ensemble' technique of acting, said of his marriage:

> ensemble is when you work as hard for the other guy's moment as you do for your own.[5]

At its best, a relationship offers huge emotional resources for dealing with the doubts, anxieties and ambitions we face in moving through life. When we work well as a couple, we offer nurture and care to each other. Any relationship is a constant, delicate balancing act. It is a problem if one *always* wants to be the one who receives care – and also if one has trouble receiving or acknowledging care from the other.

Unacceptable feelings lodged in a partner

When you can't acknowledge feelings for fear of being hurt, criticised and rejected, you will probably do your best to get rid of these shameful feelings. One way of attempting to deal with such feelings is denial.

Another way is to choose a partner, part of whose appeal is that they are able to express some of these unwanted feelings on your behalf. You can also subtly provoke a partner to have more of these feelings. Dependence, ambition, rivalry, hostility, anxiety . . . can all be better tolerated when they are lodged *out there* in someone else, such as in your partner – where you can view them critically. Analysts describe this as *projection*.

> Sally was anxious about being too dependent, and so she sneered at the feeling. It was a relief to her to choose Tim, who was rather dependent – and she subtly acted to keep him in that role. It was exhausting and infuriating to be always the competent one, managing everything – but it was also safer. If he were to become more confident and more independent, she might feel more anxious about losing him.
>
> Tim was anxious about his aggressive feelings and – while he was resentful – it also suited him that Sally was decisive, organising and angry. He felt excited when Sally was furious – but pleasantly superior: he was not like that, he was good. When Sally left him, Tim alternately collapsed or managed to find others who would organise him.

Sally bore a double dose of aggression for them both. Tim bore all the feelings of dependence and insecurity. Having broken up with the one who had carried the unwanted feeling on their behalf, each of them was left depleted.

The question for Tim is whether he can discover and tolerate his own decisiveness, potency and capacity for anger, without having to locate them *out there* in a new partner. For Sally, it is whether she might allow herself to feel more vulnerable, less than totally competent – which might allow a potential new partner to feel that he had something to offer her.

When you can't tolerate certain feelings, and push them into your partner, you will feel less close. If your partner senses (rightly) that something nasty has been done to him (or her), they will be potentially dangerous: they might even want to push the unwanted feeling back into you:

Stephen felt he had never been able to match up to his demanding father's expectations. Though extremely successful, he could still suffer painful self-doubt. When he felt unappreciated at work and despondent, he would react by criticising his wife, Mary: Mary, hurt and angry, would fight back making Stephen feel worse.

Were Stephen able to recognise his own distress and ask for the reassurance he needed instead of pushing the feeling of being *not-good-enough* out onto her – or if Mary was able to recognise his anxiety and not take it as a personal attack on her and resist going on the attack herself – they might get out of this vicious circle.

But it was hard for each of them – as it is hard for all of us – to do.

Managing difference and tolerating anger

As individuals who are separate, however well your needs synchronise with your partner, they will not always mesh – and unless you can know and communicate those differences, you will drift further apart. Fear of being abandoned and no longer loved can make you inhibit knowing or expressing what you feel – but the more you have feelings that are not recognised (in part because they are not expressed) the more you will feel uncared for and resentful: the more you hold in your simmering resentment and rage, the more dangerous it will feel – and even more reason to keep hiding it from view.

Then, like the infant in a rage, it is easy to lose sight of your partner as someone who is at all loved – though one currently causing you pain – and you can become filled with hatred. Part of your rage may be less with your present partner than with all the important figures from the past who disappointed you. It may also be with yourself, for hiding away your unacceptable anger and not asking for more.

But the anger you experience now not only is that of a baby, or young child, in a panic and rage, but also is combined with all the intellectual and physical force of adulthood. In holding onto that extreme infantile *good* and *bad* view, you can do real damage to the relationship.

Whining and coming out with anger indirectly is difficult for men and women to tolerate. Avoiding expressing disagreement – and withdrawal or defensiveness in response to a partner's complaints – makes partnerships worse in the long term. Feelings of contempt for a partner is one of the factors that most predict marital breakdown. The more you express anger fuelled with blame or rage, the more likely it is that your partner will shut down and not listen – maybe rightly so if the strength of your fury is not all to do with his (or her) failings.[6]

Managing anger well is about bearing your partner's angry complaints about you without becoming immediately defensive and not listening; it is also about being able to consider their viewpoint – but not collapsing at their criticism and letting go of your own view.

If you fear that your anger will be only destructive – or unleash something only destructive in your partner – you might want to keep your anger hidden away where it will fester, but is likely to burst out in a more uncontained way later on.

Our partner gives us the best gift of love, not when we are adorable, but when we are furious; bolshy; difficult; hate him (or her); want something different from them. And he (or she) doesn't put a barrier up, nor collapse under our onslaught, but listens to us – however grudgingly. Our partner may find our different view at that moment disturbing and infuriating, but they still allow some space in mind for it. This is a tremendous expression of love. Now, in our relief and gratitude, we can hear their side of the story, and may find some sympathy with them.

This feeling of being safely understood allows you to shift away, for the time being, from the raging, *terrifyingly bad and blissfully good* state of mind. Suddenly you are on the same side again, rather than opponents lobbing bombs at each other and not caring about the damage. The world is restored; you are partnered. You are grateful and excited and tremendously relieved. (And some of the best sex, not surprisingly, is in making up after a row.)

Conclusion

> A decent marriage . . . has to be worked for, like everything else worth having, and paid for in grinding small change, by compromise and growing older. There are no shortcuts to it.
>
> Poet and writer, Al Alvarez[7]

'*Growing older*' means more than just *putting in* the time or *accepting* the passage of time. We have to *grow older* emotionally too: by giving up some of our infantile demands and adolescent strivings and accepting that we can't *have it all* – and if we insist on doing so, we do damage to our partner and to the partnership.

We have to balance the struggle between our individual self-interest and caring for others. At our best, we are able to put ourselves in our partner's shoes and care for him (or her). We appreciate what we have been offered and value the one who provides this care for us – even if it is less than the *all* for which we might wish. At this moment – and it fluctuates – we are able to love.

Even if only out of pure self-interest – for our best happiness – we need to be able to attend to and appreciate our partner. This leaves us open to hurt if they should stop loving us, or if we lose them through death. The wonder is that, despite all this, on balance we make intimate relationships work well over such long periods of time.

Notes

1 Segal, Erich (1977) *Love Story*. London: Hodder & Stoughton.
2 Carter, Angela (2006) *Nights at the Circus*. London: Vintage, p. 347.
3 Hetherington, E.M. and Kelly, J. (2002) *For Better or for Worse: Divorce reconsidered*. London: Norton.
4 Kureishi, Hanif (1999) *Intimacy*. London: Faber & Faber, p. 98.

5 Wallerstein, J.S. and Blakeslee, S. (1995) *The Good Marriage: How and why love lasts*. London: Bantam, p. 247.
6 Gottman, John and Krokoff, L.J. (1989) Marital interaction and satisfaction: A longitudinal view. *Journal of Consulting and Clinical Psychology* 57(1): 47–52.
7 Alvarez, Al (1981) *Life after Marriage: Love in an age of divorce*. New York: Simon & Schuster, p. 17.

19

The different developmental tasks of boys and girls

While men and women may not be from different planets, we bring gender-based differences and anxieties to a sexual partnership. These can enliven a partnership when managed well – or chronically strain it when not.

Boys

Although the first experiences of their mother are the same for the baby boy and girl, the growing boy and girl have different tasks in differentiating themselves from their mother, and in the way they gain nurture.

Parents can worry that they need to prepare their young son to be tough in a tough world – effortlessly confident, popular, captain of the team. To achieve this independence, they may push their son away from the mother of his infancy, who is powerful and desired – but dangerous, in that she evokes his wish for nurture.

A father can feel particularly rivalrous when his partner's passionate physical relationship is with a baby son.[1] And he may be tempted to push his son into an early independence – so that he can reclaim his partner for himself. A mother can be uncertain about how much closeness is *good* for her son – when he is little, and particularly as he gets older and becomes adolescent. She may alternate between being too intrusive, and pulling away from him in a way that can feel, for the boy, like the loss of her love.

The growing boy learns from his father, and other men, the degree to which it is acceptable to have tender feelings, as well as tough ones. Particularly in Anglo-Saxon cultures – where tender physical affection is shown less by men than in Mediterranean ones – he may learn that expressing vulnerable and tender feelings such as admiration, desire or need is unacceptable.

Anthony Clare comments how for many men

> If (he) feels he does not have *it* – masculine strength, masculine bravery, masculine achievement – he is a castrated male. He is a woman. When men are in the company of fellow-men, they characteristically cut each other down, mock. Competition, the mark of most male relationships – in business, sport, academic life, romance, social situations – is the antithesis of the domestic, the intimate, the exposed . . . Collaborating, yielding, submitting, crying are for women.[2]

Most boys still feel under pressure to hide any feelings which might be thought *girly* or *gay*. They learn to ignore or inhibit any expression of distress. They may feel sad – but there is no place this can be safely acknowledged:

> James' father had left home. He wanted his mother to let his friends' mothers know, but he did not want to talk about it himself. He said that his 8-year-old friends would just feel sad for him but not know what to say. So they would suggest a game of football – and he could not bear that.

If a boy withdraws from possible sources of nurture, he will become more depleted emotionally. As an adult he will be less able to nurture – because he has not received much himself – and he may be alarmed at getting too close to anyone in case this internal lack is exposed. He can learn not to *show* his feelings on the surface – but this is not the same as being internally calm. In response to criticism, for example, men's heart rate and blood pressure go up and remain high, unlike women who are more likely to put their feelings into words. A man is much more likely to manage this distress by withdrawal.[3]

A man may be wary of a sexual partner who can offer nurture – and who may stir up his more infantile wishes. He may also resent those who are able to receive nurture, whether his partner or his children – because they are receiving something he cannot allow for himself.

The more resentful and inadequate the man feels, the more he can feel in danger of being *found out*, punished and deprived in turn. If the excluded partner does complain, his anxious belief is confirmed. He has been found bad and wanting:

> Patrick had always been frightened of his aggressive father and his controlling mother. He had never learned to stand up to them. As an adult he was friendly, laid-back, but unassertive.
>
> He needed his wife, Anna, to be in charge. At moments when she needed him, he panicked. He did not feel he had the internal resources to be able to provide her with this protection and care.
>
> Anna felt unsupported by him: she assumed he did not care enough to offer her more and was hurt and angry. Increasingly, she took charge. Patrick felt humiliated and angry – and got back at Anna in hidden, provocative ways: just as he had in his family of origin.

When being aware of needs, desire and vulnerability is too threatening, a man may choose a partner who will be the vulnerable one: the one who wants closeness. If his partner keeps making the approaches, as he needs her to do, she will be felt as doubly needy and smothering – since she is carrying his needs for closeness as well as her own – and he can feel even more ready to withdraw.

In his novel, *Intimacy*, Hanif Kureishi explores the feelings that leave his semi-autobiographical hero vulnerable to hurt.

> As long as she wasn't his, he could see what she was, and enjoy her. But as soon as the other stuff started with a woman – longing, missing, fearing, hoping – he was off. It was too much. Why can't he do it?[4]

For some tasks of life, switching off awareness of feelings – let alone expressing them – may be a helpful response: sometimes there is a job which just needs to be done and feelings are an interference. But often unacknowledged and undigested feelings get in the way of efficient action and decision-making.

Part of the painful humour in Nick Hornby's novels arises from his male protagonists making lists, rather than coping with vulnerability.

> I was sick to death of my job, and my indecision, and myself. But just when it began to seem as though the holes in my life were too big to be plugged, even by football, Arsenal played six semi-final games, four against Liverpool in the FA cup . . .[5]

When the task is digesting emotional disturbance, a boy – or man – can feel woefully ill equipped. This can leave men with few strategies other than withdrawal to manage distress.

John Bowlby described one man who was visiting his son in the last stages of his son's fatal illness. Despite extremely high levels of physiological arousal, the father could not acknowledge his desperate upset at being with his dying son. He could not manage to be present in the last days of his son's life – but found excuses to stay away.[6]

Had the father been able to experience his distress, to think and to grieve, he would have been grief-struck – but he might have been able to face staying with his son at the end.

The dilemma for men is that while

> men need women and children to be complete, to express their sexuality and humanity, to obtain that sense that everyone needs: the sense that one matters, a refusal to bear feelings of vulnerability make it hard for men to get what they need.
>
> (Anthony Clare)[7]

Having pushed away many sources of reassurance, love and nurture, a man can be left with few sources of comfort and closeness. Sex is one, where he will be touched – physically and maybe emotionally – in a way which is acceptably *manly*. Football – and violence – are others.

A loving sexual relationship with one partner may stir up anxiety at feeling dependent, and vulnerable to the pain of possible loss: it can feel safer to be *laddish* and not care too much, or to have more than one partner. Any such dangerous feelings – such as those of feeling unwanted or deprived – are *out there*, in someone else.

In Sergio Leone's spaghetti westerns, an archetypal figure is the young Clint Eastwood. The hero does not get close enough to anyone to reveal his name. He rides into town, faces down villains and seduces women, leaving them longing for him while he, oh-so-coolly, rides out of town.

The emotional task of girls

A girl has possibly an easier task than a boy. She can turn, from the early physical intimacy with her mother, to her father as her new love object. She can still allow herself to benefit from physical reassurance from, and intimacy with, her mother, knowing that she has this other relationship with her father which helps her separate from her mother.

Even in the twenty-first century a girl can still identify with her mother in her female ability to nurture. A young girl may attend devotedly to her dolls and feel gratification at providing care to meet a need which she feels is external: by fulfilling her *baby's* needs so well, she may feel that she is looking after herself. She may also see herself through the eyes of an admiring observer: *'such a good girl'*, *'such a lovely mother'*.

Providing care is socially approved of for girls. Even now, there are feelings which are still less socially acceptable for girls to have, such as open expressions of anger, independence or selfishness and girls tend to express them more covertly – if no less forcefully – than boys.

If a woman fails to give herself care (because to do so would be *selfish*) and she is not supposed to ask for what she wants from others, she may – with more or less success – attempt to control her partner to provide the care she wishes for. Women may then experience a pleasurable, if exasperated, superiority: *Men are so useless at* . . .

The trouble is that this is often not particularly effective in getting what she apparently hopes for since it is likely to make her partner feel increasingly coerced and resistant – and her sense of impoverishment and resentment will grow. There was a self-help book *The Surrendered Wife*, which gained some notoriety by the extreme suggestion that women hand all the finances over to their partner. But that aside, its useful central point was that women fail to meet their own needs; they dislike asking for what they want since it makes them feel vulnerable – and then attempt to control their partners.[8]

Women, like men, can deal with feelings of anxiety and vulnerability by stirring up such feelings in their partners. Her partner may have his own difficulties in offering care – but she may have difficulties of her own in allowing herself to receive it:

> Theresa was competent; funny; relaxing company; impressive. She had managed her growing family, and slowly built her career. She complained that her husband, Ian, did not look after her well.

But is there more to it than that? Might she have her own difficulty in receiving nurture?

> When she was growing up, Theresa's parents were busy with their disintegrating marriage and were never very good at noticing her needs. After they separated, they needed her to look after them.
>
> She was good friends with Ian and married him – but she never felt swept off her feet by him. At one stage he made a bad business decision, which meant they lost a lot of money, and she felt she could never quite forgive or trust him again. She withdrew into a formidable competence.

Theresa needed a nurturing, mothering partner – which presumably was what had attracted her to Ian in the first place. She also wanted one who would be competent and not make mistakes – an all-capable, fathering figure. In addition she wanted someone exciting and sexual. But if a partner were to meet her needs so fully, she would become vulnerable to hurt – for they might break up, as her parents had done. It was lonelier – but maybe safer – to keep Ian at arm's length, and trust in her own resources.

The risks of sexual intimacy

Sex offers the delights of physical passion and gratification. Touching, and being touched and held, can be immensely reassuring. It may lead to a profoundly intimate sharing. At the same time, it can stir up so many anxieties about being known so intimately.

Boys and men often feel expected to perform, to match up to fantasised expectations: their height, their perfect potency, the size of their penis, their sexual technique. Fear of failure and humiliation lurk at the very moment when, physically and emotionally, men are at their most vulnerable. Women too fear being exposed as inadequate and can retreat behind a veneer of calm – or of fake excitement.

Sex may also be used as a defence: to withdraw, withhold or hurt. There are many tender expressions for female and male genitals, but there are also others that reflect violent fantasies of war, cutting and attack. A man can use his penis as a weapon. The woman's body can feel tantalising, withholding or dangerous. In entering his partner's body, a man may have anxieties whether he will be safe, or is entering hostile terrain. Women may also be unsure whether the penis, which she takes inside, is one which is playful, caring – or attacking.

If a man needs looking after – but he must not notice it since he would feel unacceptably dependent – then he will take, but not offer in return. If a woman offers nurture in an attempt to get love and attention for herself – but cannot directly acknowledge her need nor allow herself to be cared for – she will feel deprived and angry. The scene is set for an all-too familiar battle.

The tragedy for men is that in freeing themselves from the childhood world of their mother, they cannot really enjoy and value a partner, for all that she offers – and instead may be subtly dismissive and withholding. Then men – who want reassurance as well as good sex with their partners, and who hate being criticised or ridiculed[9] – can find to their dismay that they have turned their partner into a nag, or one who turns away from them.

The tragedy for women is that though they may want looking after, if they are, they can want to retreat to the safety of being in control. Women may wish for a partner who feels a real equal, but in attempting to get her partner to do it *her way*, she may find – with no less dismay – that she has turned her partner into a subtly resentful, messy child who never gets anything quite *right*.

Both men and women can turn to a sort of laddish *not caring* as a way of managing their anxieties – but then end up feeling impossibly far apart.

The question for men and women is whether it feels sufficiently safe, despite these fears, to take the risk of openness and shared pleasure with another.

Notes

1 Emanuel, Ricky (2001) On becoming a father: Reflections from infant observation. In Judith Trowell and Alicia Etchegoyen (eds) *The Importance of Fathers*. New Library of Psychoanalysis. Hove: Brunner-Routledge.
2 Clare, Anthony (2000) *On Men: Masculinity in crisis*. London: Chatto & Windus, p. 205.
3 Gottman, John (1994) *Why Marriages Succeed or Fail: And how you can make yours last*. New York: Simon & Schuster.
   Gottman, John and Krokoff, L.J. (1989) Marital interaction and satisfaction: A longitudinal view. *Journal of Consulting and Clinical Psychology* 57(1): 47–52.
4 Kureishi, Hanif (1999) *Intimacy*. London: Faber & Faber, p. 103.
5 Hornby, Nick (1992) *Fever Pitch*. London: Gollancz, p. 117.
6 Bowlby, John (1998) *Loss: Sadness and depression*. Volume 3 of *Attachment and Loss*. London: Pimlico, p. 155.
7 Clare, *On Men*, p. 216.

8 Doyle, Laura (2001) *The Surrendered Wife*. New York: Simon & Schuster.
9 Hetherington, E.M. and Kelly, J. (2002) *For Better or for Worse: Divorce reconsidered*. London: Norton.

20

Stress and stages of life

We face all kinds of stresses through life. Even when expected, even when greatly hoped for, different events of life – such as the birth of a first baby – can put enormous strain on the relationship. Other events are less desirable, such as the serious illness or death of someone close; a life-threatening situation; redundancy; financial insecurity; the fact of ageing; the fact that life does not always go as perfectly as we wish it would.

In our can-do culture, we assume that stresses should be managed through action or possibly logical decision taking. But some changes cannot be decisively managed – they can only be digested and slowly come to terms with. Or not.

The stress is added to when you don't acknowledge the difficulties but assume you should take everything in your stride and cope. If you can notice the impact of different stresses on you, you might give yourself credit for what you do manage and pay some attention to your own needs. Like recovery from a physical wound, time is needed to heal slowly and restore your resources – and if you don't recognise your need for recuperation, you can interfere with the wounds' efficient healing.

The arrival of the first baby

Before the arrival of children, couples are relatively equal: they may have a similar level of earning, a similar amount of free time and similar expectations of each other. There may be fights about who does more housework; who earns more; who offers more but there is – more or less – enough energy and caring to go around. There is enough time for both to look after their own needs and interests, as well as have resources left to respond to those of their partner.

The arrival of the first baby changes all that. Parents of a new baby are chronically deprived of sleep. They are faced with an infant who, however absorbing and adorable, is also demanding and imperious. The baby needs looking after *now* – even if the parents are exhausted, ill, or desperate for a bit of time for themselves, or for each other. Some babies are easily satisfied, and parents have the reward of feeling that they have offered something *good*; other babies are much less easily settled and their parents are left not only feeling exhausted, but also that they are *bad* parents.

As well as wanting their best for their baby, both parents may well have feelings of resentment and envy towards him – who has so much attention and care while they are so drained and deprived. They are suddenly downgraded, from being the hero in their own drama to one of being a servant to the new hero, the baby.

Hanif Kureishi's hero catches sight of himself in the mirror, masturbating:

> When, by mistake, I glance into a mirror and see a grey-haired, grimacing, mad-eyed, monkey-like figure with a fist in front of him, and the other hand placed delicately on his side because his back hurts from lifting the children, I know I am more likely to weep than ejaculate. I was a child once, too.[1]

When a couple suddenly becomes a threesome, there are inevitable rivalries between them. In the early days of the baby's life, it is almost always the mother who plays the central role: the mother may delight in being of such central importance to her baby and she may feel caught up in an intense new love affair. She may be reluctant to share these extraordinary pleasures – as well as the demands – with her partner.

Julia found herself completely caught up with her new baby, John. He was so foreign and yet so much part of her. She could hardly bear to leave him for more than a few moments to go downstairs to find some food. The baby slept by her and Julia was sensitively alert to the rhythms of his breathing.

Her husband Chris wanted to get to know the new baby but felt clumsy picking him up and Julia kept telling him what to do and would snap if the baby started to cry. Chris resented it that the baby seemed to settle more easily with her. He didn't have the confidence to claim more time with the baby, or to encourage her to put the baby in his own room so that they could have time on their own as a couple.

Chris didn't deliberately decide to withdraw, but he had a lot of work pressures and it was easier – and in a way more rewarding – to do that than be doing what seemed a less-good job at home. Julia became more tired and more complaining. Chris withdrew more to work and his football buddies. Julia became quite depressed.

Luckily as John got a little older he became more interested in his father, kicking his legs excitedly as Chris came in the door from work. Chris, reassured, was delighted to build up his own relationship with his son. Julia was pleased too. They were beginning to adjust as a family.

Rivalry with children

As well as rivalling each other to be best loved by their child, a mother or father may also have feelings of rivalry towards their child. The more a parent felt deprived in his (or her) own childhood, the more they may struggle between feelings of pleasure that their child has the love and attention they missed out on – and resentment and envy. When such shameful feelings are acknowledged, they can still have the power to shock.

In *Atomised*, Michel Houellebecq's hero is about to leave his partner and child:

I was a bastard; I knew I was being a bastard. Parents usually make sacrifices for their kid – that's how it's supposed to be. I just couldn't cope with the fact that I wasn't young any more; my son was going to grow up and he would get to be young instead and he might make something of his life, unlike me.[2]

The power of mythic tales, whose appeal endures over centuries, is the expression of such unacceptable, deep feelings. The Greek tragedy of Oedipus begins when Oedipus' father, King Laius, cannot bear the prophecy that his son will best him, and win the love of his wife – and so he sends his infant son to be killed.

But in fact for a child to do well, his mother (and father) both have a lasting, intense love for him which in some ways, does exclude the other parent and – in the passage of time – they will both be *bested* by him. That is part of the inevitable, painful conflict of being a parent.

Children's growing independence

Of course, whatever the stresses of parenting young children, there are also immense gratifications – physical and emotional. Early on you are everything to your child: so powerful, so indispensable. For that moment, in that setting, you really do *have it all*; you are as *big as a bus*.

As your children move from infancy to childhood, adolescence and on – your position as centre of their universe is slowly lost. That slow shift from being indispensable to your children, to becoming a part of their background, however important, can feel a terrible blow. The hero of Hanif Kureishi's *Intimacy* complains how:

I think I have become the adults in *The Catcher in the Rye*.[3]

The parents in that novel are not particularly *bad*: they are thought about and are an important part of the background – *but they never appear in their own right*.

We may get great pleasure in our children's growing independence; their friends and interests; their burgeoning sexuality; their struggles and successes. At the same time we may envy them knowing that we will never have those experiences in quite that same new, fresh way again. As well as pleasure and satisfaction in the confidence of our children, we can also resent knowing that some of what they have is a result of the sacrifices we made. If they have difficulties, it can stir up our feelings of anxiety and doubt about whether what we offer is good enough.

When children become adolescent and prepare to leave home, they are breaking away from our intense preoccupation with them which – as well as a relief – can feel painfully rejecting. If we cannot acknowledge these feelings, we are at risk of acting them out more or less unconsciously by being the one to reject first – emotionally, but also sometimes in fact.

In Anne Tyler's *Ladder of the Years*,[4] her heroine, Cordelia, walked away from a family picnic and left her husband and family. Months later, she realised that what she was avoiding was the upcoming departure of her almost-adult children. She wanted to leave them before they left her. Only when she could face this fact, could she return home and share and support her daughter in her wedding.

Childlessness

Some couples choose not to have children and feel that this has been a good decision, allowing for other priorities in life. Nevertheless the effect of a choice of childlessness is not a one-off, but continues to reverberate throughout different stages of the couple's life.

Approaching middle age and the woman's menopause can be particularly hard for childless couples. For a couple who made a deliberate choice, the other option is now closed to them. They have to face the consequences – good as well as bad: they may have escaped the demands of the child-rearing years, but they are now missing out on the sense of family richness – even if they still believe their decision was right for them.

> Elly and John were together for years. They shared much together; they were good mates. Because they did not have children, they could afford to work creatively without too much worry about money; they had adventurous holidays while many of their friends had family holidays, closer to home. They were pleased with their choice.
>
> But in her forties, Elly began looking at all the kids her friends had had; how lively and fun they were – and suddenly began to feel that she had missed out. And now it was too late. Looking back, she felt she had gone along with not having children to please John.
>
> Her resentment towards him began to grow. She decided she didn't want to spend the next forty years of her life with him in the same old way – and decided to leave.

For couples dealing with a childlessness they did not choose, the sadness, longing and anger at what has been denied them are very painful. If their inability to have children was due to one partner's infertility, the one at *fault* may feel guilty and their partner may have to struggle with their feelings of resentment: and such feelings put great pressure on the couple. Infertility treatment too – whether or not it is successful – creates feelings of misery, doubt and resentment.

Mid-life

> Like many people who have not yet turned forty, I used to give the Mid-Life Crisis little credit and no respect: it was the preserve of various dunces and weaklings . . . [later] I saw that it was intrinsic and structural. It had to do with things that were already wrong and were not being faced. The Mid-Life Crisis compels corniness and indignity upon you, but that's part of the torment. . . later you see that there was a realignment taking place,

something irresistible and universal, to do with your changing views about death.

Martin Amis[5]

Middle age is the age most of our parents were when we left home – and the adolescent we were then knew for sure that they were boring and past it. Now, seeing a not-so-dissimilar, middle-aged face looking out from the mirror can be a cruel blow.

Our culture may have successfully pushed back middle age: middle age may no longer be 40, but 50, 60 – or more. Nevertheless, men and women will still notice the imperfections of face and body that dieting or exercise alone will never now make perfect. Your memory may be less good than it once was. Your sexual *pull* may feel far less assured. Men's anxiety about their sexual potency is illustrated by the demand for Viagra. You may be fitter, happier, more confident, successful and fulfilled than ever before; there may be many compensations – but there are limits to your capacities and to the time you have left.

The fact that time does not stand still because you wish it to, is a blow. Even if you are at the top of the ladder in your chosen field, there are all kinds of younger, hungry rivals who will challenge – and one day topple – you. Compared to the excited adolescent dream of success in every sphere, the reality of what you *have* achieved – however substantial – can seem less glittering and less permanent than you once hoped.

One way we may attempt to evade these blows to our self-esteem is through reverting to a resentful and self-preoccupied adolescence.

In Sam Mendes' film *American Beauty* (1999), Kevin Spacey's character withdraws from his job in a sulk and retreats to a hoped-for adolescence where 'freedom' is throwing a plate of food at the immaculate wall – which presumably he doesn't clear up – and the planned seduction of his daughter's friend. His wife (Annette Bening) tries to maintain order by keeping everything under tight control – everything clipped and in its place.

The anxious ambivalence of the hero's wish for closeness with his wife (and she for him) is shown when they approach each other – he open beer still in hand – and she chides him for risking a spill on the new sofa.

The real internal disorder, longing, and disappointment begin to be addressed in the film and the hero starts slowly to mature: he is able to be concerned about others as well as himself. He resists the sexual advances of his daughter's friend – and asks her instead about his daughter's welfare.

Redundancy

Sudden unexpected crises – such as a redundancy – may be managed if it doesn't last too long:

Laurence had been expecting his redundancy for some time – it was common in the industry in which he worked. But when it came it was still an enormous shock. He thought he'd probably be able to find some work, but he was daunted. He felt anxious, humiliated and inadequate: he hated the long days with not-enough to do. He was drinking probably too much. He didn't sleep well at night and was tired in the morning and didn't feel like getting out of bed. His wife, Steph, was alarmed too and made suggestions to help, but these made him feel furious, and he would snap at her. Laurence felt that everything that made him feel worthwhile, potent and wanted was collapsing around his ears.

He was finally able to move sideways into a job that paid less well, but was interesting. He settled down again – but wondered, with a cold sweat, what might have happened if he had not.

But not all crises resolve as that one did and couples may face something chronic and long term: for example, the disheartening impact of long-term unemployment or chronic ill-health.

The empty nest

A child's leaving home leaves a huge gap in his (or her) parents' daily life. Parents may enjoy the opportunity for more freedom, but it is nevertheless a loss – loss of stimulation, being needed, having a role and some authority – all of which takes some adjusting to.

Some women, particularly those who have put a lot of time into their children – and some men too – may feel bereft of a purpose that has made them feel worthwhile. The couple may suddenly feel pushed into each other's company again, when for many years they may have interacted with each other largely through their role as parents. Some can look at their partner and realise what strangers they are to each other – and may not be sure whether they have the interest or energy to find a new way of relating together.

Ageing and death of parents

If you are lucky, even as an adult there is a corner of your parents' mind where you are still *little, special, the apple of their eye*. In that relationship you are still the one to be looked after. Parents have known you from the beginning – as infant, toddler, through all the stages – and they hold on to that history for you.

Then gradually – or sometimes overnight – that balance changes: your parents become more frail and need you to care for them. A parent's illness can make enormous demands. The illness or death of a parent can be much more disturbing and distressing than expected. For that part of us which remains forever a child, our parents are still an all-powerful bulwark, their presence providing reassurance that everything is *all right*. While a parent is still alive, death is still safely a generation away.

And now they are there no longer. You are the *older generation*.

Retirement

Retiring from work often entails a tremendous loss of role, which provided a sense of interest, worth and the opportunity for engagement with others. This will be particularly true for those who have spent little time as an adult in activity other than paid work.

In retirement a couple no longer have an external schedule to provide structure to their day or demands that provide space from each other. Instead they may feel forced into a new – sometimes unwelcome – intimacy. Couples may well have to adjust to a lower income which can affect the opportunities available to them. There is the painful task of tolerating the increasing experiences of infirmities and deaths.

Retirement these days may be a substantial period of life – something like a quarter (or even more) of a lifetime. The question then is how to use that unknown future time in a way that feels of interest and worth. These pressures can be a spur to break-up.

Conclusion

Recognising that you are stressed, and how it impacts on you, leaves you more likely to find ways of nurturing yourself. It helps to acknowledge and give yourself credit for what you do manage. If you are able to recognise when, and how, your partner is under stress it becomes more possible to avoid interpreting their irritability as a personal attack on you.

After a break-up, it may help to understand more about the pressures you had to contend with that might have led to the marriage ending and the additional pressures you – and your partner – faced in its ending: you might find you are more impressed with what you *did* manage, and have more sympathy if neither of you managed as perfectly as you might have wished.

Notes

1 Kureishi, Hanif (1999) *Intimacy*. London: Faber & Faber, p. 110.
2 Houellebecq, Michel (2001) *Atomised*. London: Vintage, p. 223.
3 Kureishi, *Intimacy*, p. 146.
4 Tyler, Anne (1996) *Ladder of the Years*. London: Vintage.
5 Amis, Martin (2000) *Experience*. London: Jonathan Cape, p. 63.

PART 6

Moving on

A person with 'ubuntu' is open and available to others, affirming of others, does not feel threatened that others are able and good: for he or she has a proper self-assurance that comes from knowing that he or she belongs in a greater whole and is diminished when others are humiliated or diminished, when others are tortured or oppressed, or treated as if they were less than who they are.

Desmond Tutu[1]

21

Meeting someone new

Finding a new partner – as long as the relationship is a good one – is one of the factors that most contribute to people's happiness. But there are risks.

Pitfalls of rapid romance

Just as anger is often a way of avoiding grief and guilt, so can sex and the hope of romance be a way of avoiding feelings of panic, loneliness and loss. In any situation of shock and anxiety we look first for physical comfort – of being held close and soothed. The comforting elements of touch at such a time can be more important than sexual release. But rushing quickly into brief liaisons has its dangers.

After a break-up your confidence is precarious: one minute you defiantly tell yourself you're irresistible – the next you feel worthless and that no one will desire you ever again. Finding a new partner, quickly, may seem a perfect way to fill a terrible sense of emptiness; to prove to yourself that you can still score; and to punish your ex. You may cheer yourself up with the thought that if you can't or don't find the perfect replacement, then at least you can hope to have an exciting – or at least a varied – sex life.

But brief sexual liaisons take a heavy emotional toll. Hoping for such intimate attention from a relative stranger may leave you feeling even lonelier and more desperate. In one study of men and women after break-up, one-night stands led to a drastic loss of confidence in women.[2] Men pursued casual sex for longer, but after a year or two, they also looked for a more settled partnership – and if they did not find one, were at risk of becoming defeated.

Many people quickly begin new relationships, or a succession of relationships – and an extremely high number of these break down. Men are particularly likely to do so. It may be that they have more opportunity. It may also be that for men – who are less likely to have close, confiding friendships of either sex and, in addition, who may face the loss of their children – their need for intimacy and reassurance is more urgent.

Jonathan Self described his desperate rush to remarry following the break-up of his first marriage and his grief at the loss of his sons:

> I liked the idea of her, and that was enough. Before we had even been introduced, I had quite decided it would be love at first sight. My policy from the out was to overwhelm her . . . We had started living together, at my suggestion, exactly six days after Will's dinner party.[3]

Managing a new relationship, when there is so much emotional turmoil in ending the old one, is hard – for the one who is leaving the marriage, as well as for the new lover. About 60 per cent of subsequent marriages fail – not counting non-married partnerships – even though you might imagine that those who had faced the break-up of one relationship would be particularly concerned to make a new one work.

There are several reasons why a new relationship, formed rapidly, is at risk. In the early aftermath of breaking up, you have to manage the emotional impact – of accepting and adjusting to it. You are likely to be moody, anxious, fragile and preoccupied. A new partner will have to bear all your intense mood swings. There will also be difficulties to be managed between the needs of your new partner and those of your children.

In addition to the many stresses associated with leaving the marriage, there may also have been underlying stress which contributed to the break-up – and which may still need to be faced. Major life events and unrecognised depression has been found to trigger many break-ups.[4] If that was a factor in your break-up, then when the excitement of a new relationship begins to settle, those unresolved issues are still there to face. Hard for you to do at a time when you suddenly find yourself with so much else to attend to – and hard too for your new partner.

For a new partnership to have much hope of developing fully, you need to be able to bring more to it than an unquenchable need for reassurance that you are lovable, and the hope that things will get better. Given your intense need for solace and comfort, you may have little room for the *real* them – and this puts an immense strain on a fledgling relationship. In this fragile state you may not be able to really interest yourself in your new partner – and long term, most people are likely to run out of steam if they are continually providing care and attention which are not being reciprocated. And someone who is endlessly prepared to support you when your self-confidence is low, may not necessarily feel so comfortable if your confidence increases.

Of course it is tempting to rush into a new relationship – but there is a difference between needing to be reassured and the delights of company and sex, and having the emotional resources to be genuinely interested in another person. You are well on through the stages of recovery when you can really begin to do that.

Low self-worth

A still intact marriage, however threadbare, may have provided some reassurance of your worth: its ending can stir up fears of being discovered as worthless and bad. You can flail about for reassurance from outside – but you need more and more of it. You can feel like a combination of an overwhelmed baby, and an anxiously excited teenager.

It is important to find some adult, nurturing capacity in *yourself* to be able to do some calm thinking on behalf of that panicky, frantic, over-excitable *you*:

What if you were advising a teenager with drastically low self-esteem, who did not go out much and was a bit clingy, who then met someone and told you, with a blissful expression, how perfect this new love was. He (or she) was all set to move in with their new love and knew life would be perfect from now on. What would you think? Wouldn't you think this was a pretty mad way to begin?

Might you not tell him (or her) that they needed to spend time on their own or with various friends to find out who they were; to experiment with activities and interests; to find what they felt excited about; to reach out to new friends as well as to old; to learn of the importance of being alone – as well as the risks of becoming isolated? That they needed to be comfortable with themselves before they could be so in a close relation with someone else.

Only then – when they begin to have some sense of who they are, and can value themselves – would they be in a better position to choose someone who would value them too.

Only when they are no longer wholly consumed by their own difficulties but have some sort of capacity to be interested in, and value, someone else, can they be together in a partnership that is mutual and loving.

So why should your advice to yourself be particularly different just because you are ten, thirty, or even fifty years older than that teenager?

If you do meet someone new, and however excited and hopeful you feel, it is important not to burn all your bridges:

Jacky's husband had left six months before. Jacky was plucky and defiant, handing in the clothes she felt were too matronly to the charity shop and buying herself some which made her feel younger. She began going to Salsa classes, which she loved – and at an event away from home, met a man she was very attracted to – and he to her.

She loved how adventurous he seemed – so different to her ex – and heard of his plans to buy a yacht and chart it round the Med. In her enthusiasm, Jacky decided to give up her job and her house to live with him.

Living with Bill turned out to be different than she expected from the long weekends and odd weeks they had spent together. She felt oppressed by his constant presence; she felt like a guest in his house and missed her work and her friends. It became clear that it was not really working out.

Jacky was distraught. She'd given up everything for Bill! She had lost her job and her house. Jacky wanted to blame it all on Bill – but she knew that in her rush to be different, trusting and buoyant, she hadn't protected herself as much as she had needed to.

Mistrust of the opposite sex

Those who find themselves single again, after a break-up, inevitably carry the scars of hurt, rage and mistrust. The less you have been able to digest this blow, the more likely it will cause difficulty in your new partnership. If you are still caught up in a battle with your ex – whether it is in open conflict or in a simmering resentment – that hostility is likely to affect your view of all their sex.

So if your ex was just a *bastard* or a *conniving bitch* how can you begin to trust someone new? You might not want to punish a new partner consciously, but how can you really allow him (or her) to matter to you if you are still caught up in suspicion and hatred?

Advantages of taking time alone

You may feel that settling for a partnership not so different from the last one is good enough – which is what happens to many in a second relationship, particularly to men.

Those who went on to make happier second marriages had learned from the experience of what had gone wrong with their first marriage; they were able to communicate affection as well as disagreement; and they had realistic expectations of their new partner.[5] That takes thought – which is more likely to come from a decision to first settle, alone – or with your children.

If you can calm the worst of your fears, plan, and avoid rushing to the nearest safe emotional refuge, breaking up can provide an opportunity for re-evaluation. Over the years in a marriage you are likely to have made subtle accommodations to your partner – as they probably did to you too: sometimes those accommodations can feel more like distortions. Emerging from the now-defunct couple you have the possibility to stretch out this crumpled *you*, to find out what bits of you have been lying dormant and unattended.

You can gain from taking the time to find your bearings and discover who this newly single *you* is. What is important to you in life? How do you want to spend your time? Are there things you want to do differently? Or things you've always wanted to try and never have, up till now?

Since you can't yet know quite who you will find yourself to be, you can't know what sort of partner you will want to spend time with. You don't know yet how many compromises you would be prepared to make for such a person.

Would you be prepared to put up with anyone, just for companionship? You can't yet know whether you would hope, ideally, to live permanently with someone new – or perhaps only part of the time. It may be interesting for a while to play the field without any particular interest yet in settling for someone new. Just like a teenager, you may need to have a number of different relationships before you are clearer who you might want to be with.

You may hope in time to find someone special, but if you haven't yet, you have no choice but to remain single – and to manage feelings of loneliness that will hit you, however many friends you have.

There are disadvantages and anxieties associated with being single – but there are pleasures too. These include finding out about the enjoyment of – even the need for – being alone some of the time: discovering more about yourself, such as your fluctuating moods, your resources, your vulnerabilities. There is a pleasure in making decisions on your own – even if it may also help to run your ideas past others. There is a freedom in not having to look after someone else's need – unless you now choose to.

> Sarah's husband left after a long marriage. It took a long time for her to get over it. There'd been so much to attend to: she'd felt she couldn't stop for a moment. She would wake, anxious, in the night and feel more and more depleted. Being decisive and active did not work: it seemed there was no choice but to slow down.
>
> She had moments of intense loneliness and despair. However she learned that, if she didn't fight these dark moments but treated herself gently, they passed. She took some time off just to tend her garden. She didn't bully herself into frenetic activity. She saw a little of good friends. She wrote some poetry. Sarah did not enjoy the dark moments but she was no longer so frightened by them. She felt she was more open to feelings of joy. She thought she was probably more alive now than she had been in her long years of marriage.

Idealising independence

To hope for a new relationship, but not find someone, can leave you feeling sad and foolish: it may feel so much easier to give up that hope and retreat into self-sufficiency. You can idealise independence, telling yourself how much better off you are without a partner. You may stick to familiar routines, where the possibility of meeting anyone new is slight, keeping your emotional guard up, telling yourself how much you prefer it this way. It can seem so much safer to stay withdrawn.

You might decide, grudgingly, to open up only if a possible partner provides a guarantee of commitment. It would lessen your risk of being hurt, at least in the short term – though you risk discouraging those who have little interest in the heroics of breaking through a circle of thorns: for being with someone who withholds and constantly shelters from emotional risk is dispiriting.

Idealising closeness

Paradoxically it is only when you can manage a life that is single – with friends and confidants and interests that engage you; when the worst of the pain of break-up is past – that you are in a position to take the risk of getting close to someone new. You have learned that breaking up is horrible but that it can be survived – however painfully. If things go wrong with a new lover it may be terribly sad but it is not a *catastrophe*. Your self-esteem does not depend *only* on this new relationship working.

The risk is that you have to be open to feeling interested in a potential new partner and hope they will be equally interested in you – and they may not. You may start a relationship – and decide he (or she) is not right – which is likely to stir up all your anxieties about how *unlovable* you are, or what bad choices you make.

If you can't tolerate the risk of loss, then you will need to hold on tightly to a new partner; wanting to control and cling. Any activity he (or she) gets up to, independently of you, will be a threat. It may be cosy, in the short term – but it doesn't let much air in. If the relationship *has* to work, then it will be impossibly difficult to risk standing up for yourself, or having a row. How can you say what you don't like, as well as what you do? How can you ask for your needs to be met? And if it *has* to work, then by definition you are entering into a very unequal relationship: handing over all the power to your new partner.

You might hope the relationship will be *perfect* – as if it should make up for your suffering, and provide proof that you are *good, lovable* and in no way *at fault*. But even in the best partnerships there are inevitable conflicts and disillusionments – and if you can't tolerate that, it will put pressure on that new relationship.

While it may be wonderfully reassuring to feel so closely in touch with each other, it is possible that it could begin to feel over-close. And if your partner believes that your thoughts are always the same as his (or hers), you might feel there is not much room to have thoughts which might in fact be different.

Meeting someone new

The pool of others who are of similar age and single is smaller, and the opportunities for meeting in a casual relaxed way are far fewer than when you were a teenager or young adult. Friends may introduce you. Work may create some opportunities – but staying within those familiar confines can also be limiting.

Some people decide to focus in a very direct way on searching for a potential partner – through dating agencies, personal ads, the Internet or speed dating. It can be disappointing and easy to be discouraged if you raise your hopes to meet someone – and then it doesn't work out. It can feel as though it is further proof that you are no good. Having a friend to debrief with can be essential – because it is less lonely and more fun. But making connections in these ways does not have to end in romance to be worthwhile: it may be interesting to find out who is out there and what other, single, people are doing with their lives. Friendships can develop out of such connections. And some people, if they persist, do meet partners and are delighted to have done so.

Others prefer to join in activities where singles can meet on walks, activity holidays or special events. Some choose just to get out and interest themselves in the world more and see what new interests emerge from it – which may or may not a include new partner.

It can ease your sense of mistrust and grievance to have a friendship with someone of the opposite sex – because he (or she) can give you an experience of seeing life from a different point of view, which may be uncomfortable – and refreshing. Such friendships can take the heat off the driven search for *The One*.

Breaking up is astonishingly painful. It also is an opportunity for growth – whether looked for or not. If you can take time to settle without desperate flailing around for a new partner or another quick solution, then you give yourself the possibility of learning more about yourself; of growing and of having previously unknown and unexpected new chapters in your life. These new chapters may eventually include a new partner; a series of partners – or they may not.

How you manage now will affect the rest of your life. It is not only about shutting out pain and anxiety, but about finding new resources and enthusiasm. There is much you can do to influence the outcomes – but you won't have complete control. A life, if it is to be full and interesting, includes taking careful, calculated risks and moving – once more – out into the current.

Notes

1 Tutu, Bishop Desmond (1999) *No Future without Forgiveness.* London: Rider, p. 35.
2 Hetherington, E.M. and Kelly, J. (2002) *For Better or for Worse: Divorce reconsidered.* London: Norton.
3 Self, Jonathan (2001) *Self Abuse: Love, loss and fatherhood.* London: John Murray, pp. 154–156.
4 Wallerstein, J.S. and Kelly, J.B. (2004) *Surviving the Breakup.* New York: Basic Books.
5 Wallerstein, J.S. and Blakeslee, S. (1995) *The Good Marriage: How and why love lasts.* London: Bantam.

22

The future

I have not ceased being fearful, but I have ceased to let fear control me. I have accepted fear as a part of life, specifically the fear of change, the fear of the unknown and I have gone ahead despite the pounding in the heart that says: 'turn back, turn back, you'll die if you venture too far'.

Writer, Erica Jong[1]

It takes courage to begin to emerge into the world again and it is tempting to stay passive and wait to be found and rescued. But as a strategy for living, this is not a good bet. Happiness is an activity

more like wrestling than dancing . . . [we need to] stand prepared and unshaken to meet what comes and what we did not foresee.

Marcus Aurelius[2]

Happiness is not something that we are automatically entitled to, or that necessarily arrives – like a bus – if we sit and wait long enough.

Contrary to the myth, men may be even more at risk of waiting to be rescued than women. And men who are rescued by the apparent safety of a rapid – and maybe too hasty – remarriage often face an increased chance of further traumatic break-up.

Feeling alone on your raft in the middle of stormy seas – as we all can – the company of fellow sufferers is invaluable. It helps to know you are not alone, to have the support of each other, to find from them what helps. The companions you most need are those who encourage you to let go of your rage, despair, and your fear that *you'll die if you venture too far*: who encourage you to venture out – with care; who know that slips on banana skins are inevitable – and possibly even cause for humour, however bruising; a learning experience and not a *disaster*.

Some doors have shut as a result of your marriage ending but – depending on you – others can open. However alarming it may feel, as you recover from the shock, rage and grief, you now have an astonishing opportunity to rethink your life, your pleasures, how you spend your time. It takes courage. It takes not setting yourself up for failure by expecting all your initiatives to succeed. It takes resilience. It takes finding resources within yourself you may not have noticed were there before. Patience, perseverance, not taking yourself so utterly seriously, risking making a fool of yourself and lightening up – all help.

But when some initiatives work, based on your efforts – how surprisingly cheering!

In the end, life is too short to build a shrine around *what might have been . . . if only . . .* Yes, there were mistakes made along the way: it's useful to understand them in order to learn for the future. And yes, you'll make plenty of others in the future – though hopefully not the biggest mistake of all: that of being so fearful of making mistakes or of suffering any pain that you refuse to take any risks.

Relationships are fragile things. Feelings of trust, love and hope – yours and your partner's – need tending and if they are not, they wither and become stunted. You wither and become stunted.

If you come out in the end with more understanding of yourself – your vulnerabilities, needs, defensiveness – and this makes you more able to understand another, that is quite a prize. You will be more able to choose well for the future, and appreciate more and allow yourself to trust more those whom you may – cautiously – let yourself love.

It may be that, however many years later, you'll still have moments of deep sadness and regret. But that is an honourable battle wound – a part of being prepared to love deeply. I hope that, as you've built up a new life, pleasures, people you love and who love you, you will have made sufficient peace with those old wounds that when they twinge in the night, there may be regrets but there will also be pleasurable memories.

And then it's time to let go of those faithful companions of hard times – rage and grief. This can be a loss too: it can leave you feeling lighter but emptier. It leaves you the task – and opportunity – of finding how to fill this new space: with what, and with whom.

I hope that as you emerge, still unsure, you will feel less desperate: it's no longer about having to keep unwanted feelings out, but feeling safe enough to allow things in – good, bad or mixed. It is life-enhancing if you can allow yourself to take a chance, make mistakes, give things a go – and find once again your *enthusiasm*.

With luck – and with what you've learned along the way – future partnerships of all kinds may be better. With thought, practice and luck, you can learn to live and love better.

Notes

1 Jong, Erica (1997) *What do Women Want? Bread, roses, sex, power*. New York: HarperCollins, p. 45.
2 Marcus Aurelius, Roman Emperor AD 161–180 and Stoic writer.

Appendix A

Useful books: a non-exclusive guide

The thinking underlying this book is analytic, using the clinical experience and understanding of Freud, Melanie Klein, Donald Winnicott, W.R. Bion and other contemporary British analysts. If you are interested in reading more about this approach, the following books are useful introductions.

Analytic books on individuals

Segal, Hanna (1988) *Introduction to the Work of Melanie Klein*. London: Karnac.
A clear description of complex ideas.

Segal, Julia (1995) *Phantasy in Everyday Life: a Psychoanalytic Approach to Understanding Ourselves*. Karnac Books.
Description of how less conscious assumptions and phantasies affect our perceptions of others and ourselves – sometimes destructively.

Symington, Neville (1986) *The Analytic Experience: Lectures from the Tavistock*. London: Free Association Books.
A readable account of the development of analytic thinking.

Taylor, David (ed.) (1999) *Talking Cure: Mind and method of the Tavistock Clinic*. London: Karnac.
Accounts of how analytic thinking works in an NHS clinic.

Waddell, Margot (2002) *Inside Lives: Psychoanalysis and the growth of the Personality*, 2nd edn. London: Karnac.
A beautifully written account of the development of the individual.

Winnicott, D.W. (1991) *The Child, the Family and the Outside World*. Harmondsworth: Penguin.

Paediatrician and psychoanalyst gave radio broadcasts for parents in the 1960s, in thinking about themselves and their children. Still interesting, accessible and relevant.

Viorst, Judith (2002) *Necessary Losses*. New York: The Free Press. American writer and poet, who completed an analytic training, writes of the losses and disappointments we inevitably face – and the struggle to come to terms with them.

Analytic books on relationships

Mitchell, Stephen E. (2002) *Can Love Last? The fate of romance over time*. New York: Norton.
American analyst discusses the conflicts and risks in loving.

Wallerstein, J. and Blakeslee, S. (1995) *The Good Marriage: How and why love lasts*. London: Bantam.
A study of couples who have survived serious external stresses which drive other couples into breaking up.

Beck, Aaron (1988) *Love is Never Eenough*. New York: Harper Perennial.
Cognitive therapist looks at the erroneous assumptions couples can make and the need for strategies of attending to a relationship – for negotiation and clarification – rather than a reliance on expectations of *love* alone.

Children

Wallerstein, J.S. and Blakeslee, S. (2003) *What about the Kids? Raising your children before, during, and after divorce*. New York: Hyperion.
Specific advice to divorced parents around the time of the break and after.

Marquardt, Elizabeth (2006) *Between Two Worlds: The inner lives of children of divorce*. New York: Three Rivers Press.
Adult *child* of a good divorce talks about her own experience – and those of others in her study – of the impact of divorce.

Dowling, Emilia and Gorell Barnes, Gill (2000) *Working with Children and Parents through Separation and Divorce*. Basingstoke: Palgrave.
Written from the point of view of the practitioner – but might be useful for parents too.

General books

Frolick, Larry (1998) *Splitting up: Divorce, culture and the search for a real life*. London: Hounslow Press.
Former divorce lawyer points out the degree to which divorce is due to society's *commodification of relationships*, more than individual *fault*. Provides challenging, useful practical advice – particularly for the divorced father.

Hargrave, Terry (2001) *Forgiving the Devil: Coming to terms with damaged relationships*. Phoenix, AZ: Zeig, Tucker & Theisen.
Canadian psychologist writes of forgiveness in general – and his own experience forgiving his difficult mother.

Herbert, Claudia and Wetmore, Ann (1999) *Overcoming Traumatic Stress: A self-help guide using cognitive behavioural techniques*. London: Robinson.
Gives practical techniques to help.

Tutu, Bishop Desmond (1999) *No Future without Forgiveness*. London: Rider.
Inspiring book of the work of the Truth and Reconciliation Commission.

The law

Clout, Imogen (2005) *The Which? Guide to Divorce: Essential practical information for separating couples*, 8th edn. London: Which? Books.
Useful guide to the law, finance, domestic violence and other matters in the UK.

Links to useful organisations

This is a non-exclusive list of organisations offering help and advice.

The Law

Resolution: http://www.resolution.org.uk (formerly the Solicitors Family Law Association)
Association of lawyers whose stated aim is to help couples in divorce in a non-adversarial way. The website contains many clear, informative fact sheets on issues such as the divorce procedure, arrangements for children after divorce or separation and help with the Child Support Agency.

Therapeutic help

Tavistock Centre for Couple Relationships (TCCR): http://www.tccr.org.uk/
This offers a fee-paying service to couples. Based in London. It has a specific Divorce and Separation Unit offering three sessions to couples, or to an individual, facing break-up.

Society of Couple Psychoanalytic Psychotherapists: http://www.scpp.org.uk/
The website lists those who have trained at the TCCR (above). While many of its members are based in London, there are also others working mostly privately elsewhere in the UK. This site also provides good links to other marital and couple services.

Relate: http://www.relate.org.uk/
A nationwide organisation offering marital and relationship counselling. Relate offers counselling, and mediation services, for couples who are breaking up. It runs groups, for individuals going through break-up, and for help with parenting afterwards. Also, (free) help for young people (ages 10–25) whose parents are breaking up. Useful links are on the website.

Individual psychoanalytic psychotherapy

General practitioners (GPs) now often offer a counsellor who is able to provide some sessions of help on the NHS. In addition there are some, generally time-limited services offered through Psychology, Psychiatry or Psychotherapy Departments, again accessed through GPs.

British Psychoanalytic Council: http://www.psychoanalytic-council.org/
An umbrella organisation for those who have trained for intensive psychoanalytic psychotherapy. There is some provision of low-cost psychoanalytic psychotherapy through the training organisations. The website also offers a list of trained psychoanalytic psychotherapists.

UK Council on Psychotherapy (UKCP) http://www.ukcp.org/
An umbrella organisation for therapists trained in models other than the more psychoanalytic one. It provides useful links on its website.

Group analysis

Institute of Group Analysis (IGA): http://groupanalysis.org/
This runs psychotherapy groups in various parts of the UK which can offer not only support but also useful, firm feedback.

Self-help

Gingerbread: http://gingerbread.org.uk
A self-help organisation offering support to single-parent families. It offers self-help groups in various parts of the UK, online groups and help setting up your own self-help group. It runs outings for single parents with their children.

National Council for One Parent Families: http://oneparentfamilies.org.uk/
This has now joined with Gingerbread. Nevertheless it still has its own website, which has a useful helpdesk giving advice to single parents on many practical issues.

Fathers Direct: http://www.fathersdirect.com
This useful and informative website offers advice to fathers in a supportive, non-inflammatory way. See in particular their Dad pack – many useful links, including to NACCC (see next item).

National Association of Child Contact Centres (NACCC): http://www.naccc.org.uk
NACCC provides a neutral place of safety where non-resident parents can spend time with their children.

Health Visitors: http://www.healthvisitors.com
Health visitors are available to give advice on parenting both in the community and online at this website.

Bibliography

Alvarez, Al (1981) *Life after Marriage: Love in an age of divorce.* New York: Simon & Schuster.

Amato, Paul (1996) Explaining the intergenerational transmission of divorce. *Journal of Marriage and the Family* 58: 628–640.

Amato, Paul (2003) Reconciling divergent perspectives: Judith Wallerstein, quantitative family research, and children of divorce. *Family Relations* 52(4): 332–339.

Amato, Paul and Cheadle, Jacob (2005) The long reach of divorce: Divorce and child well-being across three generations. *Journal of Marriage and the Family* 67(1): 191–206.

Amato, Paul and Keith, Bruce (1991a) Parental divorce and adult well-being: A meta-analysis. *Journal of Marriage and the Family* 53(1): 43–58.

Amato, Paul and Keith, Bruce (1991b) Parental divorce and the well-being of children: A meta-analysis. *Psychological Bulletin* 110(1): 26–46.

Amis, Martin (2000) *Experience.* London: Jonathan Cape.

Beck, Aaron (1988) *Love is Never Enough.* New York: Harper Perennial.

Beckett, Sister Wendy (2006) *Sister Wendy on Prayer.* London: Continuum.

Bion, W.R. (1962) A theory of thinking. In W.R. Bion, *Second Thoughts.* New York: Jacob Aronson.

Bion, W.R. (1984) *Attention and Interpretation.* London: Karnac.

Blundell, Suzanne (2001) Fatherless sons. In Judith Trowell and Alicia Etchegoyen (eds) *The Importance of Fathers.* New Library of Psychoanalysis. Hove: Brunner-Routledge.

Bowlby, John (1998) *Loss: Sadness and depression.* Volume 3 of *Attachment and Loss.* London: Pimlico.

Bowlby, John, Robertson, James and Rosenbluth, Dina (1952) A two-year-old goes to hospital. *Psycho-Analytic Study of the Child* 7: 82–94.

Brown, G. and Harris, T. (1978) *The Social Origins of Depression*. London: Tavistock.

Bunyan, J. (1678–1684) *The Pilgrim's Progress*. London.

Cameron, Julia (1994) *The Artist's Way: A spiritual path to higher creativity*. London: Souvenir.

Carter, Angela (2006) *Nights at the Circus*. London: Vintage.

Clare, Anthony (2000) *On Men: Masculinity in crisis*. London: Chatto & Windus.

Cockett, M. and Tripp, J. (1994) *The Exeter Family Study: Social policy research findings*. York: Joseph Rowntree Foundation.

Cooke, Rachel (2006) The Amis papers. *Observer*, Review, 1 October.

Crouch, Stanley (1999) *Always in Pursuit: Fresh American perspectives*. New York: Vintage.

Davids, M. Fakhry (2001) Fathers in the internal world: From boy to man to father. In Judith Trowell and Alicia Etchegoyen (eds) *The Importance of Fathers*. New Library of Psychoanalysis. Hove: Brunner-Routledge.

Dowling, Emilia and Gorell Barnes, Gill (2000) *Working with Children and Parents through Separation and Divorce*. Basingstoke: Palgrave.

Doyle, Laura (2001) *The Surrendered Wife*. New York: Simon & Schuster.

Emanuel, Ricky (2001) On becoming a father: Reflections from infant observation. In Judith Trowell and Alicia Etchegoyen (eds) *The Importance of Fathers*. New Library of Psychoanalysis. Hove: Brunner-Routledge.

Fomby, P. and Cherlin, A. (2007) Family instability and child well-being. *American Sociological Review* 72(2): 181–204.

Fonagy, P., Steele, M., Moran, G., Steele, H. and Higgitt, A. (1993) Measuring the ghost in the nursery: An empirical study of the relation between parents' mental representations of childhood experiences and their infants' security of attachment. *Journal of the American Psychoanalytic Association* 41: 957–989.

Fraiberg, S., Adelson, E. and Shapiro, V. (1975) Ghosts in the nursery: A psychoanalytic approach to the problems of impaired infant–mother relationships. *Journal of the American Academy of Child Psychiatry* 14: 387–422.

Freud, S. (1917) Mourning and melancholia. *The Standard Edition of the Complete Psychological Works of Sigmund Freud, Volume XIV* (1914–1916): On the History of the Psycho-Analytic Movement, Papers on Metapsychology and Other Works, 237–258.

Frolick, Larry (1998) *Splitting Up: Divorce, culture and the search for a real life*. London: Hounslow Press.

Garland, Caroline (ed.) (2002) *Understanding Trauma: A psycho-analytical approach*, 2nd edn. London: Karnac.

Gottman, John (1994) *Why Marriages Succeed or Fail: And how you can make yours last*. New York: Simon & Schuster.

Gottman, John and Krokoff, L.J. (1989) Marital interaction and satisfaction: A longitudinal view. *Journal of Consulting and Clinical Psychology* 57(1): 47–52.

Graves, Robert (2000) *Robert Graves' Complete Poems in One Volume*. Edited by Beryl Graves and Dunstan Ward. Manchester: Carcanet Press.

Greenfield, Howard and Sedaka, Neil (1962) *Breaking Up Is Hard To Do*. © 1962, Screen Gems-EMI Music Inc., USA.

Hargrave, Terry (2001) *Forgiving the Devil: Coming to terms with damaged relationships*. Phoenix, AZ: Zeig, Tucker & Theisen.

Hemingway, Ernest (1934) Letter to F. Scott Fitzgerald.

Hemingway, Ernest (2004) *A Farewell to Arms*. London: Arrow.

Herbert, Claudia and Wetmore, Ann (1999) *Overcoming Traumatic Stress: A self-help guide using cognitive behavioural techniques*. London: Robinson.

Hetherington, E.M. and Kelly, J. (2002) *For Better or for Worse: Divorce reconsidered*. London: Norton.

Hornby, Nick (1992) *Fever Pitch*. London: Gollancz.

Houellebecq, Michel (2001) *Atomised*. London: Vintage.

Hughes, Beverly and Cooke, Graeme (2007) in Children, Parenting and Families: Renewing the Progressive Story. In Peace, N. and Margo, J. (eds) *Politics for a New Generation*. (IPPR).

Hustvedt, Siri (2003) *What I Loved*. London: Hodder & Stoughton.

James, Henry (1997) *What Maisie Knew*. London: Everyman.

Jamison, Kay (1997) *An Unquiet Mind: A memoir of moods and madness*. London: Picador.

Johnston, Janet (1994) High conflict divorce. *Children and Divorce* 4(1): 165–182.

Johnston, J.R. and Campbell, L.E.G. (1988) *Impasses of Divorce: The dynamics and resolution of family conflict*. New York: Free Press.

Jong, Erica (1997) *What do Women Want? Bread, roses, sex, power*. New York: HarperCollins.

Kapuscinski, Ryszard (2004) When there is talk of war. *Granta*, 88. Reviewed in *The Independent*, Review, 4 January 2005.

Kureishi, Hanif (1999) *Intimacy*. London: Faber & Faber.

Leuzinger-Bohleber, Marianne and Target, Mary (2002) *Outcomes of Psychoanalytic Treatment*. London: Whurr.

Lott, Tim (2003) *Love Secrets of Don Juan*. London: Viking.

Mahler, Margaret, Pines, Fred and Bergman, Anni (2000) *The Psychological Birth of the Human Infant: Symbiosis and Individuation*. New York: Basic Books.

Marks, Maureen (2001) Letting father in. In Judith Trowell and Alicia Etchegoyen (eds) *The Importance of Fathers*. New Library of Psychoanalysis. Hove: Brunner-Routledge.

Marquardt, Elizabeth (2006) *Between Two Worlds: The inner lives of children of divorce*. New York: Three Rivers Press.

Mitchell, Stephen E. (2002) *Can Love Last? The fate of romance over time*. New York: Norton.

Moses Kor, Eva, quoted in Lawrence Rees (2005) *Auschwitz: The Nazis and the Final Solution*. London: BBC Books.

Murray, Lynne (1992) The impact of postnatal depression on infant development. *Journal of Child Psychology and Psychiatry* 33: 543–561.

Murray, L., Stanley, C., Hooper, R., King, F. and Fiori-Cowley, A. (1996) The role of infant factors in post-natal depression and mother–infant interactions. *Developmental Medicine and Child Neurology* 38(2): 109–119.

O'Connor, Matt (2007) *Fathers 4 Justice: The inside story*. London: Weidenfeld & Nicolson.

Proust, Marcel (2000) *In Search of Lost Time: Time regained*. Trans. C.K. Scott Moncrieff, T. Kilmartin and D.J. Enright. London: Vintage.

Rawls, John (1971) *A Theory of Justice*. Cambridge, MA: Harvard University Press.

Rayburn, Tina and Foster, Timothy (2007) *I Want to See my Kids! A guide for dads who want contact with their children after separation*. London: Fusion.

Roberts, Yvonne (2004) Listen to the children, Mrs Hodges. *Observer*, 30 May.

Segal, Erich (1977) *Love Story*. London: Hodder & Stoughton.

Segal, Hanna (1986) *The Work of Hanna Segal: A Kleinian approach to clinical practice*. New York: Free Association Books.

Segal, Hanna (1988) *Introduction to the Work of Melanie Klein*. London: Karnac.

Self, Jonathan (2001) *Self Abuse: Love, loss and fatherhood*. London: John Murray.

Shields, Carol (2003) *Unless*. London: Fourth Estate.

Simmonds, Posy (1982) *Pick of Posy*. London: Jonathan Cape.

Simpson, B., McCarthy, P. and Walker, J. (1995) *Being There: Fathers after divorce*. Newcastle upon Tyne: Relate Centre for Family Studies, University of Newcastle.

Symington, Neville (1986) *The Analytic Experience: Lectures from the Tavistock*. London: Free Association Books.

Taylor, David (ed.) (1999) *Talking Cure: Mind and method of the Tavistock Clinic*. London: Karnac.

Trinder, Jo, Kellett, Joanne, Connolly, Jo and Notley, Caitlin

(2006) *Evaluation of the Family Resolutions Pilot Project.* London: Department for Education and Skills.

Tutu, Bishop Desmond (1999) *No Future without Forgiveness.* London: Rider.

Tweedie, J. (1982a) The mind veers away. *Guardian*, 12 April.

Tweedie, J. (1982b) The vision of life seen in depression has the truth in it, the bare-boned skeletal truth. *Guardian*, 17 April. Also in Dorothy Rowe (2003) *Depression: The way out of your prison*, 3rd edn. London: Routledge.

Tyler, Anne (1996) *Ladder of the Years.* London: Vintage.

Viorst, Judith (2002) *Necessary Losses.* New York: The Free Press.

Waddell, Margot (2002) *Inside Lives: Psychoanalysis and the growth of the personality*, 2nd edn. London: Karnac.

Walker, J., McCarthy, P., Stark, C. and Laing, K. (2004) *Picking up the Pieces: Marriage and divorce – Two years after information provision.* London: Department of Constitutional Affairs.

Walker, Rebecca (2001) *Black, White and Jewish: Autobiography of a shifting self.* New York: Riverhead.

Wallerstein, J.S. and Blakeslee, S. (1995) *The Good Marriage: How and why love lasts.* London: Bantam.

Wallerstein, J.S. and Blakeslee, S. (2003) *What about the Kids? Raising your children before, during, and after divorce.* New York: Hyperion.

Wallerstein, J.S. and Blakeslee, S. (2004) *Second Chances: Men, women and children a decade after divorce.* Boston, MA: Houghton Mifflin.

Wallerstein, J.S. and Kelly, J.B. (2004) *Surviving the Breakup.* New York: Basic Books.

Wallerstein, J.S. and Lewis, J.M. (2006) Sibling outcomes and disparate parenting and step-parenting after divorce: Report from a ten year longitudinal study. Presented Division 39, American Psychological Association, Philadelphia, PA.

Wallerstein, J.S. and Resnikoff, D. (1997) Parental divorce and developmental progression: An inquiry into their relationship. *International Journal of Psychoanalysis* 78: 135–154.

Wallerstein, J.S., Lewis, J.M. and Blakeslee, S. (2002) *The Unexpected Legacy of Divorce: A 25 year landmark study.* London: Fusion.

Weiss, R.S. (1975) *Marital Separation: Coping with the end of a marriage and the transition to being single again.* Basic Books.

Winnicott, D.W. (1991) *The Child, the Family and the Outside World.* Harmondsworth: Penguin.

Youell, Biddy (2001) Missing fathers: Hope and disappointment. In Judith Trowell and Alicia Etchegoyen (eds) *The Importance of Fathers.* New Library of Psychoanalysis. Hove: Brunner-Routledge.

Index

Note: page numbers in **bold** refer to diagrams/illustrations